Bad Bosses, Crazy Coworkers & Other Office Idiots

201 Smart Solutions to Every Problem at Work

★ VICKY OLIVER ★

Sourcebooks, Inc.®
Naperville, Illinois

Published by Sourcebooks, Inc.
P.O. Box 4410, Naperville, Illinois 60567-4410
(630) 961-3900
Fax: (630) 961-2168
www.sourcebooks.com

Library of Congress Cataloging-in-Publication Data

Oliver, Vicky.
Bad bosses, crazy coworkers, and other office idiots : 201 smart solutions to every problem at work / Vicky Oliver.
p. cm.
Includes index.
1. Psychology, Industrial. 2. Interpersonal relations. 3. Conflict management. 4. Interpersonal conflict. I. Title.
HF5548.8.O45 2008
650.1'3--dc22

2008018640

Printed and bound in the United States of America
POD 10 9 8 7 6 5 4 3

Dedication

For anyone who has ever had a confrontation at the office that lasted for less than five minutes only to spend the next five business days agonizing over whether you said the right thing, the wrong thing, the intuitive thing, the insensitive thing (or indeed, whether you should have spoken at all), this book is for you.

ACKNOWLEDGMENTS

A heartfelt "thank you" to all those who came forward to share their true office tales and travails with me during the writing of this book. Your unabashed candor informs every page.

I am also indebted to the Mumbles Writing Group for its cheerful critiques and suggestions throughout the writing process. The Mumbles Writing Group is a gaggle of fiction writers who graciously allowed this nonfiction writer to share a crab cake, a glass of wine, and twenty-five pages with them every other Wednesday night.

This book probably would have never happened without Bethany Brown urging me to build on the success of my first book, *301 Smart Answers to Tough Interview Questions*. Thank you too, Peter Lynch, for your careful guidance and steadfast shepherding of this project from its very inception. June Clark, your savvy counsel was often solicited, usually followed, and always appreciated.

Finally, I'd like to thank every person who, upon hearing that I was writing this book, said: "Office politics. What a great topic." Indeed it is.

TABLE OF CONTENTS

PART 2: Colleagues from Purgatory (90 Problems/90 Solutions)
And now, for the problem adults down the hallway...

INTRODUCTION

If You Can Recognize the Problem, You Can Find the Solution

The good news is you are already intimately acquainted with The Problem. That's because you have spent close to eight hours a day, five days a week, ruminating about it. You've meditated on it, bounced it around with your friends, and even managed to ignore it for a spell. But no matter what you try, nothing seems to alleviate what is on track to becoming an official nightmare. It could be your boss. It could be one of your employees. Or it could even be you.

If The Problem happens to be your boss, you may be whittling away precious sanity pondering the many obstacles you face because he's in charge. After all, Big Problems (like bosses) have a way of creating smaller management problems, issues, and headaches for the rest of us.

If The Problem is one of your employees, you might be asking yourself if there is any way to get the person demoted, fired, or even promoted to another department, just so that she will stop tormenting you!

Whether you're working for an impossible boss or laboring next to a cantankerous coworker, you will find him or her in the Table of Contents. Once you do, flip to that chapter to discover the management issues he or she is likely to cause. Read up on the problems. Study the solutions, and start putting them into practice. There's no need to spend one moment on any chapter that doesn't apply directly to your situation.

Part 1: Bosses from Hell

From the absentee boss who doubles as the Wizard of Oz to the Predator who has been eyeing you for something other than a promotion, they're all in here. You'll recognize the Credit Snatcher who's eager to pounce on your ideas like a bird of prey, the Big Sister who monitors your every move, plus every other boss who's ever driven you to the brink of quitting.

Is your boss a screamer, a nincompoop, a tyrant, a petty thief, or even a grand larcenist? In Part 1 you will meet sixteen different difficult-boss archetypes that you may already know well. The only thing you haven't mastered yet is how to deal with them. And that's where this book can really help. In the eighty Problem-Solution boxes in this part, you'll find answers, tips, and *rational* responses for handling virtually any boss-inspired conundrum.

Part 2: Colleagues from Purgatory

They're called "underlings." So why is it that 99% of the time, you feel like you're at *their* mercy? Are you at the whims of a Coddled Superstar, too spoiled to arrive at the office on time? Have you been struggling to protect an Employee Nobody Likes but You? Are you delegating big decisions to a Spineless Sycophant, all too eager to bend whichever way top management does? Do you have a Grumpy Martyr on staff, or an employee who's a Master Mumbler?

Are those who work nearest to you gunning for your job, spreading false rumors about you, desperately seeking approval, or embarrassing you with their exponential rudeness? Part 2 will introduce you to eighteen familiar and exasperating employee archetypes.

Once you've identified your nemesis, how should you proceed to work with that person? Should you challenge him or say nothing? Should you try to quarantine him like a plague victim or endeavor to change him? This section will give you step-by-step guidance in these matters with ninety Problem-Solution boxes designed to help you conquer even the messiest employee-generated management fiascos.

Part 3: When the Problem Lies Within

Let's face it, when The Problem lies with *them,* it's relatively easy to identify. But what if the same types of issues seem to shadow you from company to company? If that's been your experience, it's likely you're causing your own distress.

Skim the entries in Part 3, and practice the art of self-diagnosis. Are you wishy-washy? Do you look down on your colleagues? Do you feel like you're just not a people person? *(What, like that's a problem?)* Once you've identified The Problem That Lies Within, flip to the relevant chapter for a more in-depth analysis. You'll be able to identify ten self-sabotaging personality foibles and find tons of helpful suggestions for controlling the saboteur within.

Contrary to popular perception, life at the office needn't be an inferno of despair, drudgery, and mayhem five days a week. With the insight and guidance provided by this book, some self-mastery, and a bit of practice, you might even find that you come to *enjoy* working with some of the problem personality types down the hallway.

This is your survival manual for today's modern workplace. It will chart your best path to remedy 201 of the most common management problems you're likely to encounter, so that you can put them behind you once and for all.

PART 1
Bosses from Hell

The Boss from Hell comes in all different guises. She's either too prying or completely absentminded. She's too worried about what the higher-ups think of her department or not nearly worried enough. She manages up well or manages down well, but she certainly can't do both well. Or she's a total perfectionist and everyone in the office is terrified of her. She either forgets to compliment you on your performance or does so only in the most sarcastic tones. She may have even remarked on how nice it was that you were on time for a change.

She might be a neat freak, a control freak, or prone to freaking out at the slightest provocation. Conversely, she might be so messy that projects pile up on her desk and disappear into a black hole, never to be seen again. She's either in your face at all times or completely out to lunch. When you don't require any supervision, there she is, breathing down your neck, dragon-style. But if you desperately need to ask her a question or get her to sign off on a document, she's nowhere to be found. Naturally, anything that you ever devise, craft, create, or write will be automatically credited to her, unless you make a mistake, in which case, you can look forward to receiving all of the blame for the foreseeable future.

You wonder: can't your boss get out early once in a while, get a life, get meds, get out of your hair, or maybe, oh please dear hiring gods, just get a new job? Yet deep down inside, you know it would be foolish to count on such a blessing. So while you're waiting for the Boss from Hell to get the hell out of your life, here are some ways to deal with some of the management conundrums she creates.

CHAPTER 1

Big Sister Is Watching You

The eight employees who worked for "Susanna" were young women under the age of thirty. We didn't know how to stand up for ourselves and just say, "No, I can't work on July 4th, Susanna." We didn't realize we were being abused by a spoiled brat not much older than us. We believed we were just paying our dues, getting ahead in the big city.

You can't escape the feeling that you are being watched. It doesn't matter when you arrive at the office; your boss is there first. If you leave at 5 p.m., she asks why you're leaving so early. If you cut out two hours later, she's still bent over her desk, poring through papers. If you decide to work over a weekend, what do you know, she decides to come in over the same weekend. You can't get away from her. To do so might give her separation anxiety.

Sometimes when you're "in the zone," head bent down over your work, you'll look up suddenly—only to catch a snapshot view of your boss's chin. She seems to derive a sadistic pleasure from reading what's on your screen before you've had a chance to proof it. If you work at a company where you're expected to complete time sheets, she never fails to dispute the way you've filled out yours. There seems to be an invisible clock, and no matter what time you punch in or out, you always owe the company more.

When you have a boss who is always there, monitoring your every move, here's how to rise above some of the issues that are likely to surface.

Problem #1: The Boss Who Bugs You over the Weekend

She sees herself as the Weekend Warrior Princess. She has little regard for her own personal life and even less so for yours. She won't hesitate to call Saturday morning meetings, or even worse, continually pester you on the phone at the most inconvenient times. Is it a long weekend? She doesn't mind popping over for just a few minutes on your Monday off to talk shop till you drop.

Solution #1: Set Your Boundaries

During the week, your time is valuable. On the weekends, it's priceless. If your boss insists on meeting over the weekend, be sure to tell her in advance exactly how long you can stay. You might try scheduling your appointment around a family obligation, explaining, "My grandmother and I have tickets to a matinee. I can get to the office at ten, but will need to leave at noon on the dot." Then, just be certain to follow through.

Does your boss have a pesky habit of calling you at home? Try using the same technique. At the beginning of the call, tell your boss precisely how many minutes you can spare. Impending visits from cousins, screaming infants in the background, and bursting drainpipes may help keep phone conversations with an inconsiderate boss even shorter.

THE TAMING OF A WORKAHOLIC BOSS

Working for a workaholic entails a lot of sacrifice. You will sacrifice evenings, weekends, and your leisure time on the altar of big business, for which you will probably receive zero overtime compensation. You need to begin gently establishing some guidelines for your self-preservation. Here are some tactics to try:

- **TRAVEL LIGHT.** Forgo the cell, laptop, and Blackberry. Just leave them at home each day, and your boss will never have to know that you own them. The fewer phone numbers and email addresses you give out to people, the less likely they'll be to disturb you during your free time.
- **MAKE YOUR WEEKENDS SOUND LIKE VACATIONS.** It takes a certain level of cruelty to stop an employee from going camping over a weekend with her long-lost cousins. When appropriate, describe your weekend plans and make them sound really fun. Your boss may think twice before asking you to work on Saturday.
- **BEAT YOUR BOSS TO WORK EACH DAY.** Arrive a few minutes earlier than she does. She'll feel like you're covering for her in her absence, which she's bound to remember when you can't always be there for her late at night.

Problem #2: The Inefficiency Expert

Some workaholic bosses enjoy toiling deep into the night with nothing but their computers to keep them company. Other bosses urge you to hang out in the work pod, slaving away right beside them. If the real work that's due isn't enough to keep you cocooned after hours, your boss has no aversion to inventing work to keep you busy. Multiple revisions, endless fixes, and a fascination with reformatting may all be signs that you work for an Inefficiency Expert.

Solution #2: Hold Your Boss to a Higher Standard: Standardize All Documents

Inefficiency Experts are geniuses at inventing busywork. You're going to dig yourself out from under it by politely insisting on standardization. Call a meeting with your boss during regular working hours. Introduce the need to set up new templates for all conference reports, presentations, and client documents. (You will automatically win major points from your boss for undertaking this challenge.) Spare no effort to make the new templates easy to read and visually appealing. Then, ensure that your boss wholeheartedly approves of the new look. The very next time she tries to fritter away time on reformatting issues, gently remind her that you are simply "following the new template."

Give credit where it *isn't* due. If one of your clients happens to comment on how attractive the new template looks, why not credit your boss with coming up with the idea? It will help her get behind it even more.

Problem #3: The Boss Who Views You as Her Personal Marionette

The online job description said, "room to grow." But so far, the only thing that's been growing are your boss's plants (which you are expected to water, thank you very much). You haven't stretched; only your Rolodex file of her beauty consultants and restaurant picks has. In this day and age, it's hard to believe that doing personal chores for your boss is an integral part of your job description. You're so happy that you graduated cum laude for this incredible privilege.

Solution #3: Develop a Personal Timeline and Then Cut the Strings

To some, *The Devil Wears Prada* is a movie. To others, it's a way of life. In certain fields, administrative assistants are still treated like lackeys. It's a deeply embedded part of the corporate culture that harkens back to the old days. Your boss may have even grown up in the same corporate culture where she had to pay her dues by watering *her* boss's plants. It would be naïve to think that you'll be able to charm your way out of your heavy-duty watering responsibilities!

The only way out is to move up or opt out of the business entirely. Six months into your job, start hatching your escape strategy. Make an appointment to sit down with your boss to review your progress. Profusely thank her for the tremendous opportunity she gave you by hiring you, and express your passion for *staying*. Ask her to put you on a special project where you can both track your progress. Try to persuade her to map out a timeline for your advancement; but if she can't (or won't), don't despair.

Grab a cotton ball and wipe that pathetic "When will I be promoted?" pout off your face. Use this time to reach out to managers of other departments, including human resources. Keep your ears open for any suitable positions in the company. Often, lists of open spots will be distributed. Start applying for them. You could jump to a position that pays you more shekels and frees you from the shackles of demeaning personal-chore duty.

Management Mantra

Repeat after Eleanor Roosevelt, "No one can make you feel inferior without your consent." If doing someone's personal chores makes you feel like you're slumming, try to limit the amount of time that you're willing to do them.

Problem #4: She Wants a Play-by-Play of Every Meeting, Email, and Call

Your boss bumps into you in the hallway one afternoon, playfully punches you on the arm, and says ever so casually, "I heard you've been having some back-and-forth with Peter. You really need to start including me on your email chains." It's the second time in less than two weeks that she's suggested something similar. Translation: Your boss is on the verge of a major meltdown because she feels excluded. If you don't start cc'ing her on your correspondence pronto, she will make it her mission on earth to cut you out of the loop, perhaps permanently.

Solution #4: Bore Her with the Details

As Mies Van Der Rohe once stated so eloquently, "God is in the details." Take detailed notes of every business interaction you have, and keep emailing them to your boss until she cries, "Enough already." Your salvation lies in a moment-by-moment recounting of the minutiae. Even the most determined micromanager knows she's being paid to focus on the big picture. Have faith in the fact that, eventually, she will be called away to an important business meeting that's so far away even she won't be able to mastermind your every move. And pray that, by the time she returns, you will have accumulated some laudatory emails from those whose projects you handled so adeptly in her absence. If someone compliments you on a job well done, nicely ask him to put it in writing. Then promptly forward those beaming emails to your boss. After all, she's the one who requested a play-by-play of your every meeting, email, and phone call.

DON'T LET YOUR BOSS'S PARANOIA DESTROY YA

The bad news is, your boss seems to suffer from an acute mental disorder. The good news? At least the disease isn't contagious. Here's how to keep your head while at least one person around you is losing hers.

- **DON'T DESPERATELY SEEK HER APPROVAL.** She may start to panic that you're just as nutty as she is. Instead, praise yourself for a job well done. "Wow, I did a great job," you might say to your full-length mirror at home. "I'm awesome."
- **DON'T TRY TO GET INSIDE HER HEAD.** That can be a scary place. If she directly accuses you of disloyalty, defend yourself. If she rants against others in the department, simply listen without judgment. Keep your interactions with her focused on the business of the day rather than on the vicissitudes of office politics.
- **DON'T CHALLENGE HER.** She may turn on you faster than Jill Jekyll morphing into Hilda Hyde.
- **DON'T ASK TO BE LET IN.** Is your boss holed up behind closed doors again? Imagine there is a giant sign on the door that reads, "Do not disturb until the meds have kicked in."
- **DON'T CIRCUMVENT HER CRONIES AND SYCOPHANTS.** They are all that stands between her intensely foul moods and your head being chopped off and handed back to you on a silver platter. Her toadies are your buffer zone. If you hear that she's in one of her infamous moods, either ignore the pressing deadline or renegotiate it with her henchmen. (Hint: It helps to be on supremely good terms with those on whom you will be relying often.)

Problem #5: She Snoops through Your Papers

You always leave tomorrow's to-do list on the left side of your desk. So you're deeply perplexed one morning when you find it on the right side. Searching for clues as to who may have moved your trusty list, you bring the piece of paper up to your nose and think you detect a familiar, cloying musky scent. Hers.

Solution #5: Leave Things around Your Work Area That She'll Be Happy to Find

It may be rude, obnoxious, and tacky, but it is not illegal for your boss to snoop around. The law is a snoop enabler. It is perfectly legal for companies to comb through their employee's emails. (Beware: Many company servers keep records of all deleted emails.) At certain financial firms today, taping cell phone conversations is standard practice. Take advantage of the "open everything" policy to proudly display your to-do list. Organize the list chronologically and check off your progress as you accomplish certain goals. If you haven't finished one of your chores, transfer it to your list for the following day. Heck, while you're at it, type your daily list. Hey, if you can't hide it, you may as well flaunt it.

Just the Stats

According to a Harris poll, only 30% of the employees at large organizations believe their top managers display integrity and morality, while 48% of those working for small employers believe their top managers do.[1] Evidently, size *does* matter.

The Golden Rule

Know your boss's habits in order to outfox her. Arrive earlier in the morning than she does, thus foiling her attempts to witness your every action. Curtail the amount of time that you spend with her on weekends. Draw the line and never cross it, or she most certainly will.

CHAPTER 2

The Boss Who Doubles as the Wizard of Oz

We'd spend an hour a day asking everyone in the studio when they had last seen Mike. Mike's secretary was just as eager as the rest of us to figure out where the hell he was.

You work for a virtual boss who is virtually never around. He shuttles between offices and telecommutes between meetings. You know his cell phone, Blackberry, and European cell phone numbers by heart. In the past few months, you've become a *Time Zone Aficionado* and now sport a watch with two faces—the second one set for whichever city your boss happens to be in that week. If only your boss were where he said he'd be. He's a virtuoso at the virtual game, completely impossible to pin down.

The absence of management has created a void at your company, with some people many rungs beneath you clamoring for the Wizard's leadership, and others, several rungs above you, plotting for the Wizard's removal. You overhear treasonous statements from various bishops whom the Wizard hired in the past. You'd love to warn your boss, but are loath to do so via email.

Meanwhile, you have a job to do—or two, if you count the Wizard's. After all, there are presentations to be made and clients to court. There are underlings to direct and middle managers to appease. The churn and grind of business must go on, with or without the Wizard's input, as everyone in your organization seems to be asking for directions to the Yellow Brick Road.

Problem #6: You Can't Pin Him Down

You can't find your boss, much less ask him to comment on the new initiative. You left an urgent message with his assistant but, having heard nothing, proceeded to leave unreturned voicemails for him in New York, London, and Vancouver. Eerily, life in the maze has started to resemble a reality version of *Where's Waldo?* Everyone is desperately seeking the Wizard's feedback or his seal of approval while he appears to have gone into hiding.

Solution #6: Consider the "Next Steps" Email

The Wizard's constant absences have punched a glaring cavity into the decision-making structure. Decisions can't be made unless he's around, yet he's never around to make them. But just because there's a vacuum doesn't mean that you have to act vacuous.

Evaluate the facts. Make a rational decision. And start getting buy-in from the other top managers who are around. You might approach them, one by one, and say, "I've left five messages for Larry and haven't heard back from him. I was thinking we might tweak the initiative by doing X, Y, and Z to it. If you agree, let's start on it, and I'll be happy to apprise Larry of our progress." Then be certain to email Larry about any changes to the project along with the next steps. Send your communiqué via rush email (and fax, if you think it will reach him sooner.) Copy every single person who has touched the project in Larry's absence, including his trusty assistant.

When the boss disappears, it's even more important to keep the internal lines of communication muddle-free. You don't want momentum to stagnate or go *POOF.*

Management Mantra

"Leaders are made, they are not born," declared Vince Lombardi, the legendary Green Bay Packers football coach. If you find yourself negotiating a management gap, you may be able to parlay it into a promotion. Just be certain those around you perceive that you are filling a genuine need rather than making an uncouth grab for power.

BEWARE THE BACKLASH

Most Wizards started in corporate life as humble managers. Often, they showed wondrous aptitude for the task and were promoted multiple times, possibly beyond the point of effectiveness. If your local Wizard is expected to manage more than two offices located more than five hundred miles apart, he may resent the fact that he's not around to make decisions even more than you do. He feels his coattails shrinking and may foil your attempts to latch on to them.

To avoid a display of wizardly capriciousness, you may wish to discuss some ideas that will empower him in his absence.

- **TUESDAY-MORNING STAFF MEETINGS.** Have the Wizard call in to the meeting (and call the shots) from the road. Respect that, for most absentee bosses, less is more. Keep the meetings under thirty minutes.
- **ONE-SENTENCE WRAP-UPS.** Condense the team's questions into one sentence, and then send a text message to your boss for a quick read; i.e., "New proposal, thumbs up or down?"
- **ALTERNATE THURSDAY ONE-ON-ONES BETWEEN YOU AND YOUR BOSS (WHEN HE'S AROUND).** Sweeten the suggestion by offering to keep sessions super short. Then ingratiate yourself by actually living up to your promise.

Problem #7: Against All Expectations, the Wizard Makes a Surprise Appearance

A week ago, no one could live without him. The whole team was frantic about your boss's whereabouts. "Tell him that if he can't make it, there will be no meeting," the Senior Account Director (S.A.D.) unilaterally declared. And since S.A.D. just happens to be the third most important person on the totem pole, you took his threat rather seriously. You tried to contact your boss a few times. But as usual, he was incommunicado, and the team was forced to come up with a contingency plan. Now everyone has rallied behind Plan B. The speakers have been chosen. Rehearsals are well underway…when your boss finally circles back to you to announce that he will, in fact, be at the meeting. He's even looking forward to it.

Solution #7: Roll with It

When reporting to a Wizard, it's a good idea to plan for the unexpected. For the present, your boss is still the man in charge. (That's like having a license to drive everyone berserk and consistently getting away with it.)

The real problem is how your clients may perceive your boss's forays in and out of the project loop. No matter how much your boss's wacky schedule catapults the internal order, you never want your clients to feel that his coming and going will disrupt their special project. For, truth be told, that's the only thing they really care about!

To cushion the impact of his sudden return, consider giving your boss a ceremonial role in the meeting. For example, you might suggest that he open the meeting and introduce all the folks around the table with a brief background on how they contributed to the project. Then you or others can take your client through the actual presentation, less concerned about what the Wizard might interject.

Videotape a rehearsal and FedEx the DVD to your boss so he'll know what everyone is planning to say. Worried the DVD won't be able to find him either? Email the Wizard your notes about the rehearsal. At least he can't strike you down for trying.

Problem #8: You've Been Covering for the Wizard (but He's Never around to Champion Your Cause)

A Wizard can be a tricky ally. You'd think he would appreciate your undying loyalty and stalwart efforts to keep him in the loop. Instead, he might view your enthusiasm as a sign of insecurity, indecisiveness, or even indiscretion. Look at it from his standpoint: all six people on your cc list are now acutely aware that he hasn't been around to offer his amulets of wisdom. He can wave his magic wand at that email all he wants, but it's unlikely to go away.

Solution #8: Two Words: Paper Trail

There's a hole in the management apparatus that's the size of a Wizard. But take solace in knowing that upper management will decide how to fill the gap. Hence, the heavy burden of guilt is completely off your shoulders.

Think of your office as a tightly knit community whose inhabitants can practically read one another's unspoken thoughts. You are *not* the only person in your little office village who's noticed that you're always around to pick up the slack. Just keep doing the same great job that you have been, and chances are your day will come (hopefully before you turn as old and wizened as the Wizard). In the meantime, keep meticulous records of every meeting; copy your missing boss along with the rest of the clan; and stay cheerful. No one wants to promote a sulky martyr to Wizard status.

Just the Stats

According to a poll by MSN-Zogby, 58% of people who work for someone else say they like their boss, 18% can tolerate their boss, and 5% hate their boss (and you thought it was just you).[2]

Problem #9: You Can't Understand a Word He's Saying

He speaks in a flowery language that you find difficult to interpret. While his sentiments seem wise, you haven't the slightest idea what they mean. Occasionally, others who sat in the same meeting arrive at a completely different take on the Wizard's suggestions. You only wish that you had a PhD in whatever language the Wizard seems to be muttering. Whether he's rambling on about costs, sales figures, or returns on investments, it's all Greek to you.

Solution #9: Hire a Translator

Many bosses have poor communication skills. Long sojourns out of the country may exacerbate the problem. Your boss could be spending vast periods of time in a foreign office whose customs are quite different. Add to that a heavy travel schedule that discombobulates your boss's sleep rhythms. To the extent he's functioning at all, it's on jet lag. Or your boss might puddle jump to a different part of the United States and return with a dialect that makes him even harder to understand than usual.

Comb the office for those who can interpret the Wizard's strange dialect, and debrief with them after every meeting until you master his special lingo. For ultra important powwows, consider inviting his assistant to sit in and take notes, as she probably communicates with him more than anyone else on staff.

Problem #10: He's Losing His Power

One day, the office that he oversaw in Sri Lanka closes. Or one of his big accounts walks. The man who used to count the zeros in his frequent flyer account is shuttled back to the home office with great fanfare. There's even a big bash to welcome him home. Suddenly, the great Wizard is around all the time, but now he's just twiddling his thumbs. During his frequent absences, others on staff took over his tasks and he practically delegated himself out of existence. Meanwhile, speculation has been ripening all along the grapevine that he'll be reassigned shortly, he's on his way out, or perhaps the man sitting in his office is a mirage and the real Wizard has already vanished.

Solution #10: Stay True to the Wizard, and Maybe You'll Be Promoted

Don't assume that the Wizard's globe-trotting prowess has given him one extra erg of staying power. This may well be the first time the Wizard has experienced genuine turbulence. He may hang on to his job, or he may crash and burn. But either way, it's a good idea for you to stay loyal to your boss. If he is reassigned, you'll have an excellent chance of being promoted (especially if it's with his blessing). If he ends up losing his job and you've proved your fealty, he may take you with him to his next company. (There are worse ways to get a raise.) Even if he ends up leaving and you really want to stay, you'll get credit for staying loyal to him in a difficult situation. So instead of fretting about your own fate, try to show some compassion for his. Do your best to shield the Wizard from gawking onlookers who may wonder how he's occupying his time now that he has absolutely nothing to do every day.

HOW THE WIZARD RISES TO POWER

Many companies have zero tolerance for Wizards. In other corporate environments, Wizards thrive. Clearly, conditions must be ripe for a Wizard to amass power and move up in the organization. Here are some of these special conditions:

- **GROWING PAINS.** After a gargantuan growth spurt, there aren't enough people around to do the work. People like the Wizard are manning multiple offices.
- **AN E-CENTRIC WAY OF DOING BUSINESS PREVAILS.** Staffers are used to having little face time with decision makers.
- **A TEAM-ORIENTED CULTURE.** While the Wizard is supposed to have the final say, he knows others will rise to the challenge when he's not around.
- **THE WHOLE COMPANY IS FAKING IT.** The company is in hot pursuit of a new growth area that few of its executives understand, and/or the Wizard has been promoted to a new area that he doesn't fully grasp.
- **ONE OR MORE OFFICES ARE IN TROUBLE.** A management shakeout, buyout, or merger might devastate a particular office in the network yet leave another office intact. While the Wizard's absenteeism wreaks havoc on the healthy office, upper management tolerates the disruption because they presume he is nursing the troubled office back to health. This may or may not prove to be the case.

The Golden Rule

Flying from office to office, the Wizard leaves a void in the day-to-day operations of the enterprise. Upper management may be empathetic for a spell but will inevitably turn on him as patience wears thin. Strive to fill the gap created by the Wizard's frequent departures, and you may be promoted to Wizard status soon.

CHAPTER 3
The Doddering Mascot

My boss looked like he was about one hundred years old. But he was a crafty old coot.

His impressive title is followed by a long Latinate word such as *emeritus*. Though furnished with burnished accents of mahogany, his palatial windowed office is one floor removed from where the real action is. He's at least a decade older than anyone else in the department. He may even sport some retro affectations, such as an old-fashioned way of speaking, or a charmingly eccentric unfamiliarity with cell phones, computers, and *Xerox* machines.

He can recount stories about the firm's glory days—before the merger, before the scandal, before it became a public company, before the company moved to its current location—that no one else on staff remembers. But is he fully present in the here and now?

He's a former chairman, CEO, CFO, or president whose golden parachute landed him an office where he continues to work every day. But in the grand bustle of your company's daily operations, he is but a tangent. When everyone around you believes the man to whom you report is irrelevant, what is your best strategy?

Problem #11: You Have to Report to Someone Everyone Else Ignores

The obscure projects he foists on you have zero impact on the bottom line. He'll tie you up for months on an initiative only he considers vitally pressing. (Under his tutelage, you've become resident expert on not-for-profit even though you work at a for-profit firm.) How will you ever gain exposure to others in top management when working for this boss makes you feel invisible?

Solution #11: Remember That No Man Is an Island

Even if your boss has a tiny fiefdom tucked away in a remote corner on the floor of the company known as "no-man's-land," he is not alone. His exalted status as corporate Mascot (doddering or otherwise) means that he is still in touch with some very powerful pinstripes in the corporation. You have no choice but to throw yourself into his projects with gusto and hope that, eventually, someone other than your boss might actually see one of them.

At the same time, recognize that the isolation you feel is real. Reporting to only one person whom others deem peripheral is not the fastest route to accolades and glory. Staffers probably won't notice your efforts without some intervention. And guess what? You're just the person to intervene!

Instead of worrying about how your boss doesn't circulate, think of it as your responsibility to let him in on the rumblings of the beehive. Bring him tidbits of information about what's going on elsewhere in the company and, when appropriate, ask him to get involved. These can range from minor pieces of gossip (you've heard that Tad's secretary hoards all of the envelopes of hot chocolate—who might one speak to about ordering more for the thirsty troops?) to much larger initiatives (you've heard that the team on the 19th floor has been working every weekend for two months straight—maybe your boss should investigate). Gently push your boss to take an active interest in a new project that you brought to his attention. You and your boss will both feel a lot more relevant.

Start small and see if he bites. Begin by feeding him small appetizers of information that affect only a few people in the company. If he nibbles, feed him larger morsels. Because he doesn't directly report to anyone, your boss is freer to get involved in many different projects, if he so chooses.

Problem #12: There Is No Clear Path for Your Own Promotion

Working for a Mascot is not the resumé builder that you had imagined. The man to whom you report is old enough to be your grandfather. You doubt that he's looking out for your future when his "glory days" were a distant memory long before you were born. There is no team directly under him. And if there is a corporate ladder, it's propped against a wall somewhere in a completely different department. For the pittance the company pays you, you may as well work in the mailroom (where at least you'd have more visibility.)

Solution #12: Stop Thinking in Terms of Corporate Ladders and Chart Your Own Destiny

Riddle: How are you supposed to climb from one rung to the next of the corporate ladder when corporate ladders have virtually disappeared at thousands of companies due to management shakeouts in recent years? It's really simple. You can't! It's time to conjure up a brand new model for career advancement, one involving leaps rather than steps.

It may be smart to spend a few years at your first job (just to prove you're remarkably stable) and then leap to a different job at the same company that can help you build different skill sets. After spending a few years there, you may need to leap again—this time to a completely different job outside of the company. Imagine that you are an architect with the task of custom-building your own career trajectory. Vow to learn as much as you possibly can from each stop along the way. But once your learning curve crashes into the *proverbial y-axis,* realize that it's time to make another leap to a brand-new job where you can master even more skills.

Feel like all of this leaping is going to require one gigantic Leap of Faith? Think in future tense. To envision your own career destiny, it helps to have an end destination in mind. Picture what you wish to be doing twenty years into the future, and then work backward to figure out precisely what you need to be doing today in order to get there. Always think in terms of skill development rather than titles, and you'll be happier with your progress.

Management Mantra

"I always wanted to be somebody, but I should have been more specific," said Lily Tomlin. If you can picture your ultimate career in your mind's eye, you are halfway there. So spend a few minutes each day fantasizing about the you that you wish to become. Athletes do it. Actresses do it. Even the author of this book does it. I hope someday you'll join us.

Problem #13: You're Not Doing the Job You Were Hired to Do

You finally landed your dream job, only to watch it fade faster than a dream upon waking. You thought that you had secured a high-level job projecting market forecasts. Instead, the work your boss has you doing is so clerical that you feel you should be paid overtime for all of your late nights. You've taken two immense steps backward—to the job you had before your last job. It's difficult traveling backward in time when everyone else seems to have a career that's moving ahead. Yikes. At this rate, you'll be back at college mopping the cafeteria floors for some extra spending money before long.

Solution #13: You're in a Gray Area: Try to Make It Less Gloomy

When you were hired, chances are no one handed you a formal job description on a piece of paper. (If someone did, hang on to it. It's your ticket out.) There is a looming gray area between how you and your boss both view your role. He doesn't agree that your talents are being squandered on clerical work. He's just delighted that *someone's* around to do it.

The best time to raise your concerns is during your yearly review. Dig for the facts. Find out if things work differently in other departments. Try to have some glowing emails about your performance with you, or better yet, real results to show for all of your hard work. Highlight all of the fabulous contributions you could make if you weren't saddled with so many clerical clunkers every day.

What if you encounter resistance? Break through the logjam by consulting the Negotiating Your Way through a Perilous Performance Review Standoff box.

NEGOTIATING YOUR WAY THROUGH A PERILOUS PERFORMANCE REVIEW STANDOFF

You see yourself as an executive. Despite all evidence to the contrary, your boss views you as a peon, merely half a step up from corporate grunt. Your clerical tasks outnumber your executive tasks by three to one.

Somehow, you manage to stay upbeat. You commit yourself to the tasks, no matter how menial. Your long-awaited performance review finally arrives. Armed with glowing reports about the fabulous job you've been doing, you politely tell your boss that, while grateful for this golden opportunity, you are capable of so much more.

He fixes you with a beady eye and says, "Keeping you mentally challenged is the least of my concerns. If you're not happy here, maybe you should consider resigning." Uh-oh. Now what? Here are some options:

- **BACKTRACK.** Say something non-threatening, such as, "This review isn't going the way I had hoped," and redirect the conversation. Instead of airing a long laundry list of grievances, focus on the one demeaning task you'd like to have removed from your plate.
- **APPEAL TO A DIFFERENT AUTHORITY.** Express gratitude for all of the things that you do enjoy about your job and leave the meeting on an upbeat note. Then, candidly raise the issue with someone in HR or a confidant in your own department. Hopefully, this person will be able to provide some insight about your boss that can help you change his mind later.
- **DROP IT.** Doing so is not a display of cowardice. You still may prevail. Once a gripe is "out there," it's out there. After your boss has had some time to digest your issue, he may end up agreeing with you after all.

Problem #14: Your Boss's Feedback Isn't Relevant

Every time you hear one of your boss's suggestions, you feel like it would have been a terrific idea thirty years ago, back when the character played by Mary Tyler Moore could "turn the world on with her smile." You want your boss to approve of what you're doing, but his ideas are so behind it that you feel like following them sends potential prospects the wrong message—one delivered on crinkly letterhead via snail mail.

Solution #14: Dig Hard for Kernels of Wisdom

Very senior bosses with ceremonial titles sometimes are caught in a time warp. That's no reason to write off their every suggestion. Amidst a slew of cornball ideas might be a pearl that will help secure the business, win the new account, or wow a prospect. So often it takes only one gem. Resolve to stay open to all ideas, no matter from where they germinate. And if a great one happens to spring from the lips of your Doddering Mascot, don't forget to shower him with some good, old-fashioned appreciation.

Problem #15: He Uses His Frailty to Manipulate You

When others in the company gang up against him, the Doddering Mascot starts to walk with a limp. He has selective hearing. Isn't it fascinating how he seems to hear only the good news? If it's humanly possible, his memory for facts and figures is even more selective. Are you the only one who's noticed that underneath that frail exterior is a tough, wiry man bent on getting his own way?

Solution #15: Stay Strong (and on His Good Side)

In a business world where mentors have disappeared even faster than training programs, a Mascot can be a terrific ally if you will only let him. Although his chain of command may not be apparent, just know that he wouldn't be around still if he weren't connected to someone pretty influential at the company.

Every boss has his peccadilloes. (For that matter, so do the rest of us mere mortals.) But unlike so many other types of bosses, you are not a direct threat to the Mascot. He's survived umpteen management changes; by now, he's entrenched. Since you can't take his job away from him, he has nothing to lose by helping you get ahead. Show tolerance for your Doddering Mascot's eccentricities rather than disdain, and resolve to learn as much as you can from him along the way. It only takes one good plug from a Mascot to propel your career onto a whole different path.

The Golden Rule

The Doddering Mascot has little to lose by helping you advance. Thus, he can make an excellent advocate for you. Strive to make your Doddering Mascot more relevant by bringing him into the buzzing of the office beehive. Nourish him with honey-coated gossip tidbits, and it may help forge a beeline to your own promotion.

CHAPTER 4
Good Cop/Bad Cop

My two bosses shared an office. I'm not entirely certain if they ever spoke to each other.

It's bad enough having one boss. But you have the unmitigated joy of reporting to two. You feel like a lowly tennis ball being smashed against the court of their egos.

"But Larry said..." you report to Stanley (when he gives you a completely different directive to follow).

"But Stanley said..." you meekly relay back to Larry.

Although both cops always seem mildly interested in what their counterpart thinks, the news flash never is enough to change their minds until several sets deep into the match.

Naturally, you get along with the Good Cop (Larry) better. He's the gracious one. The one who delivers those niceties that keep you employed in the first place—good news, morale-boosting pats on the back, and juicy plum assignments. The Bad Cop never delivers any good news and wears a permanent scowl on his scraggly face. Penurious with raises and promotions, he's not terribly popular.

How are you supposed to keep everything functioning smoothly when these two sparring partners are absolute geniuses at creating a climate of dysfunction?

Problem #16: The Good Cop Says "A," the Bad Cop Says "Z"; Then the Good Cop Says...

At the last meeting, they agreed to disagree. But they definitively agreed about one thing: the direction of the presentation would be either A or Z. Now the Good Cop has finally come around and agrees that it should be Z. But in the interim, the Bad Cop has also changed his mind and believes that it should be X. Head spinning, you're not entirely certain if X and Z are all that far apart.

The uncanny ability of both of your bosses to walk away from their own opinions so late in the game drives you and everyone else in the department bonkers. You feel like at least half of your job is acting as a translator between two people who happen to sit in offices that are right next door to each other. Can't these folks who get paid a gazillion dollars each make a darned decision?

Solution #16: Time to Blow the Whistle: Get Both Cops in the Room Now!

The Good Cop and the Bad Cop may seem like polar opposites, but in reality, they're on the same team. And because they're equal in rank and stature, it's imperative that you get along with both cops. Avoid taking sides in the tennis match that is their life by politely insisting on having meetings with both of them together in the same room and resolving to stay neutral. It's really hard to argue with a neutral stance. It's kept Finland out of trouble for years.

The Inner Workings of a Cop's Mind (Good or Bad)

When the Good Cop says "A," he knows that it is subject to change per the Bad Cop's instruction. So he has less invested in A than he would were he the only boss. Ditto for the Bad Cop. He may throw the occasional tantrum when his directives aren't met. But deep down, he knows that in order to survive, he and the Good Cop must share the power. Chaos ensues as the Good Cop and the Bad Cop change their minds like chameleons (but still manage to disagree with each other). The endless back-and-forth between each individual cop and various employees is acceptable to both cops, who, unable to joust each other out of power, derive a special joy from throwing their underlings off-kilter.

Problem #17: Code Yellow: The Bad Cop Stops Talking to You

You've always found the Bad Cop to be a bit scary. Maybe it's his habit of staring right through you with his gray, marbleized eyes—as if he wants you to confess to stealing the company pencils. Or maybe it's the way that he always seems to be in a rush even when the workload eases up. The guy never was a big schmoozer, which is why you're not precisely sure when it was that your boss stopped talking to you entirely. But now that he has, you feel rather anxious about it. He only seems to communicate messages to you via the Good Cop. What, if anything, should you read into the Bad Cop's mysterious silence?

Solution #17: Don't Hit the Panic Button; Do Take a Temperature Check

A lot of bad cops have some sort of financial role (making them look grumpy more often than not). Chances are, yours is mulling over something numerical that has nothing to do with you. But just in case he is, why not conduct a self-diagnostic?

Ask yourself how you think your performance has been. Have you scored any big sales lately? Closed any new business deals? Made any cold calls? Turned in your field reports in a timely manner? What about your time sheets? If you feel like your performance has been stellar, chances are you have nothing to worry about.

What if you realize that your job performance has been off, teetering between mediocre and flat as an ironing board? In that case, you're better off using your precious time to mull over what you can do to improve your track record. Can you take a prospect to lunch? Write a killer research report? Tweak a new business plan? Redo the window display to attract new business? Rewrite the buggy code? In short, what can you do within the next twenty-four hours to dazzle the Bad Cop and shake him out of his financial woes?

How to Sell Yourself to Your Superiors

Self-complimenting is an art, one best practiced when business is booming. Here are some techniques employed by the world's savviest self-promoters.

- **RIDE THE ELEVATORS WITH AN AGENDA.** When your boss casually asks how you are doing, use your shining moment under the fluorescent glare to share something extraordinary about yourself. "I redesigned the company website," you might say, "and three clients have already told me how much they like it."
- **DRIVE YOURSELF.** CEOs work an average of sixty hours a week. Start building up your stamina. Volunteer for a new project the nanosecond another one ends. Don't lose any sleep about the toll it will take on your R&R. By the time your boss finds a new initiative worthy of your talents, you will feel well rested enough to tackle the assignment. It's never too early to begin grooming yourself for CEO.
- **HAVE GOOD NEWS? SPREAD THE WEALTH.** Have you closed a deal? Secured a contract? Signed on a new customer? Received the green light from an investor? Share your happy tidings. Scout for one-on-one PR opportunities in the hallways, at the vending machine, or in the men's room if you're a guy. (Women, take note: the ladies' room is *not* an okay place to promote yourself. In this regard, the sexes are separate but not equal.)
- **ADOPT YOUR BOSSES' MODUS OPERANDI.** The Good Cop and Bad Cop have very different styles of communication. To the extent that

you can, try to mime each cop's style and spit it right back to him. Is the bad cop a heavy emailer? Why not email him your good news? Is the Good Cop more of a people person? Leaving him chipper voicemails may help signal you're a people person too.

- **ALIGN YOURSELF WITH YOUR BOSSES' SECRET DREAMS AND ASPIRATIONS.** Beneath the fancy titles and the intense jockeying for positions of power, everyone on the planet just wants to be appreciated. When boasting of your own accomplishments, think of ways that your bosses can take your success and promote it to their higher-ups. Be the bearer of good news. You might stop one of your bosses at the water cooler and say, "The client just told me the new initiative was the best one she's seen from our department yet." (Worried that your boss will steal all your credit? *See* Chapter 8, *The Credit Snatcher.*)
- **BETTER EYE CONTACT IS THE SECRET OF BETTER *YOU* CONTACT.** Don't look away or off to the side when promoting your achievements, or your boss may conclude that you're not particularly proud of your performance. After all of your hard work, that would be devastating.

Problem #18: The Good Cop Stops Talking to You

The Good Cop is your ally, mentor, champion, beloved boss, and quite possibly the only reason you look forward coming to work. So naturally it stings when you feel like he is ignoring you. After a few days of the silent treatment, your tendency is to hunt him down to ask what's wrong. But that would be *très* unprofessional.

Solution #18: Focus on the Work, Not on Your Boss's Mood Swings

The fastest way to get back on your boss's radar is by bringing a new idea to his attention. Your presentation can be an elaborate proposal that you've spent weeks researching or a seemingly spontaneous suggestion tossed out during the Monday 8:30 staff meeting. Much will depend on the corporate culture at your office.

Two things to bear in mind: even if your suggestion seems off-the-cuff, it's helpful to back it up with some facts. For example, you might say, "Reaching young, single mothers is important to the effort. That's why I came up with a cool premium idea. What about ultra-hip diaper bags?"

Build group support for your idea with language that encourages cooperation such as, "If I can pull together a quick mommy poll to see if the idea has traction, would you be willing to run some numbers?" Give your boss a stake in your ideas whenever possible. Use phrases like, "I followed your suggestion to…" "I'd love your take on…" and "Together, I feel we can…" Dare to be innovative.

Occasionally, ask both cops for feedback on your performance. This will inspire them to think of themselves as your mentors. Approach each separately and say, "I know my formal review is several months away, but I was wondering if you could give me some informal feedback. How do you think I'm doing?" Then follow their suggestions for improvement. Although it might be more difficult to have these heart-to-hearts with the churlish Bad Cop, if you do succeed in winning him over, then your job will really be secure.

Problem #19: You're the Lowly Go-Between

If the Good Cop were an American president, he would conduct a poll before making every decision. He's an appeaser. He panders to people both inside and outside of the department. The Good Cop is a total wuss, albeit a popular one. The Bad Cop is a fighter. Cold, calculating, and persnickety, he doesn't mind a heated debate over a worthwhile cause. It's a pity the Bad Cop's viewpoint often diverges radically from the rest of the team's, and it's your job to find the middle ground.

Solution #19: Aim for Closure over Consensus

Abraham Lincoln once said, "You can't fool all of the people all of the time." You can't please them all, either. Sometimes that means displeasing one cop or the other. (And we all know which cop that's likely to be.) But if you can please both cops most of the time, you're doing just fine. Your primary job is to glean a direction that's acceptable to top management, close out on both cops' ability to weigh in and make last-minute changes, and crack the proverbial whip so everyone can get out of the office and take showers before morning. Gather just enough input from both cops to make an informed decision for yourself, and follow that direction until told otherwise.

Problem #20: The Good Cop Promises You a Raise; The Bad Cop Begs to Differ

"No raises this year, sorry," the Bad Cop says, solemnly shaking his head back and forth during your performance review just two weeks after the Good Cop promised you a raise. You feel torn between the desire to strangle your stingy boss (surely you'd get out in a few years for good behavior) and the equally strong desire to hightail it to a local pub where you can drown your sorrows.

Solution #20: Casually Snoop Around

Stay calm. Ask the Bad Cop to reiterate why you are not getting a raise. If he doesn't mention anything performance-related on your end, work out a timeline with him for when you can expect the money. Don't be shy about pinning him to both a number—5%, 10%, 12%—and the month it will become effective. Factor in the present value of money to compensate for what you are not receiving now. Then ask your boss to commit your future raise to paper. He can scribble it directly in the section of your performance review document that asks for his comments. If he does surface any performance issues, work out an action plan to turn them around. Endeavor to tie all improvements on your end to a raise within the next few months.

Now it's time for some detective work. With the studied nonchalance of TV sleuth Lieutenant Columbo, ask others in your department if they managed to secure raises. If one or two of them did, circle back to the Good Cop and ask him what's going on. Perhaps the company is about to make some cuts and your name surfaced. If so, it's even more important for you to negotiate some sort of a raise in the very near future. During company retrenchments, HR will be asked to suggest possible layoff candidates. And the very first names that will top that grim list will be those who did not receive raises. After narrowly escaping the ax this time around, you don't want your name to come up a second time for consideration.

When layoffs are in the air, negotiating a small raise three to six months down the road could save your job. The fact that you're up for a raise will be documented in your paperwork, making it harder for the company to justify cutting you from staff.

The Golden Rule

The Good Cop and Bad Cop are symbols of a dysfunctional organization. The structure allows them to get away with never having to make a firm decision. You won't be able to please both of them all of the time; so once in a while, be certain to side with the less popular but more financially astute Bad Cop.

CHAPTER 5
The Management Junkie

Our boss sent us to so many management retreats that we didn't have any time left over to get our real work done.

He graduated from a school that starts with the letter *H*—either Harvard Business School or, ironically, the school of Hard Knocks. Since graduation, he's made it his mission on earth to read every single management manual out there. He has memorized not merely seven but more than seventy spiritual laws of success that he is keen to share with his people.

He is process-oriented rather than results-focused. He's a person who believes deeply in creativity, innovation, and continuous improvement—to a fault. Your boss is the management equivalent of a serial dieter.

Whether it's subjecting his people to a retreat where they can spend the weekend crafting mission statements or forcing them to endure yet another management consultant's exercises for group betterment, your boss believes not only that change is good but also in change for change's sake.

Problem #21: Those Pesky Mission Statements

How many ways can you write, "To have fun and prosper"? You scratch your head, then put pen to paper. "To have a good time and profit." "To be more productive and innovative." "To innovate, percolate, and speculate"... Wait a second. It rhymes, but is it English? Your boss is putting your vocabulary to the test at the third outing in less than a year whose only mission is to craft a mission statement that will inspire the troops. Your own ambitions aren't nearly as lofty. You just hope that *this* retreat will get your boss off of his perennial mission-statement kick once and for all.

Solution #21: Dispense with the Hypothetical: Set Up a Problem-Solving Lab

Long-range planning sessions are meaningless if their sole purpose is to arrive at mission statement poetry. If that's what the boss wants, you are far better off finding the best writer on staff and having that person spend a few hours crafting three uplifting sentences. The more people who touch a mission statement, the more disjointed it will become, devolving into corporate gobbledygook that inspires no one. Writing by committee rarely works wonders (although the Constitution of the United States was one notable exception).

One key question to ponder: what can you do during an off-campus meeting that will inspire fellow staffers to greatness once they return? Use the time away from the office to focus on *real* problems.

Try setting up a problem-solving think tank that's not simply an exercise in futility. Have members of each department brainstorm about what their biggest problem is, and then hand over that problem to a completely different department to solve. The management information systems department might be very creative when it comes to solving the research department's issues.

Add a gaming aspect to your retreat to make it more fun. Perhaps all winners can win a trinket such as a company T-shirt, while losers have to write conference reports about the experience. Rule #1 (no exceptions): attendees are not allowed to weigh in about problems plaguing their own departments. Rule #2: silence is golden. Ask everyone to pretend they are in a virtual cone of silence. If they speak out while their department's issues are being addressed by a different team, they will be automatically disqualified.

Problem #22: A Consultant Comes A-knocking

In the grand pecking order of the Management Junkie's universe, consultants are far more exalted than full-time staff members. No matter if their ideas have nothing to do with the business model your company is pursuing. (That makes their ideas fresh.) The consultant's outsider status is the very thing that gives him clout in your boss's eyes.

Solution #22: Give Him Your Secret Password

You can't work for a Management Junkie for very long without encountering a score of different consultants, all of whom will have plenty of ideas for improvement. Try to remember that it is not the consultant's fault that your boss is addicted to consulting. The consultant hasn't been around during the past three incarnations of change. (No, that was a different consultant. Or was it two? They're all a blur.) You and the rest of the department may be jaded, but he isn't.

It's worth trying to befriend the consultant, because at the end of his long list of exercises to improve the group dynamic, he's only human. He's less likely to fault your own contributions if you make an overture of kindness. When he requests access to company goals, income and expense reports, sales figures, and conference reports, don't roll your eyes at him or act territorial. Recognize that you have a choice: you can make his life a living hell by denying him access to all of the reports he will eventually locate anyway or you can direct him to the information he needs.

Give him the password to your computer already, and tell him the location of the files! Cooperate, and he'll be far more inclined to treat you with leniency.

Just the Stats

A mission statement is a brief (four sentences or less) description of the company's organizational purpose. Typically, it explains what the organization provides to its clients but is not an advertising slogan.

Problem #23: There's a Reorganization (Again)

After promises to the contrary, your boss has decreed there will be yet another department reorganization. "No one will be let go," you are all informed, "but there will be some shuffling."

Everyone needs to move offices to be even closer to the people with whom they already work every single day. This causes massive angst from department to department, as some departments improve their real estate (bigger windows, bigger offices, more floor space) while others are moved to the wrong side of the men's room. Chaos rules as phone lines are switched and important documents are packed. Everyone is asked to meet with their new boss and teammates, a directive that some follow and others blithely ignore. The buzz in the hallways has nothing to do with new business, profits, or productivity. It's all about who's sitting where and the view, or lack thereof.

Solution #23: Create a Transition Team

Reorganizations are like surgery. They should not be undertaken frivolously. Even the most carefully planned reorganization will create ripples of discontent among some employees who will feel "burned." Why not set up a Transition Team to get back to business as usual? The Transition Team's job is to support HR. While the Transition Team won't be able to solve any of the underlying issues, it can help with some of the more routine dislocations.

The Transition Team divides and conquers, either via floor or department by department. Ask one member of the Transition Team to circle around to each person who has moved. Give each member of the team a clipboard, a checklist, and specific people to broach.

Start with the basics: Is the new phone working? What about the computer? Has the employee been able to locate all of his electronic files? Has he mastered the code to the men's room on the new floor? Does he have a key to his new office? Is there enough light in the room for him to do his work? Is his new chair ergonomically correct? Has he met with his new department head? Does he have enough work to keep him busy?

Each member of the Transition Team should complete the checklist and then turn over the paperwork to the team leader (to brief HR on who needs what). If priority is given to settling the lower-level people in the company before their managers, it will foster more goodwill overall.

Management Mantra

"The highest result of education is tolerance." Helen Keller uttered this lofty sentiment. You may not agree with your boss's obsession to reorganize, but compared to other boss peccadilloes, this one is (relatively) tolerable.

REORGANIZATIONS, MERGERS, AND TAKEOVERS—OH, MY!

There are numerous reasons a company might reorganize. Here are 16 common ones:

1. Become more customer-centric
2. Focus more on core businesses
3. Part of overall growth plan
4. Part of massive retrenchment
5. Merger
6. Takeover (hostile or otherwise)
7. Downsizing
8. Joint venture
9. Response to local and national economic forces
10. Response to competition (*e.g.*, local, national, global, Internet)
11. Desire to compete on worldwide stage
12. CEO or other visionary in company stepping down
13. Bad press—due to poor earnings, lower-than-anticipated profits, irate shareholders, or scandal
14. Lawsuit—involving either one key player or a class-action suit
15. Bankruptcy, requiring restructuring
16. A Management Junkie is in power

Problem #24: Layoffs Are in the Air

You heard a rumor a week ago that someone was fired down in accounting. And you always figured the back office was the safest place to work in your company! Before your boss has a chance to pull you aside and warn you about the impending bloodbath, you've heard that a big layoff is coming and twenty-five heads are going to roll. Even though the news is supposedly *top secret*, for some reason, the mailroom guy knows who's on the dreaded List. Names of potential victims circulate like wildfire.

Solution #24: Hold on to Your Hat

Don't panic. Doing so will set off panic vibes among your coworkers. Your only job for the foreseeable future is to hang on to your job. To do so, you will need a strategy. Try to figure out if you're on The List by quietly asking your boss or mentor. If he tells you that you're *not* on The List, work hard to maintain a high profile at the office.

Keep your head down, your door open, and your cell phone on vibrate. (You don't want to give the appearance that you're contacting headhunters, even if you are.) Recognize that The List will change dramatically several times before the final victims learn their fates, and that your boss may not actually know yours. This is the moment to make sure that you are adding value to the company. And that's impossible to do if you're holed up behind closed doors gossiping with the rest of the gang.

If someone asks you what you've heard, look her in the eye and say, "Absolutely nothing." Then get back to your work as quickly as possible. Don't be a rumor monger. Avoid the gossip swill.

THIRTEEN SIGNS THAT YOUR JOB IS ON THE LINE

Lucky thirteen. Here are some of the common warning signs to watch for as a heads-up. These thirteen signs suggest that rather than being paranoid about your fate, you are merely being realistic:

1. The receptionist is suddenly missing.
2. The annual company Christmas party or summer picnic is eliminated.
3. Work slows down and everyone around you is leaving the office every day at 4 o'clock.
4. Instead of a year-end bonus, your company announces that the office will be closed for an extra week over the holidays.
5. There is a hiring freeze in your organization.
6. All management seminars are put on hold.
7. There is a new company travel policy announced: "DON'T."
8. When clients come to the office, you are ordered *not* to order food.
9. People who never inquire about your whereabouts suddenly need an hourly accounting of your time.
10. HR managers mysteriously have their time cut back to three days a week.
11. Someone with whom you rarely interact asks if you'd ever consider transferring to a different company location far away from where you live, say, Detroit.
12. You spot a couple of people in the copying center crying hysterically.
13. Every time you pass your boss in the hallway, he scrunches his face and looks down at the floor.

Problem #25: Make-Work

You've attended more management seminars than an MBA. In group exercises mandated by the company, everyone completes one another's sentences. (You think this is called "group think" but you're not sure. Why? What does the group think?) Your presentation was even videotaped so that you can view it every day in the privacy of your office—just to see what you're doing *wrong*. When will it all end so that you can get back to the work?

Solution #25: Look at the Bright Side: You're Being Trained for Free

Think of the many skills that you can cite on your resumé, and be happy. Your future employer can't fail to be impressed that you have this training (plus relieved he won't have to pay for it). Remember that one person's boring management seminar is another person's exciting junket. So go buy a pair of rose-colored sunglasses, and imagine that the crowded business hotel lobby with the lousy coffee and stale cheese Danishes is located on a sunny beach somewhere near the south of France. Hey, it's a junket.

The Golden Rule

The Management Junkie is a true believer and the management manual of the day is his bible. You may not learn a thing from the countless exercises that will aid you in your current position. But management seminars, mission retreats, and public-speaking courses will add luster and depth to your resumé.

CHAPTER 6
The Predator

At my company, employees had to take a sexual harassment written test. If you didn't score an 85 or higher, you were out.

He's "happily married," has between 2.5 and 5.5 kids, and has stalked you from your very first day at the job. His comments on your outfits are so inappropriate as to be almost humorous. His eyes fix on one part of your body with unerring regularity. And while studies show that everyone thinks about sex once every eight minutes, he actually has the nerve to talk about it every seven.

You feel like screaming, "Hello? Everyone can hear you." But he's already aware of that. Truth is, he enjoys goading you. It's part of what makes coming to work so stimulating for him. And you're expected to report to this man, preserving a professional, upbeat demeanor, no matter what he says or does.

When the person to whom you report behaves like a lust-crazed schoolkid, what is your best move?

Problem #26: He Creates a Climate of Sexual Harassment

It's an open secret that he takes certain out-of-town clients to strip clubs. There's a pinup calendar on his office wall displaying heavily retouched, scantily clad women on motorcycles. Every guy who works under him has perfected a stand-up routine of off-color jokes, which you've been subjected to over and over again. On a scale of one to ten, the harassment level at the office is over the top.

Solution #26: Document It

If you feel victimized by what's known as "Hostile Work Environment Harassment," begin documenting evidence of it. Use your cell phone camera to snap photos of those pinup calendars. Take notes on any conversations that embarrassed you, and be sure to date them. Start keeping a harassment diary. Hostile Work Environment Harassment is more subjective than other forms of sexual harassment and sometimes difficult to prove.

Definition of Hostile Work Environment Harassment

When an employee is subjected to comments of a sexual nature, unwelcome physical contact, or offensive sexual materials as a regular part of the work environment, that environment is deemed to be *hostile*. Generally, one isolated incident is not enough to prove a hostile environment unless it is coupled with egregious, outrageous conduct. The courts will determine if the conduct is serious and frequent. When confronted with conflicting evidence as to "welcomeness," the E.E.O.C. (Equal Employment Opportunity Commission) will review the record as a whole and the totality of the circumstances, evaluating each on a case-by-case basis.

Problem #27: He Says Something Inappropriate

Your boss is the antithesis of subtle. He says, "Hi, Beautiful," whenever you pass him in the hallway instead of calling you by your name. Walk into a conference room where every chair is taken, and he'll say something suggestive such as, "Come sit on my lap." His jocular delivery makes everyone else in the department crack an indulgent smile at your expense. But the *last* thing you care to do is indulge him.

Solution #27: Express Your Discomfort

Tell the harasser that his advances are unwelcome, and don't be mealy-mouthed about it. If you are firm, that's often enough incentive to have him direct his attentions elsewhere. For example, you might request a meeting with him, and say, "I feel demeaned when you make these lurid comments. It's negatively affecting my productivity, and furthermore, it's against the law."

If one conversation won't dissuade him, broach the topic again. But if you feel like you keep raising the topic to no avail, it's time to file a grievance. Start with HR—unless your company has a specific grievance committee, in which case, start there.

The Lowdown on Sexual Harassment

Sexual harassment is a form of sex discrimination that violates Title VII of the Civil Rights Act of 1964. Title VII applies to employers with fifteen or more employees and includes state and local governments. (Check out the E.E.O.C. website for more information.)

Unwelcome sexual advances, requests for sexual favors, and other verbal or physical conduct of a sexual nature are considered sexual harassment when the conduct explicitly or implicitly affects an individual's employment, unreasonably interferes with an individual's performance, or creates an intimidating, hostile, or offensive work environment. The key word in the preceding sentence is *unwelcome*. The advances must be unwelcome to be deemed harassment.

The victim does not necessarily have to be the person harassed but could be anyone affected by the offensive conduct.

Just the Stats

According to the E.E.O.C. website, 12,025 charges of sexual harassment were filed in the United States during 2006. Of these, men filed only 15.4% of the grievances. In the United Kingdom, men were harassed more often, at least according to a 2006 government study showing that two out of five, or 40%, of sexual harassment victims were male. According to a 2007 study in Hong Kong, one-third of sexual harassment victims were men targeted by female supervisors. In the U.S., sexual harassment is also big business. In 2006, the E.E.O.C. recovered $48.8 million in monetary benefits for charging parties and other aggrieved individuals (not including the monetary benefits obtained through litigation).[3]

Problem #28: Quid Pro Quo: You Do This for Me, and I'll Do That for You

You had your eye on the position for months. But management, in its collective wisdom, handed it to the bespectacled junior with nonexistent people skills. Furious, you stride into your boss's office and demand to know why you were bypassed. "My reviews have been fantastic," you remind him, ticking off your accomplishments. "I created the 'profitability scorecard' idea that brought in the XYZ franchise. What has Herbie done lately? How could you promote him over me?"

"Let's discuss it over dinner tonight," your boss says with a sadistic wink. Or perhaps he promises you a raise for sleeping with him. Or a window office for…well, you get the basic idea.

Solution #28: Start Thinking Like a Lawyer

According to E.E.O.C. guidelines, "in investigating sexual harassment charges, it is important to develop detailed evidence of the circumstances and nature of any such complaints or protests, whether to the alleged harasser, higher management, coworkers, or others." You might have a case if you can prove any of the following:

- Your supervisor made unwelcome advances towards you.
- Your supervisor implied that if you didn't acquiesce, it would have an adverse affect on your job status.
- You say "no" to his advances, and your supervisor retaliates by demoting you.

Problem #29: The Female Harasser

She's a cougar preying on you like a kitten. The woman has mood lighting in her office that is more appropriate for a date than a meeting. First, your boss invents excuses to put you on those tasks she directly supervises. Then she finds reasons to *keep* you working on them with her after hours. During these sessions, she has the unwelcome habit of removing imaginary pieces of lint from your lapel (or even, sometimes, from your hair).

"Don't you think we make a great team?" she whispers.

Solution #29: Forgo the Mixed Message: Send a Clear "No"

Say it loud, say it clear, and repeat as often as necessary. If your boss's advances are unwelcome, tell her so in no uncertain terms. The gravamen of a sexual harassment case is that the alleged sexual advance must be unwelcome!

Management Mantra

"No" means no. Many sexual predators fool themselves into believing that "no" means "yes," but in a court of law, "no" means no such thing. Say "no" like you mean no.

Problem #30: The Group Turns against You

When you walk down the hallway, the sounds of their whispers reverberate off the walls. You feel ostracized by the female members of your department. Several months ago, you complained to someone in HR about your boss's lewd behavior and sexually charged comments. Since then, your boss has kept his distance, maintaining a chilly if professional stance. But the frigid response of the women to your case was something you never anticipated. None of these women stop by your office anymore just to chitchat. And you were guaranteed "no retribution" for speaking out!

Solution #30: Request a Transfer to Another Department

The situation has turned toxic, and sometimes it's better to purge the toxicity rather than allowing it to fester. As in cases of rape or sexual assault, the victim sometimes becomes the accused, with her character likely to fall under intensive scrutiny or group attack. Ask for a transfer.

Although it's incredibly unfair that your boss's bad behavior has forced you to leave, under these conditions, you can't get your work done. Requesting a transfer at this point might even help you prove your case. After all, your boss's conduct has unreasonably interfered with your performance.

As with every other aspect of proving sexual harassment, clear documentation is crucial. Don't allow your case to devolve into a finger-pointing exercise of He-Said, She-Said. If you have to request a transfer, line up your reasons.

Keep it professional. Wear attire to the office that sends the right message. Don't hobnob with your colleagues until all hours of the morning. You may not be able to oust a Predator, but you needn't be his target.

The Golden Rule

Due to stringent laws against sexual harassment, it is more difficult for the Predator to survive at the workplace than it was in years past. Many harassers can be tamed by the frequent and firm repetition of the word "no." Courts deem harassment to have occurred when an advance is unwelcome. As in any court case, clear documentation is crucial.

CHAPTER 7
The Inherited Boss

I've been here for seven years and had seven different bosses. Honestly, it's felt like seven different jobs.

In hindsight, it wasn't a total shock. Like storm clouds gathering on the horizon, there were multiple signs your career forecast wouldn't remain sunny forever. You spotted the first black cloud months ago. That was the day your boss, a man who always touted the open-door policy, was behind closed doors for almost six hours. When his door finally opened, two men whom you had never seen before emerged wearing matching frowns.

Several weeks unfurled without incident: the calm before the storm. Then, just a few weeks ago, you overheard two V.P.s in the ladies' room discussing "the impending management shakeout"—until they realized there was someone in the stall next door. That shut them up fast!

Last week, the sky turned pitch black. Your boss summoned you into his office, where you noticed a collection of large cardboard boxes, all neatly packed and marked to be shipped to his home address. He said, "It was really nice working with you. I wish you lots of luck." Merely one day later, everyone on staff started accusing him of screwing up big time. Amidst group gripes about how terrible your old boss was, you barely noticed your new boss's arrival. But stealthily he moved in and has already held several secret meetings with cronies from his old office in his new, windowed abode.

Problem #31: He Was Given a Mandate to Make Sweeping Changes

His reputation precedes him. At his last firm, he single-handedly axed 30% of the staff. Watercooler wags claim that even those who managed to survive his reign of terror despise him. According to interoffice scuttlebutt, he's already decided to eliminate the entire research department. (Anecdotal research predicts this will make him most unpopular.)

Solution #31: Start a Campaign to Save Your Job

Imagine that you are interviewing for a new job. The job you are pursuing is *a lot* like your old job. It pays exactly the same amount. The accommodations are identical. The tasks are all the same.

How would you sell your interviewer (otherwise known as your new boss) on hiring you? That's what you need to do now. You could prepare a report on your accomplishments. You could bolster that report with emails from satisfied customers. You could insert charts showing that since your arrival, sales growth soared. Or, depending on your company's corporate culture, you could give an oral report covering exactly the same material.

Gather your facts and figures and pie charts. Then, arrange a time to sit down with your new boss to take him through the killer report that will help you save your old job.

BRAND-NEW BOSS? TREAT IT LIKE IT'S A BRAND-NEW JOB

When a new boss arrives on staff from outside the company, the biggest mistake you can make is not recognizing that your job could be in jeopardy. Years of glowing performance reviews in your dossier will not necessarily save you. In fact, they might have the opposite effect, frightening a boss who's insecure.

New bosses often have the power to make dramatic, sweeping changes. Regardless of how long you've worked at the company, you will need to pay your dues all over again and treat your old job as if it's a brand-new one. Here are seven survival tips:

1. **STAY LATE AT THE OFFICE.** Hang around after hours. Don't feel shy about working even super late—until you scope out the new boss's daily rhythms. Is he an early riser? You'll never know unless you arrive early once in a while to see if he's there.
2. **DON'T APPEAR OVERLY ATTACHED.** Politely distance yourself from your old boss, the outgoing regime, or any particular clique. The new boss will be scanning the hallways, seeking allies. Make it easy for him to find one: you.
3. **BE CORDIAL WITHOUT BEING CLOYING.** Use phrases like "good morning," "good afternoon," and "let me hold that door for you." Avoid syrupy phrases like, "That's the nicest tie I've ever seen. What are those, miniature tennis rackets?"
4. **BE POSITIVE BUT NOT POLLYANNAISH.** If the new boss asks about your experience at the firm, frame your response as positively as possible. It's fine to mention certain organizational hiccups such as management changes. But do your best to look forward. Talk about what you hope to accomplish under your new boss's guidance rather than dwelling on the past.

5. **DON'T DAMN ANYONE.** That is, unless they've already left the company. The person who you bad-mouth today could end up getting promoted under the new regime. (Damn!)

6. **MEET AND GREET.** If the new boss doesn't seek you out to chat about life at the company, wait two weeks. Then schedule an appointment with his personal assistant to stop by and introduce yourself.

7. **BE THERE.** Make yourself available to answer any questions he may have. Keep your door (and mind) open.

Above all, recognize that it is profoundly human to want to be around those who enjoy our companionship. If you like your new boss, it's entirely likely that he'll like you back. When it comes to staffing decisions, likability trumps pure talent. Strive hard to be well liked by your new boss and you'll have a better shot of hanging onto your job. Chemistry rules.

Problem #32: He Gives You False Information

The new boss distinctly told you that his focus would be on the second-quarter results. So you felt like the office punching bag in the Monday-morning staff meeting when he socked you with twenty questions about the first-quarter results. You may have hemmed, hawed, and sputtered, but you certainly hope your points were clear!

Solution #32: Don't Take Him at His Word

He set you up to take a fall. And boy, did you fall for it. *SPLAT*. That was the sound of your ego hitting the floor. Still, there is nothing to be gained from confronting him about it. This probably wasn't the first time the man has ever fibbed; and chances are, it won't be his last. So pick up your crushed ego off the floor, and resolve to be overprepared the next time. If he claims that he's only interested in second-quarter results, make a mental note: that *means* first quarter, second quarter, third quarter, and fourth quarter.

Problem #33: He Accuses You of Doing Something That You Didn't

You return from your meeting aglow. The client loved the presentation. Several hours later, the new boss (who wasn't in the meeting) summons you into his office and closes the door. Fixing you with an authoritative stare, he clears his throat and says, "I understand the meeting this afternoon didn't go so well. The client felt put off by your _________." (Fill in the blank with "tone," "manner," or "aggressive stance.") After heated denials on your end (you couldn't have been more of a pussycat), your boss basically slaps your wrist. "Just be aware of it, okay?" he says with a withering look.

Solution #33: Defend Your Territory, but Update Your Resumé

A new boss can sometimes seem like a landlord. Every time he saunters by your humble office, he's looking at it as the future residence for someone *other* than you. He may have earmarked it for one of his allies from his last place of employment. But if you've been a steady performer and a good neighbor, getting along with peers and coworkers, the new boss may find it surprisingly difficult to oust you. Still, you should strive to think three chess moves ahead and anticipate that he may try.

One tactic some new bosses use with varying effectiveness is the false accusation. Unfortunately, you can't assume that your esteemed colleagues who attended the meeting will necessarily leap to your defense. Determining the upshot of a particular meeting is often a subjective call, and even staunch supporters of yours may be open to suggestion if your boss implies that the client really wasn't pleased.

If your boss falsely accuses you of anything, take it as a clear signal that he wants you out. Circle around to your allies, shore up your defenses, and mentally prepare for an all-out attack on your credibility. If you happen to have a good relationship with the client, take her out to dinner. (Keep mum about the boss's agenda unless you know the client really well and trust her with confidential information.) If you haven't already done so, update your resumé with your latest and greatest accomplishments. You may be fighting to keep your job. But you can still be proactive about looking for one at the same time.

Resumé fashions change. Is yours on trend? These days, executive summaries are the resumé accessory du jour with the six-figure set. But keep those summaries short and punchy. Make sure they don't repeat the same information word for word that's found elsewhere on your resumé. (That's a real resumé fashion faux pas.) Have you been in your field for under ten years? The one-page resumé is still hotter than hot. If you've been working in your field for over ten years, stick with the classic one or two-page resumé.

Problem #34: He's Interviewing People to Replace You

The reception area is clogged with a steady stream of unfamiliar people, all dressed up with someplace to go: a job interview in your new boss's office. Glancing at so many hopeful faces makes you feel panicky. You imagine that soon you'll be one of them—sitting in the reception area of a completely different company, waiting to be interviewed by a brand-new boss.

Solution #34: Don't Jump to Conclusions: Do Your Homework

Appearances can be deceiving. Your company could be expanding, in which case your boss may need to hire two or three people at your level. That said, if you notice a long line of new hires camped out day after day, you owe it to yourself to find out what's going on.

It's all in the way you ask. Slip into the role of the Agatha Christie sleuth, Miss Marple. Drop by your friendly HR department. Find the person there with whom you get along best, and simply inquire. You might say, "I've noticed a lot of interviewees waiting to meet with Mark every day. Is he intending to expand the department?" (Don't worry that your question will come off as too prying. Any HR person will understand the reason you're asking. And if she considers herself one of your allies, she'll tell you the inside scoop.)

Listen closely to what she relays. (She may need to answer your query in a guarded, politically correct way.) If she says, "Mark *has* told us that he considers you a tremendous asset to the company," you should feel confident that your job isn't on the line. If, on the other hand, she says, "I'm glad you took the initiative, Patty. Mark *has* expressed some concerns about you," then you have every right to feel insecure. Your job could be in jeopardy (see Problem-Solution Box #35).

Management Mantra

Be extremely subtle, even to the point of formlessness. Be extremely mysterious, even to the point of soundlessness. Thereby you can be the director of the opponent's fate.

—Sun Tzu, *The Art of War*

Problem #35: You're Put on Probation

One morning three months into his reign, your new boss asks you to join him in his windowed office palace. "I'm afraid I've got some bad news," he says, biting his lower lip. He closes the door and motions for you to sit across from him on the rickety, uncomfortable guest chair. An insurmountable obstacle stretches between the two of you in the form of a large, intimidating mahogany desk. "Your performance hasn't been up to snuff," he begins. "You haven't brought in any new business. And furthermore, I haven't been particularly impressed with your work product." He peers over the top of his rimless glasses at you, making you feel as small and insignificant as a bug. Beads of sweat coagulate under your armpits. You wonder what the company policy manual says about employees who are moved to vomit in their new boss's face. "You've got two weeks to turn it around," he continues, "or else, I'm afraid, we'll have to let you go."

Solution #35: Fight the Good Fight

It's usually worth trying to fight to save your job—even if you despise your boss, detest the working conditions, and perceive that there is no real future for you at the firm. It's always easier to find a new job when you already have one. With only a few short weeks to turn around the situation, you may as well throw yourself into the effort 100%. And, while you may be sorely tempted, looking for a new job once you're on probation is actually *not* a good idea. Better to salvage your old job and *then* look for employment. See the How to Save Your Job box for your best job-salvaging Hail Mary moves. Pursue them all simultaneously, and pray for a miracle.

How to Save Your Job: The Twelve Best Hail Mary Moves of All Time

First, wipe away your tears of frustration and have a moment-of-truth meeting with yourself. The situation is dire and calls for drastic measures. You will need to step waaaaaay out of your comfort zone to have a shot of salvaging your job. And even if you follow all of these suggestions, there are no guarantees. Still, every day in corporate America some plucky soul dodges a bullet. You may be able to as well.

1. **CONTACT HR IF HR DOESN'T CONTACT YOU FIRST.** Debrief. Pretend that you are a court reporter. Tell the HR manager *exactly* what your boss said. Repeat verbatim how you responded. This is a vital first step so that you, your boss, and the HR department will all be on the same page of corporate letterhead through this grueling process.

2. **CIRCLE BACK TO YOUR BOSS AND EXTRACT A PROMISE.** You want him to guarantee that if you successfully turn around the situation within the allotted time period, then he'll recommend to HR that you stay at the company.

3. **ONCE YOUR BOSS VERBALLY AGREES TO POINT 2, RETURN TO HR** (yes, a second time). Be certain the HR manager knows that you and your boss have had this second conversation about your status. Then commit the conversation you had with your boss to email, copying both the HR manager and your boss.

4. **RESOLVE ALL CONFLICTS.** Did your boss happen to mention a personality conflict between you and someone on staff? Go find that person and profusely apologize. It doesn't matter whether you were right or wrong. If you can't make it right, then *you're* the one who will be wronged.

5. **PUT IT ON PAPER.** Once fellow staffers have pardoned you, describe the results of your various conversations with them in email. It's best to write one email about each person whom you've offended so you can target the subject lines of your emails appropriately. This will also prevent the entire list of people from being circulated willy-nilly. Although it's imperative to create a paper trail, you also need to control the trail. (*Aren't paper trails just for legal beagles,* you wonder. Yes, precisely. If you're put on probation, it's not the worst thing for your company to believe that you'd defend your right to stay—in a lawsuit, if necessary.)

6. **KEEP IT SIMPLE.** You could title each one of your emails, "My conversation with _______." Streamline the body of each individual email until it's *A.S.A.P.* (*as short as possible*). You might write, "Peter and I chatted briefly about the argument we had two months ago. I apologized for raising my voice, and Peter accepted my apology. He told me that, in general, he enjoys working with me." Copy the HR department as well as your boss on all communications. If there are other people involved in monitoring your probation, be sure to also include them on the cc list. Don't "blind copy" anyone. Keep it all transparent.

7. **THE BLOCKBUSTER MOVE.** If your boss complained about your work product, use your probationary period to disabuse him of this notion. Come up with one momentous idea that he can't fail to get behind. Write the report, presentation, white paper, or killer press release that will make him recognize he can't afford to lose you.

8. **SHOW YOUR BIG GUNS.** Is there someone on staff who believes in you? It could be a colleague with whom you get along or a mentor from a different department. Take that person into your confidence. Tell her what happened, and ask if she'd mind speaking to your boss on your behalf. With this gambit, the higher up the person on the proverbial totem pole, the better your chances for survival. A good word from a senior vice president tops a good word from a vice president every time.

9. **REMEMBER THAT CLIENTS RULE.** Don't be afraid to solicit help from your clients and/or customers. An upset client who doesn't want to see you go is your best asset. Can you persuade her to sing your praises to your boss, or even to your boss's boss? That's one song your boss is unlikely to ignore (or it could be his swan song).

10. **HALFWAY THROUGH THE PROBATIONARY PERIOD, CHECK IN WITH BOTH THE HR PERSON AND YOUR BOSS.** Give each person a progress report. If they've both read your emails, these briefings should be ultra short. Ask if there is anything more that you might do in order to save your job. If either one says "yes," follow his or her directives. If they both say "no," breathe a sigh of relief. You may be able to keep your job after all!

11. **THREE BUSINESS DAYS BEFORE YOUR PROBATIONARY PERIOD ENDS, VISIT WITH THE HR PERSON AGAIN.** Politely *implore* her to go chat with your boss about your merits. (By now she should be intimately acquainted with them.) She may tell you that she already has. If so, don't forget to thank her.

12. **ON THE LAST DAY OF YOUR PROBATION, SET UP A MEETING WITH YOUR BOSS FOR FIRST THING IN THE MORNING.** If he lets you go, 10 a.m. is a great time to start contacting headhunters. If he decides to keep you, it will free up the rest of your day for you to get back to business. After all, you've just lost two whole weeks due to all of this over-communication.

Just the Stats

360-degree performance reviews have been circling through Fortune 500 companies from New York to Bangkok. These reviews, from one's bosses, peers, and underlings, may help to jettison a bad boss from power faster than if his superiors are the only ones to fill out his review.

The Golden Rule

Even with a mandate to clean house, the Inherited Boss may find it hard to expel you if you have a solid track record and strong internal alliances. In a turf war, satisfied clients and customers who are determined to have you stay are your best line of defense, closely followed by a sympathetic HR manager.

CHAPTER 8
The Credit Snatcher

Everyone thinks my boss is a star and I'm just a grunt. But this grunt is sitting chained to her desk every night, night after night, coming up with the ideas, while my boss schmoozes with the higher-ups and manages to come back with all the credit. Aaargh!

If your boss were an animal, it would be a vulture. While you're wracking your brains trying to figure out the most innovative approach to a problem, she's picking at them, thriving on the spoils of your hard labor. She is nothing but a delegator, albeit a well-paid one.

Is there an important internal meeting to present your work? Your boss asks you to leave the premises to monitor deadly focus-group research while she stays to present your magnificent opus. Is it the day to unveil the architectural blueprints to a client? Your boss has plotted with others at your company to keep the number of people down at the meeting. That particular client just happens to *hate* big meetings, wouldn't you know? Only senior vice presidents and higher are invited. Pity you're not there yet.

"What a wonderful meeting it was," she reports to you hours later with a huge grin on her face. "You're doing a spectacular job."

But are you? When your boss is the one who's stealing all of your glory, what, if anything, should you do to set the record straight?

Problem #36: She Hogs the Limelight

She rests on your laurels. You are the Cyrano de Bergerac of your company, wooing prospects with your brilliant ideas on behalf of your boss, a far less articulate and creative person. You remain invisible while she is ever promoted and perked with a bigger office, larger salary, and more impressive title. No wonder she loves you. You're keeping her gainfully employed.

Solution #36: Follow Her Example: Master Trickle-Up Theory

In business, credit tends to go to the boss, regardless of who does the work. It may seem unjust. It may seem unfair. It may seem as if your boss is a credit thief, determined to rob you of the accolades you deserve. But this is how the business world operates. This is as true today as it was when Thomas Edison said, "Everybody steals in commerce and industry. I've stolen a lot myself. But I know how to steal."

Steal a page from Edison's notebook. Edison was a truly innovative businessman who painstakingly reviewed current social needs and trends, then hired skilled practitioners to do the work for him. Yet somehow, he always managed to snag the credit. At the time of his death he held 1,093 U.S. patents and 1,239 foreign patents. And today, those from whom he stole (such as Nikola Tesla) are merely footnotes in the annals of history while Edison is revered as the foremost American inventor.

Recognize that stealing credit is one rule of the corporate game, and master the *Trickle-Up Theory.* Your work will be credited to your boss but your underlings' work will be credited to you.

There are numerous corporate career coaches on the Internet with plenty of advice on how to get the credit you deserve. Some advise announcing your good news in large meetings (so everyone will know you were responsible) rather than to your boss beforehand. Please note: this is a recipe for disaster. That's because you can only get away with it once. Dropping the credit bomb in a meeting will create an air of distrust between you and your boss. And because she is more entrenched, she will find ways to punish you for your rebelliousness.

Remember *Trickle-Up Theory* and do not attempt to fight the internal order. It can feel like banging your head against a wall, which hurts plenty and gives you a migraine. Instead, learn to flow with the internal order, and you'll feel both better and less bitter, plus you'll be considerably better off financially.

Foster camaraderie with your underlings by crediting their contributions. Don't worry that doing so will detract from the credit you'll receive from all of their efforts. The credit will still trickle up to you. That's the beauty of *Trickle-Up Theory*. Credit only flows one way (so at least the theory is easy to understand). Ultimately, you will receive the credit for all of your people's hard work, no matter what. But when you remember to verbally credit the people who work for you, then you also get a little credit for being a nice boss.

Problem #37: She Doesn't Invite You to Meetings to Present Your Own Work

You don't understand your boss's motivation for keeping you out of meetings. After all, no one can sell her own work better than the creator, right? AND YOU WERE THE CREATOR. (You had to put that in all caps so that *someone* would notice.)

Solution #37: Realize It's Not About the Work; It's About the Relationship

Very creative people sometimes have difficulty understanding how the other 99% operate. Here's a tip: your boss is not worried about the work (because she already knows that she'll get all of the credit for it). Rather, she's simply guarding the relationship she has with the client like a cat marking her territory.

In client-service industries, the clients rule with a velvet authoritarianism. Little they request is ever denied. These reigning monarchs can make or break your career with a single phone call. That's why it's a colossal mistake to marshal your way into meetings where your boss doesn't want you. Suppose that you go around your boss and get others at the company to suggest that you attend. You may succeed in getting your butt into the conference room chair, but you will have lost your boss's favor. Now, instead of viewing you as a competent underling, your boss will regard you as a rival. If she's vengeful (a trait, incidentally, that goes hand in hand with credit snatching), she can then use her relationship with the client to turn him against you. Should the client make a phone call and request for you not to be invited to future meetings, your reputation will be destroyed.

The bottom line? Unless you have a substantial internal power base, making a big deal about not being invited to meetings is akin to political suicide.

PLACES WHERE YOU CAN CLAIM CREDIT FOR YOUR IDEAS

Your boss looks like a genius every time she suggests one of your ideas. This is the law of the corporate jungle. And until you're more entrenched, there is nothing you can do to leapfrog the law. However, there are some ingenious ways to credit yourself with your own inventions. These six places are immune to your boss's claws:

1. **YOUR RESUMÉ.** Cite all of your accomplishments loud and clear. (Boasting is strongly encouraged.)
2. **YOUR PORTFOLIO.** You don't need to be a creative type to have a portfolio. Did you introduce two hot photojournalists to the stodgy lifestyles editor of your newspaper? Create a portfolio and include your contribution as part of a case study.
3. **YOUR WEBSITE.** Write a bio that trumpets your latest and greatest achievements.
4. **YOUR BLOG.** Blogging is the new self-marketing tool of the twenty-first century. Just having one gives you bragging rights.
5. **YOUR POWERPOINT PRESENTATION.** Did your boss claim credit for your brilliant investment idea? Commit it to a presentation that explains the idea, and use it to wiggle your way into a better job elsewhere. Try to get a promotion while you're at it, so that at your next job, the credit will trickle up to you.
6. **YOUR FLIP CHART.** Make a new client flip over your phenomenal flip chart—and chart your way into a new entrepreneurial venture.

In sum, the outside world is not as stingy about awarding credit as the "inside world"—the one inside your company. So no matter what's happening inside those hallowed halls, always look for ways to market your achievements on the outside. As long as you don't leak company secrets, violate any confidentiality agreements, or court your company's current clients, there are numerous ways to get the credit you deserve.

Problem #38: You Should Be Her Boss

Her predecessor was politically savvy and handled her responsibilities beautifully. So when your boss first arrived at the firm, you anticipated that she might face a steep learning curve. But that was over twelve months ago, and now your new boss isn't so new anymore. The truth is, she's lazy about learning. She stops by your mousy cubicle all the time to ask you remedial questions about things she should have mastered by now—how the intranet system works, how to fill out electronic time sheets, and how to fill out the paperwork for legal clearance. Her income expense reports are not only late but inaccurate. And when it comes to remembering who the key players are internally, she's clueless. You're not being paid enough to do your job, let alone hers.

Solution #38: Ask for a Raise

If you need any encouragement, gaze into your bathroom mirror at home every day for a week and repeat the following mantra: "I am not a Pushover. I am not a Pushover. I am not..." If that doesn't work, please spend one whole morning staring at your paycheck and visualize how much larger your boss's is. Hers could be twice the size of yours. Then ask yourself: Does that seem fair? Of course not. There is a difference between being a nice person and a pushover, one that's frequently reflected in a substandard paycheck. Your boss may be charmingly helpless. You may not even mind rescuing her (because you are so very nice). But if her numerous requests for assistance are adding up to over an hour a day of your precious time, then at the end of the day, you're being taken advantage of. Fortunately, there is a reasonable solution. Get paid to do her job.

Your strategy: First, give your new boss a long, leisurely honeymoon period to acclimate to her job's responsibilities (six months).

Then, arrange a mutually convenient time to sit down and chat. You might introduce the problem by nicely explaining that tasks such as training her on the intranet system and filling out her time sheets are taking away from the time you're supposed to devote to other tasks. But instead of leaving your work undone, you've been putting in a lot of overtime for which you are not being paid.

Ask your boss to request a raise for you, and suggest a percentage increase you deem reasonable. Tell her that you will happily continue to help her out with any of her tasks as long as she succeeds in getting you this raise. You'll get the money you deserve, and she'll avoid having to learn how to do the clerical tasks for herself. That's a win-win situation for you both.

Problem #39: She Fears You Will Unseat Her

Maybe you have a corporate angel who's been looking out for you. (Hallelujah.) Maybe the only time that your boss allowed you to attend a meeting, the client was smitten by your incredible performance. (It was pretty good, if you do say so yourself.)

In spite of your boss's stalwart efforts to keep you in the shadows while she basked in your limelight, someone noticed that you were doing an outstanding job…and that "someone" just happens to be your boss's boss. He thinks that you deserve to be promoted. Yeah, baby. That night, you jump around your living room and do a happy dance thanking the corporate gods for your good fortune.

Back at the office the next day, you are more sober. Although your promotion appears to have been sanctioned by both of your bosses, you have the distinct impression it wasn't your direct supervisor's idea. If anything, she seems more guarded than usual and even less inclined to invite you to client meetings.

Solution #39: Move into Your New Role with Baby Steps

Tread cautiously. Your boss may be (rightfully) concerned that she's as dispensable as a ballpoint pen. To allay her fears, it's a good idea to grow into your new role very slowly. Be sure to pepper your boss with numerous questions along the way, showing her that she still has much to teach you. After being marginalized by her for such a long spell, take care that you don't eclipse her overnight. Or as Dale Carnegie, author of *How to Win Friends and Influence People,* was fond of saying, "Make the other person feel important—and do it sincerely."

Management Mantra

"My grandfather once told me that there are two kinds of people: those who do the work and those who take the credit. He told me to try to be in the first group. There was less competition there." Indira Gandhi's words were inspirational. But if you wish to succeed in business today, it really helps to be in both groups. Be someone who does the work and takes the credit.

Problem #40: Your Boss Credits Someone Else for Coming Up with Your Idea

Is it permissible to snitch when your credit has been snatched? In the latest conference report, your phenomenal idea on how to structure the sale was credited to Sheila instead of you. You confront Sheila, who swears with a colorful oath that she had nothing to do with it. At least the two of you agree about that. Dammit! You're going to march into your boss's office right away and demand a retraction.

Solution #40: Start a Campaign to Track Everything

It's one thing for your boss to appropriate all of your credit. You're being paid to make her look good, and as you've learned in this chapter, this is the natural law of the corporate swamp pit. But it's downright devious for your boss to play favorites by actually crediting your good work to someone else on the team.

However, before you wrangle a much-deserved apology from the evil Credit Snatcher, take a deep breath. (Or about ten of them if you're seething.) Sometimes bad boss behavior isn't quite as malevolent as it might first appear. For various reasons, your boss may not have known that you were the one who originated the idea. If that's the situation, it's best to pop in and set the record straight in as non-charged a manner as possible. "Hey, I just thought you should know that the idea to structure the buyout as a five-year lease was actually my idea, not Sheila's." Your boss may volunteer to issue a public retraction. (If so, urge her to do so via a group email.)

Depending on your company's corporate culture, you might also use this one instance of credit oversight as an excuse to institute a series of measures to help allocate credit to the proper source in the future. Start by bringing a large artist's pad and magic markers with you to any brainstorming sessions. Draw a process chart during the session clearly showing next steps. Then assign people to handle each step, using their initials. Another technique is to discuss a routing procedure for all project documents and have an approval stamp, or a place for the person who actually created the idea to sign off on it along with the boss. In addition to allocating credit, a procedure like this also helps to assign accountability—someone to blame if the project goes awry.

Do your best ideas come to you in the shower each morning? Get into the habit of shooting your boss an email about your ideas *before* they have a chance to be watered down by the group. Last, guard your ideas while they are still in gestation. Don't discuss them with anyone on your team, unless that person happens to be your partner on the project. You don't need peer approval to move forward on any of your ideas. So guard them like a hawk until they are ready to be unveiled.

Just the Stats

A survey from Florida State University found that 37% of employees reported their supervisor failed to give credit when due.[4]

The Evolution of a Phrase: Survival of the Fittest

The corporate life is often described in Darwinian terms as a rough-and-tumble place where only the fittest prevail. Ask any executive fresh from battling the alligators in his own corporate swamp, and he'll probably credit Charles Darwin with inventing the phrase "survival of the fittest." In fact, the British economist Herbert Spencer first used the expression in 1864 in his *Principles of Biology.* But Spencer was profoundly influenced by Darwin's *On the Origin of Species.* "This survival of the fittest…is that which Mr. Darwin has called 'natural selection,'" Spencer wrote.

Darwin apparently preferred Spencer's term to his own because it avoided the implied anthropomorphism of selecting. Thus, Darwin ended up using the term himself in the fifth edition of *On the Origin of Species* with the phrase, "Natural Selection, or the Survival of the Fittest."

He gave full credit to Spencer, writing, "I have called this principle, by which each slight variation, if useful, is preserved, by the term natural selection in order to mark its relation to man's power of selection. But the expression often used by Mr. Herbert Spencer, of the Survival of the Fittest, is more accurate, and is sometimes equally convenient."

By crediting each other, both men improved on the original concept, and of the two phrases, "survival of the fittest" seems to be the phrase most nonscientists would select today to describe Darwin's theory.[5]

The Golden Rule

Credit snatching is the natural law of the corporate jungle. You can't fight it, so you might as well capitalize on it. *Trickle-Up Theory* ensures that you will receive credit for any work your underlings perform, even as all of your good efforts will be credited to your boss. Strive to gain the credit you deserve from the outside world while waiting to move up the corporate food chain.

CHAPTER 9
The Bully

The original executive producer was a people person, but we weren't meeting our deadlines. They brought in a TANK—she rolled right over us. She had a loud voice. She was totally commanding. She had no problem yelling at people.

You feel as if you are playing a high-stress, high-stakes game of Russian roulette. There are approximately six people on your team, which is headed by one big, scary Bully. Each person on the team knows that the Bully will go off on someone…the only question is who?

To dodge the bullet, different strategies are tried with varying success. Some team members pander to the Bully. They may say, "Gee, that's a swell idea, boss," when secretly, they are retching inside. They may chuckle too hard at his lame jokes, or if the Bully is female, placate her with candy and flowers.

Other team members have formed alliances with the Bully's henchmen as a measure of "job insurance" in case they are hit. Still others are skilled at the misdirect; they know how to quickly deflect the Bully's wrath away from them onto a different team member, or better yet, onto someone in a completely different department. There's also usually one member of the team who manages to absent himself from the premises whenever the Bully is on a tear. The escape artist might feign illness or telecommute from the safety of his own home until that particular round of Russian roulette is over.

The Bully walks with a swagger and keeps his finger on the trigger. More than other types of difficult bosses, bullies need to be carefully managed. The following are some proven tactics to help you take your proverbial Bully by the horns, or at least be the last man standing.

Problem #41: The Bully Uses Meetings as a Bully Pulpit

Your boss is both an idea maven and the decision maker. Pity the maven part is mostly in his own mind. At meetings, he presents his own ideas. He *loves* his own ideas. (And what do you know, he is unanimous in that.) Because he's vocal and won't back down without a verbal brawl, the Bully's ideas receive less scrutiny than other people's. Fearing reprisal, staffers are frightened to disagree with him.

Solution #41: Set Up a Meeting Facilitator Who's Not the Boss

Hypercritical of everyone else's ideas but his own, the Bully has not only the first word on any new initiative but also the last word and every word in between. If you work directly for someone like this, it may be difficult for you to enforce change without putting your neck on the line. (You're better off biding your time and waiting for the Bully to self-destruct.)

But if you happen to work in an HR capacity where you *don't* report to the Bully, or if higher-ups in the company are demanding fresher ideas from everyone, you could try setting up a facilitator for internal meetings. It might be one person or several who rotate at the task. The facilitator's responsibility is to keep the meeting moving and sometimes to intercede when someone's ideas are dismissed prematurely. The facilitator might redirect the conversation away from the Bully by saying something non-threatening, such as, "I was wondering if Sandra might repeat her idea…I didn't quite catch it." Ideally, another person in the room should be the official scribe, with his or her notes to be included in a conference report. If that's impossible, the facilitator should take notes and circulate them afterward, preferably before too much time has elapsed.

Don't get unraveled while you're waiting for the Bully to unravel. Most bullies will never win any popularity contests. Still, bullies can be wily; it would be foolish to underestimate them. Unseating them can be a slow, laborious process, even if HR managers and others in your department are gunning for them.

How the Bully Gets Away with It

Bullies are often can-do people whose tirades, tactics, and tantrums have not held them back. In certain glamorous fields, such as advertising, publishing, and the film industry, having a temper may even be viewed as a sign of creativity. The employee whiplash and inevitable high turnover that result from the Bully's torrent of verbal abuse are tolerated in the same way that one might accept the side effects of a potent drug. And make no mistake: the Bully is potent. He derives his power from a certain fissure that often exists in companies—a distinct separation between top management and those toiling away under the Bully. Since he only lashes out at those beneath him, those above rarely have a chance to feel the wrath of the Bully's temper. Even when the negative reports filter upward, the higher-ups don't always mind. The Bully may have been hired specifically to perform an unpleasant task—such as cleaning out a department. "Better him than me," the top managers think.

Problem #42: False Deadlines

If the internal deadline were any tighter, it would be a girdle. Indeed, everyone on the team feels like they are sucking it in. Here's the skinny: your boss set an unrealistic deadline several weeks ahead of the date when the presentation is really due. If the past is any precedent, you anticipate that after you and others burn out the fluorescent bulbs to meet his inane deadline, your boss will turn around and reward you by "sitting" on the work for several days. There is no real time crunch. Why is he trying so hard to invent one?

Solution #42: Either Take One for the Team or Pretend the Deadline Is Real

Setting false deadlines is one way for the Bully to manifest his power. By insisting on reviewing the material ludicrously early, he has more of an opportunity to tear it to shreds. Incidentally, everyone reporting to the Bully is acutely aware that the deadline is too tight. The problem is they are all afraid of Victor Woolf (or whatever the Bully's name happens to be). So as a group, they remain silent. In some circles, this is referred to as the *Abilene Paradox*.[6]

If you happen to be in the Bully's good graces, you might politely ask if everyone might have an extra day or two to complete their tasks. Start by reviewing a calendar and working backward from the date when the final presentation is due. Talk in terms of "we." You could say something benign and team-oriented such as, "If we can show you the proposal on Monday instead of Friday, it will give everyone the weekend to fine-tune their ideas, and you'll still have a whole week to review them."

If the Bully agrees to your terms, everyone on the team will have more breathing room (plus they'll only have to work over the weekend if they so choose). If the Bully verbally slaps you, you'll gain sympathy from fellow staffers (earning you karmic chits that you can cash in later). However, if you are not in the Bully's inner circle, simply act like his imposed deadline is real. Why stick your neck out only to have him snap it in two?

Problem #43: You Are the Object of Your Boss's Ridicule

You don't mind some good-natured joshing at your own expense. But there's nothing jovial about your boss's barbarous banter. He has a nasty habit of picking on you about something that you just can't help, such as your high-pitched nasally laugh, squeaky voice, or diminutive height. While everyone else on staff curries favor by guffawing at your boss's jokes, now you feel profoundly self-conscious about doing so. Recently, the brute even raised the stakes by calling you a hideous name. (It was so funny, you forgot to laugh.)

Solution #43: Stand Up for Yourself: Confront the Bully

Once a Bully locates your Achilles' heel, he'll continue to probe around the area until he brings you to your knees. You are far better off showing some spine rather than rolling over. After all, no one ever cowered her way into greatness. Make an appointment to sit down with your boss, and be sure to conduct this meeting behind closed doors. Look your boss squarely in the eye and tell him that if he doesn't quit making fun of your laugh, you will post a blog about him on SaveTheAssistants.com, using his real name. When his jaw drops to the floor, laugh like a hyena and tell him that you were "just joking." He'll think twice before picking on you again.

Just the Stats

According to a study conducted in the United Kingdom by the Manchester School of Management, bullying often accompanies an autocratic, confrontational, macho management style. That said, women are just as likely to be bullies as men. Examples of bullying include: fault finding, humiliation, ridicule, and the "spreading of gossip and rumors about you."[7]

Problem #44: You Are the Boss's Whipping Boy

First, he's on your case for speaking up in meetings. Then, he picks on you when you're too quiet. He seesaws about what he's looking for, alternately commenting that your presentations are too longwinded or barely skimming the surface. He's told you in no uncertain terms that he hates the S.W.O.T. (Strengths, Weaknesses, Opportunities, Threats) analyses you spend hours crafting. The last time you counted, his criticisms about you outweighed his compliments by seven to one, while you distinctly remember reading in some popular management manual that it's supposed to be the other way around.

Solution #44: Stay Cool: You May Even Be His Favorite

Many office bullies enjoy teasing those whom they secretly admire. It's almost as if there's an inverse relationship between the Bully's volume (thunderous) and his range of emotions (miniscule). Since he has no idea how to express true appreciation or gratitude, sometimes the only way he can "show the love" is by barking. And his proverbial bark really may be worse than his bite.

Studies show that for someone's behavior to even be *considered* bullying, it needs to be perceived as such by the intended target. If you lower your expectations about your boss, and recognize that once a bully, always a bully, two outcomes are likely. First, his behavior will bother you a great deal less (because you'll realize that he can't help himself), and second, you'll stop trying so hard to please him (because you'll realize that, on some primal level, it's impossible).

If he treats you like his whipping boy, that's one thing. But why whip yourself into a frenzy over such a loser?

Management Mantra

"To thine own self be true." William Shakespeare said it best. Only you know your limits: what you can and cannot accept. If the Bully's tirades bounce off you like Teflon, give yourself a huge hug. Clearly, you have superior coping skills. But if his outbursts have begun to chisel into your self-esteem, it's time to either speak up (to your boss), speak out (to someone in HR), or at the very least, belt out a rousing rendition of *Take This Job and Shove It* before you arrive at the office each morning.

Problem #45: You're So Peeved That You Can't Stand the Sight of Him

His belligerent banter used to be directed at someone else on the team who quickly hopscotched to a better job in the organization. (You found this Houdini-like feat inspiring.) Directly afterward, the Bully's head-butting seemed relatively contained. But in hindsight, you realize that he was simply taking a breather to size up his next victim: YOU. Now your boss tosses his vitriolic tongue-whippings your way with abandon. You keep waiting to be rescued by a corporate Dudley Do-Right type. But while fellow staffers seem simpatico, for some reason, no one on your team ever jumps in to save you. Grapevine gossip advises against heart-to-hearts with this particular Bully. Rumor has it that he cannot be tamed. And you're wary about discussing your problems with anyone in HR. (They all love him—go figure.)

Solution #45: Time-out for a Vacation

Don't do anything drastic (unless you consider signing up for a really luxe cruise drastic, in which case, go right ahead). Try to stay away from the office long enough for the Bully to locate a new target. He can't live without one for long.

While you're away, meditate on what your life would be like without this particular boss running roughshod over your feelings. If you decide to "fire" him, at least you'll do it calmly, befitting one who has just returned from vacation. (You never want to burn your bridges.)

And what if you decide that you can't quite live without that paycheck? Imagine that you have just purchased a suit of armor and take a steely approach. Refuse to let your boss inside that armor because that would give him access to your sense of self-worth. Your self-esteem is your most precious asset, while the man to whom you report is nothing but a !#$&%!

BULLY CHECKLIST

Left to their own devices, most human beings would rather avoid confrontation. Bullies are built differently. They may have grown up in abusive homes with cold, unloving parents as role models. While no formal study exists tracking the young bullies of the playground to see if they later devolve into workplace bullies, there is plenty of anecdotal evidence to suggest that they do. Here are some methods your local Bully may be using to get his own way:

- **THROWING TEMPER TANTRUMS OVER MINOR INFRACTIONS.** Was the wrong sandwich ordered by mistake? Did the secretarial staff substitute regular cola for diet again? The Bully's in touch with both his Inner Brat and his Outer one.
- **PITTING COWORKERS AGAINST ONE ANOTHER IN THE QUEST FOR HIS FAVOR.** But today's Office Pet is tomorrow's Pariah. (The Bully retracts his favor in a blink.)
- **BEHEADING THOSE WHO DISAGREE WITH HIM.** For some reason, everyone calls him "Henry VIII" behind his back.
- **ISOLATING ONE PERSON ON THE TEAM AS HIS TARGET.** The Bully then proceeds to verbally flog his victim in public.
- **RUNNING THE OFFICE ACCORDING TO HIS MOODS.** Up. Down. Down. Up. His moods fluctuate faster than a metronome.
- **BEING PROUD OF HIS OWN BAD BOY BEHAVIOR.**

Just the Stats

According to an Employment Law Alliance poll, 44% of U.S. workers say they have worked for an abusive boss, and 64% believe that bullied workers should be able to sue to recover damages.[8]

The Golden Rule

Bullies are tough, but when you face them down, sometimes they blubber like crybabies. Pick and choose your battles. If you are the target of a Bully's ire, carefully weigh the career pros against the health hazards of withstanding his abuse. Temporarily absenting yourself may help you dodge a bullet. The Bully always requires someone to torment; and if you are not around, his bull's-eye may shift.

CHAPTER 10
The Coward

He was a big believer in that Wall Street habit of delaying bad news for as long as humanly possible.

Did your company's bread-and-butter account just decide to butter their bread elsewhere? Did your mother-ship company just dispatch a fleet of pinstriped executives to "rescue" your top management with a boatload of advice about what your office is doing wrong? Did your largest supplier just go belly up? Don't expect your boss to tell you!

When it comes to sharing bad news, he has the stiffest of upper lips. ("Loose lips sink ships" is his favorite motto.) And while he may give lip service to sharing good news with his people, the truth is, he operates from fear.

When times get tough, the Coward gets going. Like the Wizard, he's been known to take long journeys away from the office (although in his case, it's so that he can wait out a political storm from a distant shore). However, unlike most Wizards, the Coward has serious traction. Since he rarely takes sides, his is the one stance every side finds unobjectionable.

When your boss is a Coward, should you show strength, weakness, all of the above, or none of the above? What is your best survival strategy?

Problem #46: He Doesn't Convey Bad News until It's Too Late

He sneaks back from an important sales call, quietly closes the door to his office, and doesn't emerge for three days. "What happened?" everyone wants to know. The gossip mill churns, but the rank and file are merely whispering amongst themselves. Even the Coward's closest colleague doesn't seem to know the upshot. On day four, the Coward sends a memo thanking everyone for their esprit de corps. Three weeks later, you learn that your company didn't win the account. Six weeks after that, you *still* have no idea why.

Solution #46: Figure Out the Cost of Delay

The Coward has difficulty letting people in, especially when he has only bad news to share. (He is, after all, a coward.) But if you're in a capacity where you can actually help your boss contain the damage, you need as much lead time as possible. Somehow, you will have to persuade him to open up to you. One way is to talk to him about costs. How much money does the company lose when negative news doesn't reach you in a timely manner? In short, what is the price of delay? Here are some examples:

- **Rumors start.** Hallway chatter distracts employees, causing productivity to dwindle. If you want to get mathematical about it, you could guesstimate how many employees gossiped for how many minutes each day and what the cost per hour is.
- **The press hears about it.** Bad news leaks through the vents in the ceiling. Had your boss explained what happened a bit earlier, you might have been able to spin it to the press. Since he didn't, the press has now drawn its own nefarious conclusions. Employee morale plummets twenty-six stories (or however tall your office building happens to be).

- **The competition hears the bad news.** Before the word is out at your own company, your rivals have heard the scoop. This gives them a huge edge in the marketplace, which can eat into your company's profits.

THE 411 ON WITHHOLDING INFORMATION

To put it mildly, your boss doesn't like to share. In a world where Too Much Information (T.M.I.) is the rule, your boss won't even release the minimum information (t.m.i.) Maybe your job involves damage control. But you can't control the damage because you don't even know that there is any damage. Doesn't your boss realize that by keeping mum about big problems, he's curtailing your ability to do your job?

The answer is complex. Your boss has learned that in the Information Age, the control of information is a source of power in itself. He may be forestalling the release of the bad news until he can reach a particular person—such as his boss, the company lawyer, or the company spokesperson.

If his bad news is subjective, your boss may be waiting for some objective confirmation before releasing it. (How bad was the meeting? Was it as bad as he thought? Is the client relationship salvageable?)

If your company received negative publicity, your boss may be deliberately procrastinating in order to assess the fallout before publicly reacting to it. If results from a particular sales period were depressing, he may even be holed up in his office for days, praying for a miracle.

In addition to all of these perfectly valid reasons for keeping a tight vise on the flow of information is one overarching fact: at heart, your boss is a coward!

Problem #47: Instead of Sticking Up for You, He Makes You Play the Heavy

Last week, he applauded the new strategy and even went out on a very short limb by calling it "breakthrough." Since then, he's had several meetings with the higher-ups and finally circles back to you with their feedback, all negative. You challenge him on their assessment. He says, "You're absolutely right. I don't want to be the go-between on a project that's this important. Do me a favor and just talk to them directly, okay?"

Solution #47: Play the Heavy, but Stay Detached

Your boss's power stems from his ability to stay detached from the outcome of any particular project. By directing you to talk to the higher-ups without him, he's sending you into the wolves' den. If they tear you from limb to limb, he's not going to be there to protect you. The only armor you can bring is the cloak of detachment. If you're detached, you're invincible; and ironically, very powerful people respect that. Use linear logic rather than unbridled passion. If it helps, imagine that someone else worked on the project other than you. Stay focused on the fact that you're talking about work. (Never think of any project as your "baby.") Another gambit: imagine that you are on your deathbed quietly looking back on your life. Would you even remember this silly project? Of course not. Stay detached.

Just the Stats

Of the people interviewed for this book, just as many complained about working for cowards as working for bullies. While bullies inspired fear, cowards inspired nothing but disdain. Spinelessness is a universally unappealing quality in a boss.

Problem #48: He Regularly Shafts the People on His Team

Your boss speaks a dialect of Double-Talk. There are two verbs in this special language: to *compliment* and to *diss*. To your face, he compliments the work. Then, if anyone else complains about the work, he agrees with him or her, effectively dissing the work behind your back. Finally, when you approach him to ask why your proposal died, he compliments you on your work ethic—and assures you that you're doing a spectacular job.

Solution #48: Create New Alliances to Get Better Results

Most fields are results-intensive. At the end of your performance review period, you're supposed to have real results to show for your efforts. That works out beautifully—as long as your boss and others in your department like your ideas and suggestions. But what if you keep presenting ideas that are never bought? You will need to figure out a way to get one of your projects approved by the forces-that-be, or you will be cut faster than you can shout, "Hey, wait a minute. I'm really valuable."

Start thinking like a contestant on a reality TV show, such as *Survivor* or *The Apprentice,* and form an alliance with someone whose projects do get approved. (To pull this off, it helps if you've befriended the person long before your moment of need.) Tell your office buddy that you'd sincerely love the opportunity to work with her and, hopefully, learn from her. What if she's more talented than you? Make the idea of working together more appealing by offering to do more of the grunt labor—

background research, financial modeling, typing, proofing, whatever she assigns to you—while she concentrates on the juicier parts of the assignment.

Your boss and others will have a harder time rejecting your work when it has the fingerprints of an A player all over it.

Problem #49: He Promotes You to Bad Cop

You're so elated to be at a new level of responsibility that, for the first few months, you barely notice how often your boss manages to hide behind you. But after the initial excitement simmers down, you can no longer deny it. He makes you deliver bitter pills of bad news to fellow staffers while he liberally dispenses carrots and pats on the back. What a wuss!

Solution #49: Convey That You're Just the Messenger

The Coward hates confrontation of all kinds. Thus, it's unwise to confront him about how frustrated you feel with the current arrangement. He'll automatically assume that you can't handle your new job.

When you must tell people bad news, simply let them know that it's coming from the boss. Here's a script for you to experiment with. "Brian asked me to let you know that your proposal needs to be massively retooled. I'm sorry to have to tell you this, because personally I thought some parts of it had a lot of merit. Please don't shoot the messenger."

Play with these words, amend them, and tweak them until they are your own. But be certain that whatever you do say conveys the idea that the message comes from your boss, not you, and that personally, you empathize with the recipient. At the same time, make sure that your words can't be twisted to make them sound as if you disagree with your boss's viewpoint. Dial down your temperature to lukewarm when you deliver the script, and you'll be just fine.

Learn from the Coward's modus operandi. Stay in his shadow for as long as you can. If he asks you to deliver difficult nuggets of information to the people in your department, coat those nuggets with as much sugar as you can muster. Publicly defer to the Coward whenever possible. Make sure that everyone knows the Coward is still numero uno.

SINK OR SWIM: WHAT COWARDS CAN TEACH YOU ABOUT SURVIVAL

Many bosses regard their employees as children, whose time, development, and homework assignments require regular monitoring. In return for this degree of supervision (a.k.a. micromanagement), these bosses offer their people a certain amount of protection. By contrast, the Coward views his employees as adults who need to fend for themselves. Do you need help on an assignment? The Coward has no problem lending a hand, but if his direction is questioned by anyone in a position of authority, he will duck out quickly. The only thing the Coward feels truly impassioned about is his own survival, which is virtually guaranteed, as he's dispassionate about everything else. Thus, you can learn a lot about survival from the Coward.

When strong opinions boil over into heated debates and the people at your company start taking sides, monitor the Coward's actions closely. Listen to what he says. How does he manage to cool tempers and massage away the tiny chips lodged on people's shoulders? How does he redirect the conversation to more neutral territory? Are there any particular catchphrases that he uses? Make a mental note of them and recycle some of his winners whenever you find yourself in a spirited debate.

Problem #50: He Criticizes You through Third Parties

Your boss mentions a problem that he has with you to someone else in passing. That person immediately reports it back to you. While you can't imagine why your confidant would lie to you, you're not entirely sure what to do with this supposedly "confidential" information. It's annoying to hear negative feedback from a third party. Can your boss really be this passive-aggressive?

Solution #50: Either Ignore the Remark or Change Your Ways (Just Don't Have a Meeting about It)

Pretend that you were a fly on the wall during that particular conversation and overheard something you weren't supposed to. Behind closed doors, your boss revealed his true personality. But just because your boss had one moment of unbridled aggression at your expense does not mean that you should turn around and aggressively try to find out what he meant. Instead, thank your confidant for sharing the information. And take a couple of days to dissect what you heard. If you think that your boss's criticism of you was legitimate, take the necessary steps to change. But if, after careful consideration, you believe that his charge was unfair, just put it out of your mind. So far, his negative opinion of you hasn't risen to the level where *he* feels he needs to have a discussion.

Management Mantra

"Take a chill pill." Be less passionate about the work. When you have a Coward as your fearful leader, you have no choice.

The Golden Rule

Albert Camus once noted, "There is always a philosophy for lack of courage." That philosophy is survival. And, make no mistake, the Coward is a survivor. His aura of detachment protects him from political upheaval. In most office tempests, he will end up the last man standing. Rather than disdaining him as so many do, try to employ some of his techniques to bolster your own chances of survival.

CHAPTER 11
The Temporary Boss

*The man who drove me absolutely batsh*t with his directives wasn't even my official boss.*

He arrives like the Stealth Bomber. Surreptitiously, he's ushered into the company's largest empty office (like no one will notice that someone new is in residence). Several days pass. Nobody from top management bothers to introduce the stranger to the troops. One day, he stops you in the hallway to ask you for something trivial, such as a pen or a paper clip. You fetch it.

After your initial non-introduction, if you happen to be unfortunate enough to be sitting near him, then you're in his line of fire. And he's very high maintenance. He needs file access, the code to the men's room, the employee phone list, a list with everyone's titles, lunch menus, and a key to the back door. Where can he obtain office supplies, he asks impatiently. Who works in the management information systems department, and why haven't they installed his computer yet? Can you lend him a yellow pad?

You're eager to tell him that you're not a secretary, but fear that doing so might come off as rude. Instead, you shake his hand, shower him with your best *Candid Camera* smile, and introduce yourself by your first and last name. His shifty eyes dart to one side as he says rather gruffly, "I'm Steve." You've just spent hours attending to his every whim. Yet this *Steve* won't even tell you his last name.

Who is this intruder? And precisely how long is he planning to stay?

Problem #51: He Draws Everyone into His Orbit

If men are from Mars and women are from Venus, this alien must be from Pluto. He circles through the hallways, demanding new reports, old conference reports, and proposals, along with a forest full of other paperwork from everyone he passes. Is he a freelancer? Consultant? Mercenary? Ax man? You're practically working for him and you *still* don't know his last name.

Solution #51: Recognize That You Are Dealing with a Force, Possibly a Dangerous One

If top management didn't sanction him, he would have never been awarded that gorgeous corner office. Yet there is still no word from the higher-ups, and this just adds to the confusion. You heard it here first: this new man with no last name could very well be your future boss. So first, make certain that he feels at home in his new temporary office. And then, once he stops hounding you for supplies, read the box called "The Two Types of Hired Guns."

Management Mantra

"Patience is a virtue." If you don't happen to be a patient person by nature, do your best impersonation of one. Take deep, cleansing breaths. Take up transcendental meditation. Say "om" a lot.

The Two Types of Hired Guns

Who is the celebrity with only one name who seems to be hiding in the biggest window office on the floor? He's either a BIG HIRED GUN or a small one, but either way, you should recognize that guns of all kinds are dangerous.

If he is a BIG HIRED GUN, it means that the man who is shooting orders left and right might be elevated to boss status shortly. Why hasn't anyone shared this fact with you? Isn't it rather germane to your life? Simple: Top management needs to keep a lid on the news for just a tiny bit longer because there is one insurmountable technicality. The BIG GUN is still officially employed somewhere else. Or he may be under contract to a different firm. Technically, he's not supposed to be working for any firm that competes with his old one until the contract expires. So, for the present, he's freelancing under the radar. Hence the bizarre aura of secrecy surrounding the arrival of someone who is clearly a big shot.

If he's a small hired gun, it means that he's a consultant—a temporary employee who has been brought on board to solve a particular problem. The problem might be an engineering glitch or a system-wide breakdown, such as a disappointing series of fiscal quarters that could necessitate a reengineering of the entire company (*See* Problem #22: *A Consultant Comes A-knocking*). Whether you're dealing with a BIG HIRED GUN or a small one, it's smart to acquiesce to his demands and do your best to get along with him. Your future happiness pretty much depends on it.

Problem #52: You and the Hired Gun Get Off on the Wrong Foot

Work has been ambling along at the pace of a tortoise. Bored, you access the *General Hospital* chat room from your computer and converse with participants about Luke and Laura's fate. Next, your best friend calls to ask whether she should dump her Lothario of a boyfriend. "Yes, yes, yes," you counsel her for the fortieth time. She shares his latest escapade. "Just dump the guy!" you say with disgust. Suddenly a towering shadow looms in your doorway with the silhouette of the Hired Gun. "Can I borrow a Post-it Note?" he asks, smirking from his high loft of smugness. You slam down the phone on your friend and rifle through your messy desk drawers, looking for a Post-it notepad. The Hired Gun glances at your computer screen, now filled with postage stamp-sized photos of your two favorite soap opera stars. "Nice to see you're working on the important stuff," he says, walking out and shaking his head with dismay.

Solution #52: Take Your Foot out of Your Mouth

Consider it an axiom of Murphy's Law that the very day your new Temporary Boss finally wants to talk shop, he'll catch you doing something you shouldn't. While it's true that "you never have a second chance to make a first impression," every day presents a new opportunity to erase a negative one. Seize it. Why let a false start sour relations between you and the Temporary Boss? "I've been taking a short break before I plunge back into those sales reports," you might say with a grin. "And any time you'd like to talk about them, my door is always open."

HOW TO IMPRESS A TEMPORARY BOSS

- **ACT DEFERENTIAL.** Assume that he is important from day one. It will give you a leg up on fellow staffers who may be waiting for top management to give him the official blessing before they start sucking up to him.
- **BE HIS SHERPA.** Is he lost? Give him a floor map. Offer to introduce him around. Do you really want to ingratiate yourself? Point him to the secret stash of office supplies.
- **UNEARTH THE COMMON BOND.** Does he have an intriguing piece of art on his wall? Be sure to draw him out about it. Does he have a photograph of the Chicago Cubs sitting on his desk? If you're a baseball fan, mention it right off the bat.
- **REMEMBER THAT KNOWLEDGE IS POWER.** Stay up-to-the-minute about upcoming meetings, company initiatives, and new procedures. Be the person he approaches with questions about how things really work inside the company.
- **KEEP YOUR TECHNOLOGICAL EDGE.** If your Temporary Boss is under thirty, this won't impress him much. But if he's any older, he may feel slightly technophobic. Teach him how to FedEx packages from his desktop, and you will have made a new and (quite possibly) very important friend.

Problem #53: He Wants the Dirt

"Can I see you in my office?" the Temporary Boss asks you one morning. Ushering you into his mammoth temporary space, he quietly closes the door and requests an honest assessment of how smoothly the department is running. You'd love to tell him that it's a "well-oiled machine"—except that would be candor-challenged. Instead, you mutter something vaguely positive, but he presses you for details. He wants to hear your impressions of your current boss and fellow colleagues.

Solution #53: Take the High Road

The Temporary Boss is conducting a diagnostic of the company. He may appear to be particularly interested in your opinion of certain individuals. But even if you dislike some of the people he mentions, it's tactical to be tactful. Don't rave about someone who's incompetent, but don't get down in the mud either.

If you must damn someone, do it with faint praise. Instead of calling someone a "hack," you might observe that he seems to be "a solid performer." If you think that someone is a rageaholic, you might rephrase that as "he certainly keeps people on their toes." If someone appears to be floundering, you might express that she's a "Newbie," if true. (Of course, if you think that someone is absolutely terrific, use this opportunity to say so.) While this may sound counterintuitive, the one thing you *shouldn't* worry about is what others might be saying about you.

Instead, concentrate on making a good impression. When you can be gracious about fellow coworkers and bosses, you end up making a stronger impression yourself; and with a new boss, that's what really counts.

Just the Stats

The Prisoner's Dilemma is an aspect of game theory that teaches how collusion influences outcome. Because the prisoners can't collude, they end up with an outcome that's worse for each person individually. If you know for a fact that the Hired Gun is having individual meetings with everyone on staff, it may be to your benefit to collude with your allies on what you all wish to tell him. However, if for some reason everyone's already in lockup (thereby making collusion impossible), remember to be lavish with your praise and stingy with your criticism.

Problem #54: No One Can Make Heads or Tails of His Calculations

The freelancer mad scientist is another type of Temporary Boss that can make laymen lay down and cry, "Uncle!" He's a brilliant engineer intent on putting the buttoned-up managers at your company through a creative process known as hell. He has no interest in teaching those with a non-technical background the finer points of whatever it is he's working on. Thus, there is no way for anyone to coordinate the flow of work. When deadlines are missed, there is zero accountability.

Solution #54: Hire a Techie

Don't squander precious money on mental health professionals or so-called management experts. They'll have no success in managing the mad scientist either. He'll shut them out of his metaphorical lab and won't understand why they are bombarding him with so many unanswerable questions, such as, "What?" and "When?" Instead, hire a Techie who is *not* a genius to work under the mad scientist. The Techie should be able to understand the mad scientist's methods well enough to transliterate them to civilians. Filter all management concerns about timelines and deadlines through the Techie. The Techie will need to make himself available to the "suits" to answer their questions about important details, such as feasibility, accountability, and profitability.

Problem #55: He's on a Completely Different Timeline

Hired Guns get paid handsomely to perform their consulting magic. They might earn thousands of dollars a week or even per day. This sometimes leads to a problem with deadlines that's the polar opposite of the mad scientist's. (*See* Problem #54.) In this scenario, the Hired Gun must accelerate the timeline. He needs everything done, like, yesterday, because he knows that his freelance contract will expire in a few short months. He must show results—super fast.

Solution #55: Sit This One Out

There is usually some padding built into internal deadlines (in case errors are made necessitating time-consuming revisions.) Thus, you might be able to squeeze a few days out of the timeline. On the other hand, it is *not* your job to defend the deadline. Doing so will likely infuriate the Hired Gun, who is under unrealistic pressure to show results at warp speed. Recognize that this is his problem, and take care not to make it yours. Does he wish to see the materials tomorrow? Does he want everyone to work through the weekend to speed up the process? Does he insist on calling a bunch of internal meetings on Friday night at 6 p.m.? Outwardly, appear empathetic, but know that the same barriers to speedy completion will still exist no matter who's snapping his fingers. This isn't your fight. Take a back seat and let others jump into the fray.

The Golden Rule

Upper management may appear to ignore the Hired Gun, but never follow their lead until you've ferreted out his true status. Treat him with deference and respect, for it's highly likely that this temporary employee may soon be the man to whom you report.

CHAPTER 12
The Spin Doctor

We'd do pitches together. He was the big macha. I was the blocking and tackling guy. I knew the numbers. We'd go into a meeting. He would completely and utterly lie…about what our expertise was…how we could help the company. He'd sell them on these false concepts.

He has the soul of a used-car salesman. He'll say anything to close a deal, promising all sorts of resources your company doesn't have. He considers bait and switch two legitimate tools of his trade and sees nothing controversial about conning his customers. Possessed with the salesman's slickness of patter, he is irresistible.

You live in secret dread that, one day, an irate customer or company head will expose your boss for the imposter he is. And when the day of reckoning finally comes, you reckon that you may be held equally accountable. But every time you approach your boss to ask about his penchant for doctoring the truth, he looks at you as if *you're* the one who's sorely misguided.

In his heart of hearts he believes that outrageous fibbing is one of the costs of doing business. Truth be told, he even gets a secret charge out of it. As they say, "It comes with the territory."

Problem #56: He Makes It Up as He Goes Along

A potential client inquires about your company's global network. Just as you're explaining that the network is 100% domestic, your boss mentions some affiliation with a foreign office you've never heard of before. According to him, the two offices work together "all the time."

Will a prospect sign on the dotted line, just as long as your boss promises to oversee the business? He swears up and down that he'll be a devoted watchdog, and before the ink on the contract is even dry, he's delegated the task to the B players back at the firm. Do the numbers argue eloquently against a deal? Your boss has no aversion to manufacturing a second set of completely different numbers. He pulls them out of thin air. You don't know whether to call him Pinocchio or Merlin the Magician.

Solution #56: Backpedal Gracefully

The Spin Doctor, a gregarious and charismatic frontman, has put you in the awkward position of having to follow up on his promises. You'll need to map out a strategy for how to deliver the unvarnished truth to your client, and there's only one way to do it: piece by piece. Occasionally, you may need to put your own spin on his spin—pretending that you heard something quite differently than how the Spin Doctor actually phrased it. Blaming a change on outside forces, such as a tumult in the economy, may help soften the blow, as will courtly manners on your part. Take great pains to answer your phone and be a sympathetic sounding board for your client's fury.

Problem #57: Your Customer Remembers It Differently

Your boss possesses so much charisma that potential customers repeat his outlandish promises to you verbatim. "How come you're giving me your standard discount rate," a customer may challenge, "when *he promised us* a 40% discount? You were even there when he said it. Don't you remember?" You hasten to assure the distraught customer that you'll investigate the "error" and promptly find your boss to discuss a strategy. "Just fix it," your boss says with a wink. "You know the drill."

Solution #57: Lucy, You've Got a Lot of Explaining to Do!

Most customers resent being treated like marks. If you find yourself working for a boss who constantly lies to customers, your company may be suffering from poor word-of-mouth and a lack of repeat business. Seek novel solutions to mend the immediate problem and restore your customer's confidence—at least in you. If the promised discount rate will take too large a chunk out of your commission, look for other ways to close the gap. Can you comp your customer with free service calls for a few months or offer him deeply discounted add-ons to the original purchase? First, neutralize your customer's ire by addressing his complaint. Then work to repair the relationship. Always remember that the fastest way to a customer's heart is through a golf course.

Just the Stats

According to *The Columbia Guide to Standard American English,* the term *spin* originally derived from a ball game such as bowling or billiards. "Seeking to gain an advantage, the player puts spin on the ball to make it react differently from a ball without the spin and to make it deceive (or persuade) the receiver."[9]

Problem #58: He Has You Working on a Project That May Be Nonexistent

One of your deals hits a huge pothole in the road. The tire bursts; the steering wheel needs adjustment; the deal is permanently stalled. But your boss keeps talking about the deal as if it's still happening. Confused, you explain that it was your understanding that the deal died weeks ago. Your boss stares at you as if, surely, you must have lost your mind. Either that, or you recently had a lobotomy, poor thing. "Keep working on it until you hear differently from *me*," he commands.

Solution #58: Ask for Group Support

Spin Doctors are eternal optimists—to a fault. They live in a fantasy bubble that floats on nothing more than the fumes of their hot air. However, while natural ebullience may sometimes explain a Spin Doctor's bullishness for a project that is clearly moribund, there could be other reasons why he might deliberately fib about a project's feasibility.

Is bonus season around the corner? Is his contract up for renewal? Are there cuts to be made at your firm in the near future? If so, your boss may believe there is a perfectly valid reason to delay bad news for as long as possible. Before you attempt to set the record straight, consider whether doing so will help or hurt your own career at the firm. If speaking out will smear your reputation, you might be better off taking your boss's lead in the short term and just following his instructions. There is always the tiniest chance that continuing to work on a dead project might revive it. (*Surely you believe in reincarnation. No? Oh, c'mon.*)

However, if working on the fictitious project is taking away from the time you have to devote to real projects, ask others from the department to help you out on the fictitious assignment. Doing so will help to expose your boss's motivation. It will be harder for him to string along a whole of team of people working on a nonexistent project rather than you alone.

Problem #59: He Promised the Client the Moon and the Stars (and the Cooperation of the Back Office)

Your boss managed to close the deal by overpromising. (Surprise, surprise.) But this time, he actually had the chutzpah to suggest that your back office would process the order in under a week! (The back office of your company is so tardy, it makes the government look like it runs fast.) Worse still, your boss waxed poetic about the speed of your back office to one of your company's largest customers on the eastern seaboard. When you visit the back office to check on the order, the crisis deepens. The order is completely bungled. You fear it will take at least two more weeks to sort out the mess.

Solution #59: Tell the Customer about the Delay Before He Asks

Aretha Franklin had the right idea when she sang about respect. Most customers are more forgiving when you treat them with some. Tell your customer that you caught a series of errors on the order, and you'd rather take the time up front to correct the mistakes. Sweeten the news by throwing in a small freebie, and the conversation may be less distressing (to him, anyway). For example, you might offer to waive the service charge for two months as a result of this inconvenience.

Major crisis averted, it's also wise to poke around a bit and ask others with whom you work about their own experiences with the back office. If it turns out that there is a pattern of recurring negligence, why not research some training programs or refresher courses that will help the back office team ease the glitches? Be proactive, and you may end up solving two issues. The back office will run better *and* your boss may perceive you as a managerial type. If you can snag a promotion from the jaws of near fiasco, it could help whisk you out from under your boss and his Spin Doctoring ways.

Management Mantra

"What I have become is a product of what I've seen." Those words, spoken by someone named *Anonymous*, illustrate an excellent point. Bad habits are contagious. If you are working closely with someone of dubious character, you will need to figure out how to escape from him, lest you *become* him. (See the two boxes on networking at the end of this chapter.)

Problem #60: You Are Dependent on the Spin Doctor for His Leads

His petty deceptions make you cringe, but you're stuck working for him. You are, after all, dependent on his Rolodex file. If you don't cover for him, you'll have no choice but to start cold calling new prospects, and "please leave a message at the sound of the beep" gives you the bleeping heebie-jeebies!

Solution #60: Master the Art of Networking

"Networking" is an inelegant word. When you hear the word, visions of posh dinners do not dance through your head. From a syntax standpoint, the word "networking" sounds like it involves "work" plus two extra syllables of drudgery. Yet, done correctly, it can help you attract talented prospects to your cause, win coveted new business, or sell thousands of widgets. If it can do all that, surely it can help rescue you from an unethical boss.

Start the networking process by getting yourself on the A-list. Fortunately, you don't need red-carpet credentials. All you need is industrial carpet expertise and a laptop. Sign up for upcoming trade show and industry conferences. Join a trade association or several. Start hanging around other successful people (it's the world's best way to attract leads). Believe in serendipity and be poised for opportunity to strike.

Once you've already spent a pleasant evening chitchatting with a prospect at a networking function, it's a cinch to ask him for an in-person meeting. Cultivate your own leads and contacts, and you'll no longer be dependent on your local shyster—er, boss—for his.

MELTING-THE-ICE WORDS AT A NETWORKING GIG

Many novice networkers get all tangled up in their words because they have a mistaken assumption about what they're supposed to be doing at these functions. The point is not to be fascinating, riveting, titillating, or even mildly interesting. (Well, that's a relief.) The only real charge is to make contact.

If you don't regard networking as flirting, you can begin talking to anyone about the world's most banal topics, and just see where the conversation leads. Here are some words and phrases to start the conversation flowing.

- *Are you a wine person or a beer person?*
- *Did you catch* Dancing with the Stars *last night? Who won?*
- *Did you come out with some people from your office?*
- *Did you try the mini-hamburgers? How were they?*
- *Do you know anyone here besides the host?*
- *How do you know so-and-so (the party host)?*
- *How many networking parties did you go to in December? Were any of them any good?*
- *Is it freezing in here, or is it just me?*
- *What did you think of the honored speaker?*
- *You look familiar. Did your child happen to go to Camp Hillard?*

HOW TO BECOME A PROSPECT MAGNET

Don't chase after your prospects. Instead, have them chase after you. It's easy, once you master the divine alchemy of prospect magnetism. Provide all prospects and potential new business contacts with a product or service they really need, and watch them hunt you down to solicit even more of your ideas. (It's so much classier than chewing up their voicemail tapes always begging them for a meeting.) Here are three ideas to pursue:

1. **TEACH YOUR CLIENTS HOW TO BUILD THEIR BUSINESSES.** If your prospects like what you have to say, they'll keep coming back for more.
2. **BECOME AN EXPERT IN YOUR FIELD.** Have leads approach you for your knowledge instead of the other way around.
3. **THINK IN TERMS OF REPEAT BUSINESS.** Can you offer a seminar to your leads in three parts? (That equals three visits from them.) Can you help them build a business-boosting plan based on seasonality? (That's four visits.)

In short, what can you do for your customers that will necessitate meeting with them multiple times throughout the year? Strive to be high touch instead of highly annoying.

The Golden Rule

Spin Doctors spin the facts to entice clients and win new business. However, while the spin can sometimes make new business prospects dizzy with excitement in the short term, too much spin can unravel a deal once the client inevitably discovers that he's been hoodwinked. For the present, you will need to refine your own spin lingo as you search for new solutions to pacify irate clients. If you are working for a Spin Doctor, seek to network your way far away from him while you still can.

CHAPTER 13
The Insatiable Narcissist

I have three kids plus the most demanding child of all—my boss.

She doesn't care about her employees' hobbies or hubbies. In her mind, her employees only exist when they're at the office, catering to her needs. Everyone working under her is simply a reflection of her—her dreams and aspirations, her triumphs, her failings. It's all about her, her, her.

But enough about her. Let's talk about you.

Are you having a bad day? You'd best hide or it could make *her* look bad. Do you need to leave the office early? You'd better get someone to cover for you, lest she need you that evening.

The Narcissist isn't like Big Sister, incidentally. You can't score points with her simply by hanging around all the time. No, the Insatiable Narcissist only needs you when she needs you. But whenever that magical moment strikes, you had better be there for her because her needs can be quite intense.

Problem #61: She Wants You to Be Her Yes-Ma'am

Your boss doesn't care if you're a Yes-Man or Yes-Woman, as long as you say "yes" loudly, frequently, and as obsequiously as possible. She employs you after all, doesn't she? (The correct answer is "yes.")

Solution #61: Manus Manum Lavat (One Hand Washes the Other)

Seneca, the Roman dramatist, philosopher, and politician coined the phrase "Manus manum lavat" to explain how politicians view favors. Literally, it means, "One hand washes the other." Your boss expects you to say, "Yes, Ma'am" to all of her ideas (no matter how lame). In return for your sycophantic sucking up, she will favor you by saying "yes" to some of your ideas—particularly when her own idea well has run dry.

Worried that the constant kissing up may hurt your integrity? *Yes, Ma'am.* You're right to be concerned. While kowtowing will work wonders with your boss, fellow staffers may start calling you "Brown Nose" or even worse behind your back. On the flip side, those who challenge your boss's ideas won't be around for long. They'll soon be replaced with new people who will call you "Brown Nose."

Management Mantra

"Don't mix business with pleasure." Any sign that you are could be misinterpreted by your boss as taking away the focus from her. So keep your cell phone, calendar, pager, and *iPod* out of sight. Without her, you have no life.

Problem #62: She Thinks You Should Be a Mini-Her

While your boss is one of the more self-involved people on the planet, she likes to think of herself as a mentor. She responds well to those who ape her personal style and attempt to cast themselves in her image. Sometimes she makes suggestions for how you can improve yourself—your image, voice, or managerial style—so that you can be more like her. Some of these suggestions will be in your control. Others won't be.

Solution #62: Follow One or Two of Her Suggestions; Thank Her for the Rest

Your boss only has two modes: call them "on" and "off." When she is *on*, her own river of self-esteem is flowing. She has a rapturous desire to be embraced and adored, no matter what she says. Is she criticizing your work outfits? Advising you to get voice lessons? Bemoaning the fact that your hair is too long? She honestly believes that she's doing you a favor. She's in love with herself and assumes that you are as well. *Hey, isn't everyone?*

Instead of feeling miffed by her brazen criticisms, swallow your pride and thank her. Act as if she's giving you the golden keys to your self-betterment, and then follow only the suggestions you agree with (and can afford to implement).

Incidentally, when the Narcissist is *off*, she may spiral into a dangerous self-hating mode. As annoying as she is when she's spouting advice about how you should be more like her, she's far worse to deal with when she's beating up on herself. She may even cry or become maudlin. When that happens, do everything in your power to avoid her.

Problem #63: She Needs Constant Attention

Is top management ignoring your boss's multiple emails? She'll turn to you for her affection fix. She may even confide something supremely personal to gain your sympathy. It may be of a psychological nature (why she and her husband got divorced, for example). Or she may break someone else's confidence (she knows for a fact that the CEO and CFO are having an extramarital affair). At first, you feel as if she must really respect you to take her into her confidence. But as time goes on, you realize that she is merely using you when others aren't around to pay attention to her.

Solution #63: Adopt a Gratitude Attitude

Vulnerable to huge drops in their own self-esteem, narcissists will sometimes let you in more than other bosses will. They crave constant stroking and have the charisma to attract the love they need to buoy up their fragile sense of self-esteem.

Your boss has shared so many confessions with you that it may seem as if she wants you to be her shrink. But whatever you do, don't hold a mirror up to her soul. She's not looking for any compelling psychological insights into her character or motivation. (There's considerably less there than meets the eye.) She just wants a superficial pat on the back plus your undying deference.

Your best strategy is to thank her for keeping you employed and shower her with appreciation for any shards of guidance she manages to toss your way. Phrases that appeal to the narcissistic temperament include: "What a great idea," "I couldn't have done it without you," and "Thank you for getting behind this project."

The Myth of Narcissus

Ovid's tale depicts a youth who shunned contact with Echo and other beautiful nymphs. One day, a fair maiden who had been spurned by Narcissus uttered a prayer that he might experience for himself the barb of unrequited love. A sympathetic goddess granted the maiden's wish. Shortly thereafter, fatigued by an animal hunt, Narcissus stooped down to drink and espied his own image in a lake. He promptly fell in love with the reflection staring back at him—his own bright eyes, curly locks, and ivory skin. Unable to tear himself away from his own image, he forgot to eat and drink and gradually lost his color, vigor, and beauty. Pining away from the curse of self-love, Narcissus eventually died.

Problem #64: She Has Grandiose Visions for the Department

Last year, the sales projections were unrealistic. Yet, somehow, your department leapt over tall projections with a single bound and surpassed them. This year, the projections are even more unrealistic (plus the two superheroes of the department left to join another firm). How does your boss arrive at these pie-in-the-sky numbers? Does she secretly want you to fail, so you can all eat humble pie at the fourth-quarter Year-in-Review Conference?

Solution #64: Never Say "Never"

For someone so self-absorbed, the narcissistic boss is often surprisingly productive. She sees herself as a larger-than-life heroine in the drama that is her life, and the company as a glorified extension of herself. She has oversized visions for the company. And every so often, her dreams *will* help to propel your department to greatness. She may speak in terms of profit and loss, but in reality something much more important is on the line: her own fragile sense of self-esteem. Try to learn from her how to stretch your own visions to become an even bigger success.

Just the Stats

It's called *narcissistic personality disorder*, and it affects approximately 1% of the population. (That may sound like a tiny percentage, but it is still 300,000 people.) Lying is the most common complaint about narcissists who will misrepresent themselves in order to be better liked by whomever they are trying to engage. According to the *Diagnostic and Statistical Manual of Mental Disorders (DSM-IV), narcissistic personality disorder* is marked by "a pervasive pattern of grandiosity (in fantasy or behavior), need for admiration, and lack of empathy."[10]

Problem #65: She Contrives to Keep You in Your Place

When you first started working for her, she took you under her proverbial wing. You were pleased that someone so high up in the pecking order actually seemed to care about nurturing your own development. You envisioned staying in the nest long enough to finally lay a golden egg. But gradually, as you assumed more responsibility, she seemed determined to clip your wings. She no longer values your input and says "no" to each and every one of your suggestions. She manipulates conditions for the express purpose of holding you back. You used to be her pet chickadee. Now you're afraid she'll soon be singing "Bye, Bye, Birdie."

Solution #65: Get Out from under Her

Narcissists first idealize and later devalue. The narcissistic boss will end up discarding the initial object of her affection. That's because under the deeply rooted insecurity, narcissism is ultimately about control. At first, the narcissistic boss seems to respond favorably to you. Naturally, you assume that it's because she loves your work product or your ideas, but in reality, she just wants your approval. However, once she's confident that she has it, she will begin to turn against you. It's a fact. Once she gains your affection, she will spurn you. You need to find a way to move up in the organization (so you will no longer be reporting to the Narcissist). Or find a new job before she cuts you loose and you have to look for one.

Keep your contact base fresh and start attending networking functions. Make it a priority to attend at least one networking function a week until you network your way into a better job situation. (*See* "Melting-the-Ice Words at a Networking Gig" in Chapter 12, *The Spin Doctor*).

The Golden Rule

Narcissists crave admiration and will reach out to their underlings in order to obtain it. However, once a narcissist hooks you, take care, for she will quickly recoil from you. For your own sanity and self-preservation, it's best to leave her before you are forced to.

CHAPTER 14
Enraged and Addicted

He was reminiscent of Wall Street during the '60s. He'd get drunk over lunch and start screaming obscenities, commenting on the women at the next table, even calling the waiters "a-holes." People who worked for him complained about him constantly, but because he had been at the firm a long time, he was basically untouchable.

She's possessed by some not-so-secret demons.

Her temper is legendary, and underlings consider her a "rageaholic." This, it turns out, is an apt term because her anger is fueled by an addiction to either alcohol or drugs.

Even with handlers who are professionally equipped to take the edge off of her remarks, the rageaholic boss loses friends and influences people to keep their distance.

People just can't stand working for her. And once a client has been on the receiving end of a rageaholic's ill-timed outburst, it's only a matter of time before he voices an official complaint.

Eventually, the higher-ups at the company have no choice but to either put her in a gilded cage (where a polite gatekeeper ends up acting as her front man) or show her to the door, hoping that she won't bite them on the way out.

Problem #66: You're Frightened of Her

You've watched her combust at staffers on the flimsiest of pretexts so often that now you just want to keep your distance. Not hailing from an abusive clan yourself, you tend to shut down when people lash out at others for no reason.

Solution #66: Don't Seek Her Approval

Outbursts of uncontrollable rage are particularly tough on employees who view their bosses as authority figures with the power to approve or disapprove of their actions. Suppose your own mother was warm and nurturing. She used feedback as a tool for positive reinforcement. In the best case, that meant praise. In the worst case, her criticism was constructive.

Flash forward to the present. By mistake, you take a job where you find yourself working for someone who never has a kind word to say. She publicly chastises anyone who commits the most minor offense. It can feel surreal, almost as if your boss dropped down from a completely different planet. Then again, if you're looking for your boss to enhance your sense of self-esteem, you're looking for love in all the wrong places. Instead seek ways to bolster your own feelings of self-worth.

Just do the work to the best of your ability, and take pride in your product. Look for mother love and morale boosts outside of the office.

Problem #67: Every Little Slight Is a Tirade Waiting to Happen

At the office Christmas party, your boss finds herself seated at table 70 with the rest of her department instead of at coveted table 2 with the top brass. She glares into space for the whole night, refusing to answer questions with more than a monosyllable. The morning after, she rails on the people in her department, claiming their work isn't stellar enough to merit more than a nod from top management. Clearly, she's taking out her own frustrations on the group. Either that, or she has a wicked hangover.

Solution #67: Your Boss Is a Diva of Destruction: Keep Your Distance

Your boss has no control of her emotions. Her emotional I.Q. is dangerously below average. And her outbursts are noxious. You may believe that no one who is truly important at the firm will ever hear about her temper tantrums, but the plain fact is they already have and it is for this reason they are avoiding her. Follow suit. Limit your interactions with her to the minimum face time possible that you need to maintain appearances and get your work accomplished.

The Difference between a Rageaholic and a Bully

On the surface, the rageaholic shares certain behavior patterns with the Bully, such as the penchant to scream just because she's in the mood. But there is a big difference between the two types of bosses. The rageaholic can't keep a lid on her emotions, while the Bully is attempting to use his notorious temper to achieve results. He picks on people selectively. She doesn't, presumably because she can't help herself.

She might be an alcoholic or a substance abuser. She might have an undiagnosed thyroid condition. She could be an ex-smoker, struggling to free herself from nicotine's addictive allure. Whatever the reason, her actions are unprofessional.

While the rageaholic and the Bully are both people abusers, the upper echelons at most companies view them quite differently. Top management sanctions the Bully; that is, until the complaints about his temper outnumber the accolades he earns due to his bullish performance record. He's nasty, but at least he's in control. But top management always shuns the rageaholic. She's nasty and out of control.

It's a good idea to stay as far away from her as humanly possible, lest the sound of her screams taint you as she's being ushered out the door.

Problem #68: Before Lunch, She Tells You One Thing; After Lunch, It's a Different Story

Your boss takes long, leisurely lunches where the alcohol flows. While she returns from lunch considerably livelier than she was earlier, it's also with a different spin on the project of the moment. She reverses herself on decisions made a few short hours before she left. You feel like you could use a drink—and you don't even drink.

Solution #68: Pick the Story That Benefits You Most

She speaks out of both sides of her mouth. You have no choice but to pick the side that benefits you the most and pursue that direction. Worried that she'll call you on the carpet for flouting her directives no matter what you do? Kick the habit of being dependent on her in the first place. Never ask for permission. Instead, simply inform her of your intentions. If she has a real problem with any of your decisions, she'll let you know. (It's not as if the woman has any compunctions about raising her voice.)

A Twelve-Step Guide to Fixing Your Self-Esteem Issues, without Resorting to Shrinks, Career Coaches, or Medications

Need a self-esteem quick fix? Here, for your reading pleasure, is the Do-It-Yourselfer's Guide to self-esteem repair. While some of these ideas will appeal more to women, and others to men, please note that all of these suggestions require time away from the office. As the saying goes, "Out of sight, out of mind."

1. **TAKE OUT YOUR AGGRESSIONS BY TAKING UP KICK-BOXING.** For extra energy, think of your boss's scowling face every time you kick. Oh, that feels good.
2. **START A SUPPORT GROUP THAT SUPPORTS HIGHER LEARNING.** When you hear the name "Twain," do you think of Mark or Shania? (If you answered "Mark," give yourself three points. If you answered "Shania," pretend that you answered "Mark.") Escape from the relentless pendulum of your boss's mood swings by starting a reading group that focuses on the loftier fare of literary classics.
3. **PUT YOURSELF IN SOMEONE ELSE'S CAPABLE HANDS.** The strain you feel from your neck all the way down your spine could be a sign that you're taking your work woes home with you. Release them—by having a professional massage therapist knead them out of your system. Deep tissue massage is a proven way to relinquish those little office tensions that have a way of building up over time.
4. **BE KIND AND UNWIND.** Random acts of kindness have a way of rescuing us from the self-absorption that's one of the many negative side effects of working for a rageaholic. Your boss screams at you for absolutely no reason, and so you keep replaying the scenario in your mind, wondering what you did wrong. When you do something nice for someone else, it interrupts the negative video clip titled

Work Hell that plays over and over in your mind's eye. An act of kindness can be as simple as helping an old lady read the ingredient list on an item in a grocery store. Or it can be as meaningful as deciding to become someone's adopted older brother in one of the many mentoring programs designed to help underprivileged kids.

5. **MEDITATE—ON YOUR PERFECT COLORS.** Wearing the right colors can subtract ten years from your age, and that can really lift your spirits. Are you a *summer, spring, fall,* or *winter*? Get your colors done and find out.
6. **RECHARGE YOUR BATTERIES BY CHANGING YOUR LIGHT BULBS.** When the physical space around you begins to deteriorate, you need to maintain it, or else you will start to feel burned out on the inside.
7. **COMPARTMENTALIZE.** Don't let the mess that's going on inside your head spill onto the floor of your home. Throw out your clutter or give it to thrift. Put loose papers in drawers.
8. **GO ON A DATE—WITH YOURSELF.** Why wait for others to approve (or disapprove) of your movie selection? Reserve a day to do all of the things that you want to do, solo. Take in a museum. Treat yourself to lunch. Catch a date movie all by yourself. Aren't you fabulous?
9. **SOLVE A MYSTERY. WHATEVER HAPPENED TO…?** With the Internet, it's surprisingly easy to locate just about anyone. To prevent apoplectic shock on behalf of the person you're contacting ("Why is she contacting me after all of these years? Do we have a love child?"), send the person an email first.
10. **TRY ON A BRAND-NEW PERSONALITY.** Browse in a vintage store and buy a garment from the 1920s or 1930s. Maybe it will be a flapper dress (if you're a woman) or a smoking jacket (if you're a man.) Adopt the character of the person who you feel must have worn it last.
11. **I'M OKAY, YOU'RE OKAY KARAOKE.** Experience the healing power of music by belting out your favorite tunes at a karaoke

bar. There's no faster way to inject some testosterone into your self-esteem.

12. **BECOME A STAR—BY ASSOCIATION.** Get yourself invited to a celebrity fund-raiser and challenge yourself to talk to the honoree. When you rub shoulders with the great and the near great, some of that celebrity stardust rubs off on you.

Take the time to nurture your own sense of self-esteem, and it will pay you back. Your boss's tirades will bounce off you faster than a tennis ball on a grass court. You may hear your boss scream, but the sound of her shrieks will no longer rattle you. That's because you will find yourself in a completely different place: one where you are free, free, free from her at last.

Just the Stats

Estimates vary, but according to some reports, approximately 23 million Americans suffer from alcohol and drug addiction. Yet only a scanty 20% seek help for their problem. *Heavy drinking* is defined as five or more drinks on one occasion at least five times a month. Alcohol and drug addiction cost American businesses roughly $100 billion a year in lost productivity.[11]

Problem #69: You're the Cleanup Guy

At the slightest provocation, your boss raises her voice at vendors and suppliers. You've watched them go slack-jawed from the shock. Her righteous indignation sometimes forces your company's vendors to back down. But at other times, they've been known to complain bitterly about her tone of voice, finding it too snarly for their tastes. By comparison, you seem like a saint. You are even-keeled and unflappable. Thus, your boss has elected you for an ultra-special assignment: to clean up after her! Every time she loses her temper, she dispatches you to apologize for her or to explain away her actions.

Solution #69: Brush Up on Office Diplomacy 101

Congratulations. You're on your way up. Even your boss recognizes that she needs to be "handled." Think of yourself as her press secretary of internal and external affairs. To accomplish this task seamlessly, you will need to become expert at apologizing on her behalf.

Excellent manners on your part will go a long way towards erasing the terrible impression she makes. Charm and a bit of wit may help you overcome the initial awkwardness. After you've apologized for your boss's flagrant outburst, give the official press report. "Tiffany profoundly apologizes for the outlandish remark she made at the last meeting," you might begin. "She wants you to know that she simply got carried away in the heat of the moment. She also asked me to convey that, of course, our company will approve the extra surcharges without delay. If you fax me the paperwork, I'll see to it that it's signed by the end of the week."

Don't be surprised if everyone just wants to deal with you directly—it's so much simpler.

Send lavish gifts to those whom your boss has insulted. Get into the habit of taking subtle credit for her generosity. For example, if you know for a fact that one of your chagrined vendors has a sweet tooth, send her a box of *Godiva* chocolates. Before it arrives, ask her if she received it. When she says, "What gift?" you can tell her it's a little something that you *and* your boss thought she might enjoy.

Problem #70: Your Boss Misses Important Meetings

Your whole department has been scrambling for weeks to pull together a presentation for a bank. Your company is asking for big money: a loan worth several million dollars. The CEO has been leading the charge, night after night, for weeks on end. But when the day of the presentation finally arrives, she's nowhere to be found. Urgent calls to her cell phone are not returned. You and the rest of the team have no choice but to attend the meeting without her. A few hours after the meeting ends, the CEO arrives at the office, raging about the broken subway system. But, to your knowledge, there was no subway breakdown that day.

Solution #70: Cover for Her; but If It's a Pattern, Drop a Hint to Someone Who Can Help

One missed meeting is not a sign of an incurable addiction. But if your boss habitually misses meetings, that's one habit worth trying to break. Never go up against an alcoholic boss one on one. Denial will be her likely response, followed by anger if you really press her. Alcoholics can be quite cagey about inventing all sorts of excuses to explain away their problems. And you so much want to believe the excuses because, oddly enough, there's something that's truly compelling about an addict's personality. Someone teetering on the razor's edge of destruction often has a reverse charisma that can be quite bewitching.

But if her self-destructive pattern continues unabated, eventually it will jeopardize business. And at that point, you will have no choice but to speak up. Find an HR person and tell her that what you are about to reveal is confidential. Have her discreetly check the facts without bringing up your name.

She and others in her department may be able to recommend a rehab program for your boss. Rehabilitation centers are gaining a lot of credibility these days as one way to curb the ever-mounting problem of addiction in the U.S.

Management Mantra

"This, too, shall pass." It will pass because, sooner or later, your boss will self-destruct. And chances are, it will be sooner rather than later.

The Golden Rule

Uncontrollable outbursts of rage that seem to have no direct cause are often telltale signs of an addiction. Never accuse a boss of being addicted to drugs or alcohol, as she'll be inclined to deny it. Instead, adopt a "wait-and-see" attitude. If the situation worsens, a confidential but frank discussion with someone in HR is your smartest tactic. While it's a big step, handled correctly, it's your best move. As companies struggle to hold on to good talent, *rehab* is no longer the four-letter word it once was.

CHAPTER 15
The Sheltered Sultan

The universal factor common to all failing businesses I have counseled or acted as financial advisor to, is the inability or unwillingness to see the handwriting on the wall and to take early action that could actually save the company.

As a Young Turk, he led your company through a turbulent period several years back that earned the fierce loyalty of those under him. But recently, the company's core business hit a rough patch, and tongues have started to murmur that your intrepid leader has lost his edge.

He stubbornly refuses to tinker with the way the business operates. Even when confronted with hard evidence that market share is shriveling and customers are departing in droves, he resists trying new approaches.

He sees little value in analyzing the competition. He doesn't have a real interest in keeping tabs on what's going on in the outside world. Insulated from some of the harsh realities by cronies and yes-men who lull him into a false sense of security, there is no one on staff with the clout to tell him that what got the business here will not take it to the next level.

In some primal way, he understands that the business is broken. But can he be pushed to take the hard steps necessary in order to fix it?

What, if anything, can you do to help this Sheltered Sultan find his way back from the slippery slope before your company slides into bankruptcy?

Problem #71: He's Dumb about Intelligence

Your boss doesn't know what he doesn't know. And he doesn't care that he doesn't know it. The only thing he knows for sure is that he doesn't want to squander a lot of money for up-to-the-minute information on changes in the marketplace. He believes that whatever worked in the past will continue to, even though it's obviously *not* working. He's unconcerned about whatever it is his competition is doing, until they are literally inside his company cafeteria, eating his lunch and drinking his diet cola.

Solution #71: Give Him the Three-Minute Download

Imagine that you were an esteemed cabinet member employed by a president of the United States who hated to read. What would you do? You would stay up-to-date on polls, significant market trends, and reports from the State Department, the FBI, and the CIA, as well as other pertinent data. And you would fill in your boss at every available opportunity. Essentially, that's what you need to do now. The manner in which you do it needs to be palatable to your boss, though, as it's unlikely that being Minister of Information is part of your formal job description.

Why not give a mini-PowerPoint presentation on your findings? If your boss chafes, experiment with other formats. You could email him the pertinent information. You could announce it in a meeting. Or you could share it with someone on staff who has your boss's ear and ask her to be the messenger.

Whether you deliver the news flashes verbally or orally doesn't matter so much, as long as, somehow, your boss receives marketplace intelligence in a timely manner.

Splice and dice the information for your boss into manageable chunks. It's unlikely that someone who hates to read will appreciate receiving long, undigested articles via email. So K.I.S.S. up to him, by Keeping It Simple, (Stupid). Highlight the key points, and then recap your learning in a few bulleted points.

Problem #72: Tunnel Vision

Your boss is the consummate insider. His planning is limited to updating the annual budget without focusing on any new input from the outside world. Instead of soliciting feedback from the real people who are using your company's product or service, he surrounds himself with true believers who protect him from having to deal with change. He's 180 degrees removed from customer-centric. He fears the man on the street. Your Sheltered Sultan may look like the CEO of your company, but he has the mind-set of Marie Antoinette.

Solution #72: Take Off the Blinders

Take it upon yourself to review the failing product or service with fresh eyes. Imagine that you've been asked to write a Harvard Business School case study about it. Here are some of the issues that you may need to detangle. Is the problem with the product or service? Or is the trouble with your customer base? (Are your customers aging? Are they dying? Are they loyal or fickle?) Has anything changed about the marketplace in the past year? How has the competition reacted or failed to? Is the business sufficiently diversified? You may have to import an outsider to develop the perspective your company urgently needs to focus on the problem.

What are the logical next steps? Should you shake up the product mix? Do you need to tinker with the price or alter the distribution plan in any way? Does the original business model still work? While you're digging to get to root of the problem, consider whether you will need to reexamine vendor policies or take any other drastic cost-cutting measures such as renegotiating the company lease.

Just the Stats

"Eight out of ten entrepreneurs go out of business." That is commonly cited as gospel. But is it true? Some say it isn't because it counts exiting a business as a failure, when sometimes, companies exit a business to take their profits. One fact that is true: compared to other business people, entrepreneurs tend to be heavy risk takers.

Problem #73: What Global Economy?

How has your company reacted to the pressures of globalization? For the answer, just check out the company website. There's absolutely nothing gripping about it! It displays the addresses of your various offices along with photographs of your core product line. But consumers can't buy products directly from the site or provide any feedback about the experience. Your closest competitor, a relatively new company that embraces technology, has recently upgraded its website to sell goods and services around the world. Meanwhile, that diehard lunatic—er, that would be Luddite—known as your boss, merely shrugs off this major development, to the intense frustration of everyone working under him.

Solution #73: Help Set Up a Website That Works for You

Never discuss in the abstract the onslaught of globalization and how ill prepared your company is to handle it. To a technophobic boss, visions of an Orwellian world where Big Brother not only watches you but logs on to your website and complains about your company's product line can be most disconcerting!

Challenge yourself to learn how to develop a twenty-first century website. Not your job? Start a committee that will find an outside firm to design the site. Here are some questions to ask at that initial meeting. How will the navigation system work? How can you make the site customer-friendly? Should it have a shopping cart function that lets visitors log on and pay via credit card? How often can the site be updated under the contractual arrangement? Have the firm create a test demo of the new and improved company website and have all committee members experiment with it to iron out the kinks *before* previewing the demo to your boss and other staffers. Gather the committee's input and make changes. Then ask everyone in your company to visit the test site before it goes live.

Once the company website is up and running, do your homework. Research simple ways to spread the word. Should your company invest in keywords? Can you add a blogging function to the site? In short, what can you do to make your website fun, friendly, engaging, and more interactive?

Management Mantra

"Ignorance is not bliss." Ignorance could cost your company its lead in the marketplace, its entire customer base, and the livelihood of every single employee at the company. We live in a 24/7, Internet-based world where changes happen at a frightening speed. Smash the window of your boss's ivory tower if you have to. These days, anyone who refuses to keep up is falling behind.

Problem #74: He's Distracted

Your boss used to work sixty-hour weeks; even when he wasn't around, he could be reached for consultation. But in the past two years, he has endured a series of personal setbacks (or triumphs, depending on your point of view). He's either finally tied the knot or cut the marriage noose. For some reason, you can't seem to get his attention to discuss the rapidly declining business.

Solution #74: Focus Your Energy on Focusing Him

Don't be nervous about looking like a Nervous Nellie. Your boss is being negligent. Should he continue to ignore both the market and the vital competitive factors, he could wake up one morning to find that his principal business model is unprofitable or even obsolete. You are simply trying to bring these matters to his attention before it is too late for him to react. Air your concerns with others at the company. If they share your point of view, eventually the top officers will schedule a mandatory emergency meeting with your boss. That should shake him out of his bliss long enough to bring him to the table.

Problem #75: No One at the Company Wants to Look in the Mirror

Denial starts at the top and filters down. The core business is starting to crumble, and the existing management of the company is to blame. Why can't everyone just see that? Hmmm. Maybe it's because the very people who need to diagnose the problem are those who caused the problem in the first place. Just a theory.

Solution #75: Acceptance

As with any misfortune, accepting the situation is the first step to turning it around. However, being honest about your company's dire straits also bears a great risk as it could involve the loss of one's employment. Over a century ago, Upton Sinclair once said, "It is difficult to get a man to understand something when his salary depends on him not understanding it." Existing management will need to attempt to identify those elements of the business that should survive and restructure within them. Sometimes this might involve the sale of various parts of a company's operations, and to do the responsible thing, management may need to put itself out of a job. (See the following chapter on Swindlers, Defrauders, and Company Cheats.)

The Golden Rule

Today, it is dangerous for a business to ignore the marketplace. Competitors don't require nearly as much time to catch up as they did in years past. In the Internet-based global economy, changes occur in nanoseconds. Do one thing a week to bring your Sheltered Sultan up to up to date so he will be unable to resist advancing into the twenty-first century.

CHAPTER 16

Swindlers, Defrauders, and Company Cheats (Know Anyone Like This?)

There is an old saying, "In the end, all businesses fail because they run out of money." The lengths that some managers will go to so their businesses will not run out of money are often incredible.

He can stretch a business expense until it's the size of a Lear jet. In fact, he frequently mixes business and pleasure—at cocktails, golf courses, and spa resorts. Either he lost his moral compass a long time ago or temporarily misplaced it in a yacht leased back when prospects looked rosier.

He views the business as an extension of his lavish lifestyle rather than a real corporation with investors. Thus, when it comes to treating his investors as partners, he can be secretive in the extreme. His investors may find him to be somewhat paranoid, but his secrecy doesn't stem from any deep-rooted psychological condition, unless it's the psychology of greed.

Your boss's wheeling and dealing could very well get him into trouble. Depending on how flagrant his actions are, he could even go to jail. You need either to help him clean up his act or start planning your exit strategy. Is your boss crooked? Here are some red flags to watch for.

Problem #76: A Vendor Starts Screaming about Not Getting Paid

It begins innocently enough. One day, you notice an unfamiliar number flashing on your caller ID at work. You pick up the phone, only to hear a vaguely familiar voice yelling at you at ear-piercing decibels. The disembodied voice is shouting phrases such as, "past due," "talk to my lawyer," and "those charlatans you work for." You politely interject, "Excuse me, I didn't quite catch your name." It turns out to be one of the vendors who your company uses all the time. The reason he's calling you, he explains, is because your bosses haven't bothered to return any of his phone calls during the past three months.

Solution #76: Work Out a Discounted Payment Schedule

Before arriving at a solution, it's always a good idea to figure out what the problem is. Ask your boss or bosses why this particular vendor wasn't paid promptly. Perhaps the goods he provided were of inferior quality and your company is demanding a "make good" on the next shipment. Maybe the vendor refused. If so, delayed payment might be a valid recourse. But if it turns out that the vendor wasn't paid due to a cash-flow problem at the company, someone at your office will need to work out a discounted payment schedule with him.

You might assume that he won't be open to negotiation because he sounds so irate on the phone. But in truth, he might be perfectly willing to renegotiate—with a guarantee that he'll get paid within a reasonable time frame. Clients forsake their payment obligations every single day for a slew of different reasons. Chances are, this vendor has experienced this very problem before.

Two points to bear in mind if you're the one who ends up doing the negotiating: (1) there is a present value of money (so the sooner you can pay him, the cheaper it might be) and (2) all threats aside, your vendor probably *doesn't* want to spend a lot of money on legal action. He may grumble, he may grouse, he may rue the day he decided to get involved with your company. But if you are empathetic, you may well succeed in working out a payment schedule you can both live with.

Recognize that the word travels at the speed of gossip. Every time your company slips out of one of its payment obligations, it infuriates another vendor and your company loses face. Vendors talk among themselves, and eventually your business will be blackballed among a whole series of service providers. Pay your vendors every penny they're due, unless your company is cash-poor and begging for alms!

Problem #77: He Practices Voodoo Economics

Sound financial planning is not your boss's area of expertise. One morning, you nicely ask him to explain a line item on an invoice-expense report. Instead of answering your question, he pricks you with a pointed remark, and suddenly you feel like you have to walk on pins and needles. Or you observe a number on an asset balance sheet, which should have been recorded as a loss, marked as a profit instead. Or you notice that a profit is recorded in the correct column but is off by a decimal point. Were these simply careless oversights or premeditated attempts to swindle the company? Perhaps one of the business managers at your organization takes you aside one day and tells you *not* to charge one client for time spent but to put your time against another. What should you do?

Solution #77: Remember That Emails Count as Legal Documents

Shoot a series of politely worded emails where you simply ask the questions. Watch your tone when writing emails of this sort. Rewrite them a few times until you're positive that Emily Post would approve. There are ways to hoist a red flag without raising your boss's hackles. If your boss ignores your emails or doesn't provide a satisfactory answer, you can surmise that you may be on to something. At that point, you would be well advised to *drop* the queries and concentrate on extricating yourself. As a general rule, if your company is pursuing questionable business practices, you should consider leaving. Begin sending out job feelers. From the Pandora's box of a troubled company, sooner or later, the truth will pop out.

Four Clever Ways to Research the Company Where You Work

1. **Vault.com.** Research whether any past employees were disgruntled enough to say anything negative about your company in the employer reviews.
2. **Sec.gov/edgar/searchedgar/companysearch.html.** Punch in the company name, ticker symbol, and state to find all filings. When the list of filings comes up, choose the most recent 10-K report. This is the company's annual report and should include a good description of the business.
3. **Buy one share of stock in your company to receive quarterly reports and annual reports.**
4. **Check out your company's website.** Look for a link about investor relations.

Problem #78: Barter Is His Stock-in-Trade

Everyone at the firm is a martyr to barter. Your firm does a lot of legal work for an airline, for which it receives airline tickets that can be used for up to five years. Pity no one at the firm travels very far (when they do, it's via taxi). Meanwhile, the firm needs cash now—for office furniture and equipment. What was your boss thinking?

Solution #78: Investigate Barter Exchanges

Barter is the exchange of goods and services for other goods and services. There are numerous barter exchanges on the Internet where you can trade something that you receive in exchange for something else without any money changing hands. You could suggest to your boss that you swap those airline tickets for something your company needs right away, such as office furniture. Or you could sell the airline tickets on *eBay*.

Just the Stats

Quickie quiz: Is Uncle Sam pro- or anti-barter? Answer: He's all for it, as long as he sees a part of it. Why should he be left out of the loop? Savvy tax accountants agree: barter does not offer a tax loophole. You need to report the value of the goods bartered on Schedule C, Profit or Loss from Business Form 1040. Check out the IRS website for more details and search for Schedule C.

Problem #79: Your Company Asks You to Take a Pay Cut

Your performance during the past six months has been so robust that you feel as if you've been single-handedly propping up your entire department. Tragically, you're absolutely right! Your results have been stellar. It's just everyone else who failed miserably, which is why your boss is asking you to consider the unthinkable. He wants you to agree to a salary rollback to prevent more heads from rolling. You open your mouth to object but feel too stunned to speak.

Solution #79: Ask for Stock Options or Other Perks

When the proverbial ship is sinking faster than the Titanic, upper management sometimes asks the valuable players to make sacrifices to help keep her afloat. If you accept the suggested salary cut without a squeak, your survival at the company will be virtually guaranteed—at least until the next round of staff cuts.

On the flip side, depending on how much money you need to support yourself, a salary rollback can cause instant motion sickness. Just thinking about it is making you gag, and it's only partly from the choppy atmosphere at the office these days. This is the way that your company chooses to repay your loyalty?

When you hear news that threatens to rock your world, don't feel compelled to make an instantaneous decision. Go home and sleep on it to gain some much-needed perspective. Once you've piped down, take out a pen and paper and do the math. First, figure out if you can survive on the penurious salary. Then force yourself to get creative about it. What sort of compromise could you live with? Are there other ways the company might compensate you? Can you take advantage of the opportunity to ask for stock options? Could you request to work out of your home one day a week? Can the company perk you with transportation to and from the office? In short, what can they do that won't make the salary rollback pinch quite as much?

Titles: The World's Cheapest Perks

If you opt to ask for stock options and are refused, negotiate for something else with a monetary value. If you can't get something that's worth real money, ask for a better title. Titles are absolutely free to the company but add pizzazz to the most mundane-looking business card. Are you an associate? Ask to be anointed senior associate. Are you a senior associate? Ask to be called vice president. Are you a vice president? Ask to be crowned senior vice president. Are you senior vice president? Ask to be promoted to grand pooh-bah. Think of title inflation as compensating for the deflation of your salary. The bigger the requested salary cut, the more impressive your new title should sound.

Problem #80: The Company's Bankrupt

You always suspected that your company was in trouble, and now your secret fear has been confirmed. The company is declaring bankruptcy. You wonder what this might mean for the company's prospects, both in the short and long term. Uncertain of the proper protocol, you can't decide whether to circulate your resumé immediately or hang out for just a little longer to see through the whole painful process. (You may have carped and quibbled about your bosses once or twice during the last 182 pages of this book, but that doesn't mean you won't miss them all dearly.)

Solution #80: Let Your Clients See the Light at the End of the Tunnel

If the life of a company is like a book, the *last* chapter you'd want to be in is chapter 11. But the plain fact is, declaring bankruptcy will force the company to restructure its balance sheet. Certain financial obligations (such as the lease) can be dropped, which can be helpful if the company has shrunk recently. While the business continues to operate, it will be protected from creditors. And ultimately, the company will be financially stronger than before—with a big *if*—if it can prevent the domino effect of client departures once those clients hear the bad news.

Someone from your company, such as the owner or CEO, will need to reassure clients that the business is fundamentally sound and it is simply the debt (bank loans, leases, and bills) that needs to be restructured. Make inquiries to be sure this is happening. The protection the company will receive under bankruptcy will allow it to serve clients better than before. Some of the "sick" branches of the business will be pruned to focus on the healthy parts, which include their accounts.

The owner or CEO should call one-on-one meetings with each client to report the news. Reassurances will need to be given that the restructuring plan is sound, the underlying business is strong, and that the company will not go under. If this doesn't happen, take to the boats!

Management Mantra

"The whole is worth more than the sum of the parts." Why does the U.S. government allow troubled companies to stay in business? The rationale behind chapter 11 is that the value of a typical business is far higher than the sum of its parts. It's generally more efficient to allow a faltering company to stay in business than to sell off its assets individually.

WORDS THAT MAY HELP CAST BANKRUPTCY IN A BETTER LIGHT

Chapter 11 is a chapter of the U.S. Bankruptcy Code that governs the process of reorganization under the bankruptcy laws of this country. A chapter 11 filing is an attempt to stay in business while a bankruptcy court supervises the reorganization of the company's contractual and debt obligation.

The court can grant complete or partial relief for most of the company's debts and its contracts so that the company can make a fresh start.

Believe it or not, chapter 11 is all about optimism. And the more optimistic you can sound when discussing it, the more clients you will retain. Here are some words and phrases to get you started.

- *A year from now we'll have a robust balance sheet.*
- *It's time to focus on our core business.*
- *Look at the bright side.*
- *Our key employees have agreed to stay on, and we hope you will too.*
- *This is a blessing in disguise.*
- *We're bringing equity into the company.*
- *We're going to increase the equity of the business by getting rid of the debt.*
- *We're going to trim the deadwood and save the trees.*
- *We have a temporary cash flow problem.*
- *You won't recognize us.*

The Golden Rule

Not all troubled companies have a swindler at the helm, but having a swindler in charge will bring down a company quickly. Trouble also has a way of accentuating a leader's worst character defects. Declaring chapter 11 will necessitate making some hard decisions, but it is a show of faith about a company's long-term prospects. A plan will be put into effect whereby the unhealthy parts of the enterprise will be trimmed so that the healthy parts can thrive. If your company is on the cusp of bankruptcy and you are asked to take a salary cut, look for ways to negotiate a perk that will make the salary rollback more palatable. Lest they forget, remind your bosses that loyalty goes both ways.

PART 2

Colleagues from Purgatory

The colleague from Purgatory never ceases to torment you. She might bombard you with questions all day long. Or she might lounge at her desk eating bonbons while you do all the heavy lifting. She might devote considerable energy to buttering up the higher-ups or stoop to new levels in an effort to undermine you. She's either wagging her tongue, spilling everyone else's torrid secrets, or wagging her tail at you, trying to tease out yours—thus infuriating every single person on the team. She might sing aloud to her *iPod* until you beg her to stop or smell so poorly that you have no desire to stop by her office to work with her. But work with her, you must.

If you need her to make a decision, she waffles more than a waffle iron. Yet if you dispatch her to iron out an issue with a client or supplier, she bungles it so badly that if you didn't step in to save the day, you would all get burned. You have never met a weaker link with such a strong sense of entitlement. And if you didn't know for a fact that she had a beeline to the big boss, you would fire her, transfer her, demote her, or at the very least, put her on probation.

You have courted, coddled, and kowtowed to her. And she has repaid you by skipping out early, outing company secrets, or just checking out entirely. Is mentoring this coddled, frazzled, mumbling, bumbling, stumbling, intensely paranoid colleague really part of your job description? Or was she put in your life to teach you something? While you're grappling with that greater philosophical dilemma, here are some ways to handle some of the stickier conundrums that are entirely her fault.

CHAPTER 17
The Coddled Superstar

She was a prima donna who kept prima donna hours. In late, out early, and on her cell phone the whole damned time. Naturally, she was the first person on the team to be promoted.

She is talented, and boy, does she know it. Perhaps she's worked at the firm for a couple of years and now feels a sense of entitlement along with seniority. She slides in the door at ten minutes of ten, out the door at five, and has leisurely lunches lasting over two hours. When you politely knock on her office door, she always seems to be on a personal call and she's not shy about asking you to leave!

You have caught her doing the crossword puzzle, paying her bills, checking her online horoscope, and making dinner reservations—and all that before lunch. The only thing you rarely see her doing is working for the firm. You believe her talents are being squandered and would love to put her on a new business project or a key initiative. But with her self-imposed flex time, you're not 100% certain that you can count on her to see the project through.

When the Coddled Superstar you have working for you is too spoiled for her own good, are there any sure-fire ways to discipline her?

Problem #81: She's Always Late

She flounces into every internal meeting ten minutes late, mumbles an apology, and takes the seat closest to the door. She's not only flouting your authority, she's disrespecting everyone else in the room. Inevitably, some kind soul at the table will feel compelled to repeat the information that has been already conveyed to the group for the benefit of the late arrival. (And it was so fascinating the first time.) The Coddled Superstar only has to sit through one meeting. Those who were considerate enough to arrive on time have to sit through one-and-a-half meetings.

Solution #81: Time Is Money: Start Charging Those Who Are Late

Start a kitty that people must contribute to each and every time they're late to an internal meeting. If your company happens to raise funds for a particular cause, a kitty is a terrific way to penalize people for showing up late to meetings and raise real donations at the same time. You can either charge by the minute or a flat fee. For example, you could charge $1 for every minute late or a flat fee of $10 no matter how late the person arrives.

A fun twist on the idea is to start a kitty and use the proceeds to throw a terrific party for the whole department at year-end. Add a theme to it, and everyone who arrives at the meeting promptly can hobnob about the upcoming party while they're waiting for the Coddled Superstar to make an appearance.

Management Mantra

Woody Allen once said, "Half of life is showing up." The other half is showing up on time. Don't let late arrivals show you up. They assume that you'll say nothing about their untimely rudeness, because people seldom do. But if ten people sit around a conference table for ten minutes waiting for a meeting to start, that's one hour and forty minutes of wasted time. No time like the present to put an end to that.

Here, Kitty, Kitty: How to Start the Kitty Idea at Your Company

Find the person empowered to approve the kitty idea and sell it to him or her. It might be someone in the HR department. If not, start there anyway, as HR will certainly know where to direct you. Then follow these easy steps:

- **Ask which charities your company supports and figure out the logistics.** Can your company cut a check for the amount of cash collected? How often should the kitty be counted? Who will be the keeper of the kitty? (It should be someone who tends to arrive at meetings on time.)
- **Enhance the kitty proceeds with spare change.** Place kitty cans in the company cafeteria. Round up the amounts charged for all cafeteria food to the nearest dollar and toss the spare change into the cans. A few cents here and there really add up over time.
- **Assign captains for the fundraising drive.** This can help build support for the cause and keep morale high.

Problem #82: She's Working 24/7—On Her Personal Life

You've memorized the names of his seven brothers, two cats, and pet hamster. You know that cheesecake is his favorite dessert and that he was born during a leap year. No, these aren't your boyfriend's vital stats; they are your *employee's* boyfriend's vital stats. You know every little thing about him because your underling talks about him nonstop. And then some. And then some more. And then, *Oh, please, won't she ever stop jabbering about him?*

Solution #82: Send a Message

You don't want to be cruel, but in the words of a well-known song, sometimes one has to be, in order to be kind. Consider the following: while the Coddled Superstar has been sitting on her laurels chatting about her boy wonder, who at the company has been picking up her slack? Maybe it's time for you to start paying more attention to *that* employee.

Start rewarding the hard workers in your department with better projects and assignments, and give Little Ms. Superstar some of the boilerplate assignments for a change. Do you have a clerical project that you'd love to whisk off your desk? Why not assign it to her today? When she asks what's going on, you might suggest that you're worried about giving her more challenging projects since she seems to be very wrapped up in her personal life at the moment. If that doesn't convey the message, wait until her annual review and mention it again.

Towards Peaceful Coworker Coexistence

What if the garrulous Superstar happens to be at your exact level rather than a direct report? You can still "send a message" by politely telling her that you need to get back to work. If the two of you are buddies, why not suggest catching a drink after hours to catch up on her love life?

Just the Stats

The top four excuses for wasting time at work:

1. Not enough work to do
2. Underpaid
3. Coworkers too distracting
4. Not enough time over the weekends or at night[12]

Problem #83: He Disses You in Front of the Whole Staff

You get along with your colleague and intuitively trust his judgment. But he has a creative temperament that asserts itself when the pressure is on. Your company has been short-staffed for months, and you've had to rely on this whiny, sensitive soul even more than usual. One day he just snaps at you—and it's in front of everyone else.

Solution #83: Apologize to Him Behind Closed Doors

If an overworked colleague erupts, it's rarely because he's questioning your authority. It's because his shock absorbers are worn down so thin that he just needs to get home and get some shut-eye. Think of it as a mini-breakdown.

While it may sound counterintuitive to apologize to someone for something that clearly wasn't your fault, an amazing thing happens when you can bring yourself to do so. An intimate bond is forged. All you have to say is something akin to, "I blame myself for your outburst earlier today. Clearly, I've been relying on you too much. If you have any issues with me, I'd appreciate hearing about them in the privacy of my office. If you don't, let's just shake hands and get over it."

Chances are he'll apologize to you on the spot. But even if he doesn't, he'll reconsider before publicly chastising you again.

Call a "time-out" just like you would with a little kid having a tantrum. Send your colleague home for the rest of the afternoon. He'll get the rest and recuperation he needs and will return rejuvenated on the following morning. It's often worth blowing the schedule to have a well-rested and grateful colleague back in your corner.

Problem #84: Her Smoking Breaks Add Up to More Than a Lunch Break

She dashes out of the office at 9:30 a.m. to smoke a cigarette. By ten minutes of ten, she still hasn't returned. At 11:15, she needs to run outside again, and this time, it's with your secretary and another direct report in tow. It's the modern-day version of *Upstairs, Downstairs*. While they gab and puff away downstairs, absolutely no work can be accomplished upstairs. At noon, it's time for your colleague to fly downstairs again. She saunters towards the elevator bank, cigarette hard pack in hand, off to a lunch break that will stretch for over an hour. If only you could figure out a way to keep her around, preferably alive, and not reeking of tobacco.

Solution #84: Pile Her with Work

There's no point in discussing her two weaknesses—smoking and time allocation—without a cogent plan. What could you possibly add to the canon on the hazards of smoking that she doesn't already know? And on the topic of time allocation, she's likely to counter that, somehow, she manages to get her work done.

A cleverer idea is to avoid the conversation altogether and start piling her with projects. If she grumbles that she has too much work on her plate, that's the moment to suggest that if she took fewer breaks throughout the day, perhaps she might get her work done faster. (Please note it's impossible to pursue this strategy simultaneously with the strategy suggested in Solution #82, so you'd better hope that the Coddled Superstar who's working 24/7 on her personal life isn't also a smoker! If she is, you might be better off taking her aside and gently informing her that the minimum number of hours she needs to spend a day on your projects total seven, not four point five.)

Problem #85: She Grooms Herself More Often Than a Cat

She has a standing round mirror on top of her desk and a mounted mirror on her wall. Periodically throughout the day, she checks herself out in *both* mirrors. What a vanity case! When you enter her domicile, she's either correcting her lip line or curling her lips to inspect the pallor of her teeth. You've also seen her fluff her hair, apply mascara, and even paint her nails right at her desk. Since when did it become socially acceptable to perform one's entire grooming ritual without getting up to go to the ladies' room?

Solution #85: Give Her a Mouse to Play With

While self-grooming at the workplace is unprofessional, there are certain environments, such as the fashion and publishing industries, where everyone bucks professionalism and does it anyway. It's hard to rail against it when the corporate culture turns a blind eye to public grooming and treats the entire workplace as if it's one giant female locker room.

However, if you notice one of your employees grooming herself every time you stop by her office, you might take it as a sign that the woman is underemployed, and *that's* something you are empowered to change. Try to devise ingenious ways to put her makeup and fashion expertise to good use. Ask her to write a report on trends impacting your industry and post it on the company's intranet server. Once she finishes her white paper, examine the backlog of work that never seems to get done, and start assigning her those projects. How are subscriptions faring? What can be done to boost ad sales? Can she invent new ways to generate renewals? Make sure that she's so busy she won't have time to run to the ladies' room, let alone groom herself at her desk.

The Golden Rule

Coddled Superstars are often spoiled by the high regard in which their bosses hold them, and after a time, may seek to take advantage of their special status by abusing the system. Showing up late to work and even later to internal meetings are two flaws that are easy to rectify. However, if the Coddled Superstar takes excessively long breaks, either at lunch or to attend to personal business, it could be a sign that she is chronically underemployed. If that's the situation, it is your responsibility to challenge her with long-term projects that no one else has the time to do.

CHAPTER 18
The Grumpy Martyr

We had nickname for him...John of Arc.

He views his work as a religion and considers himself one of the true believers. His work involves plenty of sacrifice, and rarely does he work a weekend without letting you and everyone else know about it. (He has to spread the word because you and other miscreants are never around on Saturdays and Sundays to witness just how hard he works.)

His gripes about the ill effect work is having on his health are just the beginning of a long chain of complaints on the topic. He laments endlessly about the projects, the processes that are in place to get things done, the outcomes, and his fellow staffers. However, when it comes to fixing a particular problem, he shows little willpower. (The truth is, he'd much rather complain.) The Grumpy Martyr feels underappreciated and unloved, but his very actions are so repellent that most staffers go out of their way to avoid him. Then he wonders why he can't get their cooperation.

While the Grumpy Martyr can be extraordinarily difficult to deal with, there are ways to finesse him so that he won't demoralize the rest of the team.

Problem #86: He Has an Exaggerated Sense of Self-Importance

In his mind, the whole office was in shambles before he came on staff. And there is some truth to that.

Let's suppose that your company throws events for organizations. The Grumpy Martyr fusses endlessly about the condition of the lists (disorganized), the choice of venues (lackluster), and the quality of the food (inedible). His constant complaints about, well, *everything* galvanize everyone on staff to reevaluate their own contributions. Lists are culled; venues are radically improved; even the catered chicken seems to lose its rubbery texture. The whole level of service improves by 300%. Much positive word of mouth is the happy result, and your company begins to attract more prestigious organizations as clients.

A year after the Grumpy Martyr's arrival, everyone on staff is extremely pleased; that is, except for the Grumpy Martyr! He's still grumbling about the shoddy lists, venues, and food. Nothing is ever good enough for his perfectionist palate.

Solution #86: Encourage Him to Work Alone

The Grumpy Martyr's insufferable sense of self-importance inflicts the greatest damage when he is paired up with other staffers. His penchant for magnifying his own contributions while minimizing the contributions of others threatens to depress team spirit. He functions best when he is off by himself, grousing about outside vendors and suppliers. If you can find an area of the company where the work is not team-oriented, this is the best spot to house your local martyr. He can moan about how no one is there to help him out, but the sounds of his grumbles won't distress others or prevent them from doing their work.

Towards Peaceful Coworker Coexistence

What if you can't encourage the Grumpy Martyr to work alone because you're supposed to work with him on a project? You may be dismayed to discover that he's quick to find fault—both with you and others. As annoying as this habit can be, it's best not to complain about him, as doing so may quickly label you as a rabble-rouser. Take a vow of silence. Know that he's kvetched so often to so many people that by now, everyone just ignores him. If you are the target of his complaints, you probably don't have to worry about job security, as long ago, anyone who mattered at the firm simply put in their *earPods* whenever he was around so they wouldn't have to listen to him.

Problem #87: No One Works as Hard as He Does

"What did you do over the weekend?" he asks on Monday morning, all bright-eyed and seemingly interested in your life outside of the rat's maze. You fill him in on the thrilling details—movie, potluck supper with friends, read the Sunday *New York Times* cover to cover. "Why, what did you do, John?" you ask.

"Me? I was in the office the entire weekend," he says, fluttering his shutterbug eyes at you for sympathy. As it's the eighth Monday in a row that he's claimed to have worked overtime, you feel a pang of guilt. Is he really rolling in weekend after weekend when no one else is? What's that about?

Solution #87: Express Concern That He May Be a Workaholic

You need team members who will bust their butts for the company on selected occasions, such as for important meetings, pitches, customer feedback sessions, and training boot camps. But working around the clock for no reason will quickly burn out your best people. You should do your utmost to politely discourage it.

Do you believe that one of your colleagues is addicted to work? Kindly take him aside and ask him if he thinks that he might be a "workaholic." (These days, the term is almost a compliment, so he's unlikely to feel insulted.) If he confesses that he is, you might convey that working too hard is hard on the heart and the arteries. Tell him that, selfishly speaking, you want him to take more time off in between heavy work stints so he'll be alive when you need him to do the heavy lifting. Then, pat him on the back as you direct him to the

Workaholics Anonymous website: www.workaholics-anonymous.org. He may follow your advice. Or he may choose to ignore it. But either way, you've communicated that working 24/7 when it's completely unnecessary won't earn any special indulgences from you.

Is He Overworked or a Workaholic? Take This Quiz

Statement	True	False
1. His mouth runneth over about how hard he's been working. But things at the office are relatively slow.	T	F
2. He'd rather infect the whole office with his nasty cold than take a day off to recuperate. *Achoo.*	T	F
3. He's a terrible delegator. When forced to share the responsibility for a project, he devises all sorts of objections about the person to whom he's supposed to be delegating.	T	F
4. He seems to have no family life, or if he has a family, they live in a different state.	T	F
5. He rarely takes vacations, even though your company has a use-it-or-lose-it vacation policy.	T	F
6. He compulsively checks his Crackberry—er, Blackberry. (It's easy to make typos when typing with one's thumbs at three in the morning.)	T	F
7. He's a control freak without the fancy title to justify his controlling nature.	T	F
8. He wants others to help him out, until they actually do try to help him out.	T	F

Add 3 points for every True answer and subtract 2 points for every False answer. Did your Grumpy Martyr score 9 points or higher? He's a confirmed workaholic.

Just the Stats

The word *workaholic* was popularized in 1971 by Wayne Oates's book, *Confessions of a Workaholic*. The term implies someone who is addicted to work (and ignores family and other social relations as a result). To date, there is no generally accepted medical definition of *workaholic*.

Problem #88: He Feels So Persecuted

He's a savior. (In his own head he is, anyway.) But you and others are nothing but ingrates. The whole company desperately needs him for his fantastic insights, but alas, you are all too ignorant to realize it! While he's killing himself to save the company, no one shows him a drop of gratitude.

Solution #88: Give Him Enough Rope to Hang Himself

The Grumpy Martyr is a master at casting blame but avoiding responsibility. He questions authority but resists taking the lead to fix the problems he so readily identifies. If the problem is solved any differently than the way he recommends, it will still continue to exist as far as he's concerned. However, if staffers follow his advice and actually end up solving the problem in the manner he suggests, he'll quickly find another problem to complain about. If you can't get him to work by himself in the company, your next best gambit is to give him all of the responsibility for a particular project. If he succeeds, his repetitive chorus of complaints will be silenced, at least temporarily. And if he fails, he'll have no one to blame but himself.

Management Mantra

"Martyrdom is the only way a man can become famous without ability." When your Grumpy Martyr is torturing you with his constant harping, George Bernard Shaw's inspirational saying may help to keep things in perspective.

Problem #89: He Grouses Twice as Loudly as Everyone Else

The Grumpy Martyr finds something to cavil about in every project. But he has no real interest in fixing the many problems he flags. For to fix the problems would take away his reason to be. In the definition provided by *Wikipedia,* a person with a *martyr complex* "desires the feeling of being a martyr for its own sake…because it feeds a psychological need." How does one successfully manage a person who wants nothing more than to feel victimized?

Solution #89: Limit the Time He Can Spend on the Soapbox (and Have Him Memorize a New Script)

Recognize that his agenda is to complain, and stop inviting him to meetings, if necessary. Be honest with him. If you hear fellow staffers carp about him behind his back (and you will), tell him what they have been saying. You might reveal, "Some of the people you work most closely with have mentioned that you rarely have anything positive to say about their efforts. As a result, they've requested to no longer work with you. You're going to need to turn this around."

Strongly suggest that he first seek them out to make amends and then stay mum in meetings—unless he can balance his negativity with positive statements. There is an art to giving criticism. Teach him to start by saying something positive. Follow up with the areas that could use some improvement. And then end by saying something positive. If he needs a visual aid to remember this technique, tell him to picture a sandwich.

Problem #90: He Complains about Not Getting Support, but Won't Accept Any

The Martyr always picks a fight with the process. Possessed with a controlling personality, he disparages those who disagree with him. Thus, staffers have learned the hard way to avoid working with him. When someone new, and therefore uninitiated, offers to help the Martyr, his or her efforts are roundly criticized. The Martyr will convey that his coworker is incompetent or difficult, when in fact, it is the Martyr who is incompetent at working with others and extraordinarily difficult! The Martyr's nastiness towards the one person who can tolerate working with him reinforces everyone else's fervent desire *not* to work with him.

Solution #90: Put Up with Him and Shut Up

The Grumpy Martyr is his own worst enemy. You needn't become one of his enemies, for he already hates himself enough for both of you. Eventually, his antics will succeed in alienating all of the rank and file, and he'll be surrounded by enemies. In the interim, they will nod their heads at whatever he says, simply to avoid quarreling with him. Yet privately they will ignore him.

You need to take a broader view and force yourself to listen to his rants, no matter how disagreeable. Some of his concerns will need to be addressed for the successful completion of the project; and at this juncture, you may well be the only person who's paying any attention to him.

The Martyr's loud pleas for attention ultimately have the opposite effect. Staffers end up ignoring him, as his constant quibbling makes him unpleasant to work with. Never promote this person to a position of power, unless it also involves a transfer to Siberia. (Even if it does, double-check to be certain that he won't have to interact with other people there.)

The Golden Rule

The Grumpy Martyr has a grotesquely magnified sense of self-importance. He believes that he alone is vigilant while others on staff just don't care. If you are working side by side with him, the best thing to do is to simply nod your head and screen out his thunderous chorus of complaints. But if the Grumpy Martyr reports to you, either teach him how to deliver constructive criticism or place him in a people-free department where his loud grumbles will inflict no harm.

CHAPTER 19

The Employee Nobody Likes but You

She'd show up at the office every morning on her rollerblades, sweating from head to toe. After that, she'd never change her clothes. The people I worked with drew straws about how to talk to her about her sweat problem, because it was pretty severe. Unfortunately, I drew the shortest straw.

The woman is a collection of nasty habits. You wish to talk to her about business, but instead find yourself pondering how often she takes a bath. Her clothes reek of stale, grimy smells, or is that merely body odor? Her smelly lunches disgust the other employees, all clamoring for you to suggest that she eat *outside* of the office. She also can be inconsiderate about people's personal space, sometimes blasting her *iPod* in common areas, or worse, singing along to the music. And yet, she is talented—a fact that's lost on many in your department who appear to be mounting a witch hunt against her.

When a team's gripes about a particular member of the department won't simmer down without your assistance, what is the proper response? Everyone talks about grooming someone for upper management. But is there a way to groom someone to be a more considerate coworker?

Problem #91: Her B.O. Has You Double-Checking Your Own Armpits

You can smell her from a mile away. Her body perfume (you use the term loosely) has notes of sweat mixed with embedded grime and a slight hint of cat litter. And you're not the only person around who's sniffed the stench! Other staffers have approached you to inquire if you might discuss the problem with her. They don't want to be rude, but they also don't want to work closely with her; and somehow, you're supposed to politely share that.

Should you leave a bar of soap by her desk? Begin gifting her with deodorants and perfumes? Or take a deep breath (through your mouth) and discuss the problem with her. These are the things they *still* don't teach at Harvard Business School!

Solution #91: Air It over Lunch

Every difficult conversation in life goes down a bit easier over a terrific lunch; although in this case, you may want to steer clear of anything too garlicky or spicy. This tête-à-tête is likely to be tough on your employee because there is no way to raise the issue without her deducing that others have been gossiping about her. Mentally prepare yourself for the worst but hope for the best.

Endeavor to take the "sandwich" approach when delivering this piece of criticism. (*See* Solution #89.) That is, start with a positive piece of feedback, address the B.O. issue in the middle of the conversation, and then end with another positive piece of feedback. For example, you might say, "Carla, I have some good news and some bad news. The good news is that your great spirit and dedication haven't gone unnoticed. Everyone, including me, is super pleased with your performance. The bad news is that there is one tiny area of improvement I've been asked to talk to you about. Some people on staff have noticed that your grooming habits may need to change. One or two of your coworkers asked me to talk to you about body odor and cleanliness issues. There's some literature I'd like you to read about it." You might finish by saying, "Again, in general, we couldn't be happier to have you on our team, plugging away." Then, simply point her to the information in the "Twelve Grooming Tips" sidebar.

When giving feedback of this type, do try to be sensitive to how your employee may react. She might cry and get very upset. Or, conversely, she might appear to shrug it off but then spend the rest of the meal sulking. You might want to bring a small packet of *Kleenex* with you, just in case.

TWELVE GROOMING TIPS: OR HOW TO PREVENT YOUR COWORKERS FROM FAINTING EVERY TIME YOU DRAW NEAR

Everyone has some room to groom. It's a rare employee who couldn't benefit from a little extra grooming advice when it comes to readying herself for the workday. But a few people have a particular odor that drives away fellow staffers and has them diving for the nearest Exit sign. The following twelve tips can help you erase that malodorous scent, so you can start with a clean slate: your body.

1. **SHOWER POWER.** Nothing conquers body odor better than a meticulous scrub under a hot shower. Are you a sweat hog? Take two showers a day, one in the morning and one before you retire at night.

2. **DON'T SUBJECT PEOPLE TO SMELL HELL.** Opt for deodorant soap instead. *Dial, Lever Brothers,* and *Zest* all manufacture deodorant soaps in a range of fragrances palatable to both you and the coworker in the next cube over.
3. **RUSH TO BRUSH.** Invest in a body brush, and use it to scrub away those invisible pieces of grime that tenaciously cling to legs and back. If a brush feels too harsh, buy a loofah.
4. **SAY "TA-TA" TO THAT TORRID TAR SMELL.** Some dandruff shampoos flake out when it comes to the way they smell. Compensate for their deadly, tar-based odor by using a light conditioner on your hair directly after shampooing, or a teaspoon of sweet-smelling mousse.
5. **DON'T GIVE DIRT ANY PLACE TO HIDE.** Shave daily—if you're a man, unless facial hair is minimal. (If so, every other day is plenty.) Women need to shave legs at least once a week, even in winter. Female underarms are best left bare with a touch of deodorant.
6. **ATONE WITH TONER AND GET SQUEAKY CLEAN.** Walk into any dermatologist's office, and how will she clean your face? With toner, of course. The alcohol content of most toners will strip skin of even the most stubborn makeup shards. Do you exercise regularly? Swathe a toner-infused cotton ball down your neck and upper chest area twice a day after washing your face. You may be surprised at what you find.
7. **TOOTHPASTE OR TOOTH POLISH?** That is the question. Contrary to popular belief, the brand of toothpaste isn't as important as just using some of the white stuff twice a day. Invest in some mouthwash for yourself, and watch your coworkers breathe a sigh of relief.
8. **STICKY SITUATION OF THE DAY.** Does your back feel clammy after a long day of slaving under the fluorescent glare? Do

you have a ring around your abdomen at the place where your underwear hugs your waistline? Powder off those problem areas. Buy a body powder that contains cornstarch. Use deodorant on the area first, and let dry completely. Then dust with a light sprinkle of powder.

9. **THROW OUT YOUR MOLDY OLDIES.** Most women don't realize that makeup has an expiration date. The packaging may not declare precisely when that date is. But if you've been using the same foundation for over three months, it may have developed a yucky, "old-lady" smell to it. Certain sunblock lotions can also turn rancid after a few months as ingredients start to separate. Not only is there a loss of product efficacy, the ingredients begin to smell poorly.
10. **NAIL THAT GROOMING THING.** Dirty fingernails are unseemly. If you're a woman, there is no substitute for a professional manicure. If you're a man, at least commit to using a nailbrush twice a week.
11. **REFUSE TO SMELL LIKE A PERFUME COUNTER AT A DEPARTMENT STORE.** Go light on the perfume and cologne. Ditto for makeup, which often contains various perfumes that don't complement the perfumes found in other makeup products.
12. **KEEP IT CLEAN.** Change your underwear every day. Your mother may have told you to do it "in case you're hit by a bus." But what if you aren't? Be considerate of fellow coworkers by remembering to change your underwear anyway. Do you smoke or own pets? Be especially conscientious about ridding your clothing of any remnant smells. Assume that the people with whom you work have a fantastic sense of smell, and do your utmost not to offend it.

Problem #92: Her Clothing Screams Something Other Than Business

Her clothes are from a different time and place. The time is supposed to be morning and the place is supposed to be the office. Yet, for some reason, she arrives one morning dressed in a purple *Spandex* warm-up suit. Naturally, you assume that she rolled in straight from the gym. But, as the day wears on and she neither changes her outfit nor explains it, you arrive at a completely different conclusion. Obviously, the woman is oblivious to the dress code. Come to think of it, her violations have been flagrant. At various times, she's worn a teddy to the office, a glitzy evening dress, plus one outfit that either resembled pajamas or prison attire.

Solution #92: Issue a Memorandum Detailing the Uniform

Even high fashion direct from the runways of Paris sometimes sends a mixed message. If it's a year when athletic gear and flapper dresses both happen to be in, who can blame anyone for being confused about what's appropriate? You may find a colleague's outfits to be loud, tacky, and possibly shocking. But you can't automatically assume that she knows she's in violation of the corporate dress code.

Leave nothing to chance. Take the time to detail the corporate uniform in a memo. Distinguish the male dress code from its female counterpart. Do you wish staffers to dress up for client meetings? If so, let them know. Does your office subscribe to Casual Fridays? Identify precisely how Friday's outfits may differ from those worn during the rest of the week. Are blue jeans acceptable attire on any day of the week?

If an employee's dress-code violations continue after the dress-code memo has been released, address it with her in person.

Management Mantra

"It's funny that it all becomes about clothes. It's bizarre. You work your butt off and then you win an award and it's all about your dress. You can't get away from it."

—Reese Witherspoon

Problem #93: She Has a Nervous Tic

When she gets nervous, she coughs uncontrollably. Or her lisp becomes more pronounced. She may repeat the same word or expression over and over. Or lose herself in the middle of a long preamble about… (she forgot). By now, you're so used to her tic that it no longer throws you. But clients and new staffers sometimes have a great deal of difficulty understanding what she's trying to say.

Solution #93: Speak to Her in a Calming Voice

If you happen to be partners with her, it's perfectly acceptable to jump in and translate her lisp-laced rumblings for the clarification of the group. But if you're her supervisor, it's often more compassionate to let her stumble through the sentence on her own without jumping in to speak for her. You can aid her enormously by remaining patient and adopting a soothing tone of voice. Try to rephrase the question in a way that will elicit a clearer response from her. You might gently coo, "That's okay, Sally. Nobody here is in a rush, so take your time. I think you were beginning to tell us how the third-quarter results looked surprisingly positive. Now what do you attribute that to?"

Problem #94: She's Famous for Her Email Flamers

The people in your department are refreshingly e-centric. They would rather communicate via email than speak to one another in person. You receive up to sixty emails a day, a few from those above you, and many more from those below you.

Generally, the e-culture works, although the number of emails a day can be daunting. But there is one employee who shoots nasty emails to the other coworkers at the slightest provocation, always copying you. You hate reading them and imagine you are not alone, as her finger-pointing is always directed at others.

Solution #94: Pick Up the Phone

Email etiquette, or "netiquette" as it is sometimes called, can be a bit tricky. The tone is often the first thing to go, when it should be the last thing to sacrifice. There's never enough time to write an email right the first time.

If an employee has a pattern of sending nasty emails, call her on the phone and let her air the grievance. Sometimes the very act of verbally venting one's frustrations allows them to dissipate. You might open the conversation by saying that you read her recent round of emails and you're calling to try to get to the bottom of the issue she seems to have with so-and-so. Then simply hear her out.

If that doesn't work and she continues to *e-spew,* go find her in person and explain that even internal emails need to maintain an aura of professionalism and politeness. Beyond that, they should be positively friendly.

Just the Stats

PEW Internet & American Life Project conducted a tracking study of Internet use that highlighted some intriguing findings: 64% of men and 69% of women said that email at the office was "most effective for editing documents." A smaller percentage (32% of men and 39% of women) believed email was "an effective way to ask questions." Only 5% of men and 6% of women surveyed felt email was a smart way to "raise a problem with a boss." And only 4% of both men and women found it useful for "dealing with sensitive issues at the workplace." If you have a problem with an employee, coworker, or direct supervisor, pick up the phone to discuss it, or better yet, go visit her in person.[13]

Towards Peaceful Coworker Coexistence

Is one of your coworkers slamming you via email? Take the ultimate *C.Y.Y.K.W.* (*Cover Your You Know What*) strategy. Resist your first tendency to shoot back a nasty email in return. Take a deep breath and devote your attention to the cc list. Is your supervisor on the list? If so, then *she's* the intended audience for your coworker's rant. Seek out your supervisor and defend your actions to her one-on-one. Make sure that she understands your point of view. (This is more easily accomplished when you remain calm.) Then, write a diplomatic email back to the person who flamed you, copying only him and your supervisor.

"Hi, David," you might begin. "Thank you for expressing your concern about the pilot program for the ACE initiative. But, as Susie and I just agreed, it is very much on schedule." Then sign it with a breezy "cheers" or a smiley face, and move on with the rest of your day.

THE LIGHTER SIDE OF COMMUNICATION

Electronic emoticons, such as those shown below, receive major frowns among intellectuals and serious writers. But smilies do have a place in corporate America. Maintaining an upbeat tone in one's emails is vital. If there is any doubt about how an email could be interpreted, there are worse things than inserting a smiley face to express a lighthearted tone. (It's not like the email is going to win a Pulitzer Prize anyway.)

Btw: the creation of smilies is a burgeoning field, and today there are even smilies to express highfalutin' concepts such as "John Lennon's glasses." With all due respect to John Lennon and his glasses, here are some shortcuts that you may find more useful for your business communiqués.

:)	*a smile*
;)	*a wink*
:(	*a frown*
:/	*perplexed*
btw	*by the way*
fyi	*for your information*
bcnu	*be seeing you*
lol	*laughing out loud*
rofl	*rolling on the floor laughing*
ttfn	*ta-ta for now*
ttyl	*talk to you later*

Problem #95: Deviant Behavior

She sings aloud to the tunes blasting on her *iPod* while other denizens of the cubicle culture try to work in peace. Or perhaps your company has a central computerized music system that employees are allowed to enjoy from the privacy of their own workstations. But her workstation happens to be situated in a public area, and complaints about her tragic taste in hip-hop have been mounting. Or she brings a smelly tuna melt to the office each day and insists on popping the concoction into the microwave, where it bubbles over into a fetid mess. The communal work area should be clean and odor-free, preferably with some gentle white noise in the background. Is that too much to ask?

Solution #95: Be the Buffer

Your charge is to put the kibosh on inconsiderate behavior, discourage mean-spirited gossip, and foster team camaraderie. When someone in the department complains that his personal space is being infringed upon, express your sympathy but also try to foster tolerance. Be a nurturer, not a naysayer.

Not every person on the planet was raised in exactly the same manner. Some staffers were to the manor born while others never mastered a bread plate. An employee who croons aloud may not realize that her behavior is disrupting other people's concentration. If an employee brings a tuna melt to the office every day, chances are she is unaware the smell may be loathsome to those around her.

Agree to raise the complaint with her, but also do your utmost to dispel the mounting fury on the part of the tattler. Remind the aggrieved party that one woman's tuna melt is another person's banana yogurt. Be fair-minded and tolerant of people's foibles, and you will have a shot at becoming a beloved manager.

The Golden Rule

Those who have adapted to the corporate culture may sometimes band against a certain employee who doesn't seem to fit in. Don't be swayed by the mob mentality. Following the mob will only lead to anarchy, which ultimately could cause your own downfall. Instead, strive to be known for your fair-mindedness and tolerance. It's difficult for even the most hard-hearted of individuals not to be awed by a show of generosity. This need not involve a display of wealth; sometimes it only entails a show of restraint by refusing to chime in with the chorus of discontents.

CHAPTER 20
The Veteran Hack

Even if they weren't talented at the job they were supposed to be doing, their personality would often redeem them. I'd never go to management and try to get them fired. That would take too long and rock the boat too much.

He's not going to win any awards for his sparkling creativity. He probably won't win the Nobel Prize in this lifetime. But at least he's easy to get along with—if you can only bring yourself to appreciate the Hack's finer qualities. He's solid, dependable, your go-to guy in a crunch. He makes no waves, which may well be the reason he's survived umpteen management shakeouts.

Want to know the secret of his success? Look no further than his bulletin board, no doubt adorned with photographs of his wife, kids, and pet Rottweiler. He has his priorities in order. And, frankly my dear, his job comes last.

Would he lay down and die over some blueprint he drafted? Recite the Riot Act over a poetic turn of phrase in the seventeenth paragraph of his article? Storm out of a meeting because some higher-ups altered a line of his precious code? You bet he wouldn't! But he sure wouldn't mind catching that 5:55 to the 'burbs.

Problem #96: He's Nothing but a Hack-in-the-Box

He likes to think inside the box, giving the corners a wide berth. He considers himself a problem solver rather than a creative genius, and few would quarrel with that self-effacing self-assessment. His ideas may never cause goose bumps to zip down your spine. But at least he'll never embarrass the company by delivering shoddy work. A consummate journeyman, he's dedicated to delivering ideas on time and on budget. He doesn't have a self-destructive gene in his body. He's dependable, dammit!

Solution #96: Don't Underestimate Your Veteran Hack

It's unfair to think of the Veteran Hack as complacent when he is merely efficient. The fact that he's been around forever gives great comfort to clients who know their businesses will be adequately serviced. Fact: most clients don't have a lot of time, and they certainly don't want to take any foolish risks. It's worth it to your company to keep the Veteran Hack around purely for the stability he provides to the client relationship.

Think of him as a rock. Would you want to move a big, heavy rock to more fertile terrain? You shouldn't want to. Most rocks are better left alone.

In Defense of the Veteran Hack

Most hacks are veterans who have survived a few turf wars in the halls of corporate America. Hacks are B-players with the stamina, follow-through, and closure skills to help the A-players' dreams materialize. Hacks are not "big-idea" people. Rather, they are craftsmen committed to meticulous execution. Hacks and geniuses can easily coexist; both play a vital role in organizations.

Problem #97: Younger Members of the Department Disdain His Tried-and-True Ways

The familiarity of his ideas breeds nothing but their contempt. To younger staffers, he's an emblem of everything the enterprise shouldn't be—old, fat, outdated, and boring. The fact that the Veteran Hack often manages to sell through his lame concepts makes the younger members of the team hold him in even greater disregard.

Solution #97: Take Down His Naysayers a Peg or Two

There is no room for unbridled arrogance at the workplace. Those who are arrogant must be humbled before their haughtiness marinates into pure, unadulterated jerkdom. Even if you respect the ideas of someone who is unabashedly insolent, it behooves you not to always buy into them. You don't want that person to start feeling like a Golden Boy who walks on water while everyone else sinks.

Towards Peaceful Coworker Coexistence

What if you find yourself working side by side with someone who constantly belittles the efforts of the Veteran Hack? Refuse to take part in his Hack-bashing. Take care that fellow staffers don't associate you with the naysayer. Don't be seen going out to lunch with him. Occasionally, let the Veteran Hack know how much you appreciate his guidance. Impress upon him how much he is teaching you. A little gratitude goes a long way.

Problem #98: He Doubles as a Spy for the Big Boss

The Veteran Hack may have risen to prominence during a previous era in the history of the firm. Perhaps his relationship with the big boss is the very reason the Veteran Hack is still around, hacking out his boilerplate ideas so many years later. He may hit a round of golf with the boss every so often. For somehow, while the big boss is rarely at the office, he seems to hear about every political brouhaha and communication mishap.

Solution #98: Have Him Sell the Boss on the Phenomenal Job You're Doing

Why leave your fate at the company to chance when you have all of the survival skills you need at your disposal in the form of the Veteran Hack? Ingratiate yourself with this good ol' boy. Convey your sincere appreciation for his many talents. Cherry-pick little pieces of good news for him to communicate to the big boss. But be stealthy about your agenda.

If the Veteran Hack clues into the fact that you know he's a spy, he may justly feel like you're using him. Don't ask him a lot of questions about his golf or poker game, or about any other interactions he may have with the big boss.

Treat the Veteran Hack with the same arms' length cordiality and deference with which you treat your external clients. Think of the Veteran Hack as your *internal client,* someone to be courted at all costs.

Problem #99: Around Him, Morale Plummets

The Hack has a long, successful track record of total mediocrity. His ideas get bought while other fresher, more innovative solutions get turned down. In fact, once the brilliant ideas get squashed, the Hack often rises to the occasion, coming up with the safe choice that saves the client relationship and solves the assignment. He has a whole attaché case worth of skills that no one else in your department possesses. However, the Hack is not suave when it comes to internal politicking. He can come off as a bit of an egghead when it comes to judging other people's ideas. He isn't trying to be obnoxious, mind you. He just knows for a fact that their ideas will never work, for X, Y, and Z reasons.

Solution #99: Tell Him to Zip It

The Veteran Hack is an integral part of the department in the same way that bread and butter is an essential element of breakfast but hopefully not the only sustenance available at the meal. Fortunately, the Veteran Hack rarely rises to the level of decision maker. When he speaks out against someone else's idea, he's only trying to be helpful. But it can have the opposite effect, making morale crash. Ask him to hold back on expressing negative opinions, and instead look for ways that people's ideas might be reshaped to improve on them.

Management Mantra

Voltaire, that eminently quotable French philosopher, once said: "Good is the enemy of great." And many times, it is. When you settle for the first good idea that comes to you instead of digging deeper to see if you might arrive at another even better idea, you're on the road to hackdom. That said, "Don't let great be the enemy of good" is also a fine maxim to keep in mind. If the search for excellence is preventing you and other team members from reaching your benchmarks, it's crucial to act. Remember always that hacks and geniuses can be friends.

Problem #100: You Can't Teach an Old Hack New Tricks

When it comes to ideas, he's all for recycling. If it worked before, it will work again. He not only distrusts changes of all kinds but believes that change for change's sake is a dangerous notion that should be crushed. Many on staff cast nasty barbs about the Hack behind his back, but because he's a master craftsman who can be relied on in a pinch, the higher-ups like having him around.

Solution #100: Team Him Up with Someone Younger and More Experimental

If your company has a team culture, consider shaking up the teams. Don't always pair the young whippersnappers with each other. Instead, capitalize on the Veteran Hack's ability to get things done by matching him up with someone who's a little fresher but could benefit from the Hack's discipline. They could end up generating ideas that are truly groundbreaking because they're cool *and* get bought. Who knows? The Hack and the Genius might really end up enjoying working together. Stranger things have happened.

A DOSE OF CREATIVITY FOR THE HACK

Creativity is like a muscle that one flexes in a gym. With various exercises, the muscle can be toned and refined. (Although if one is starting with zero creativity, he's unlikely to morph into Albert Einstein overnight.) A particularly flabby creativity muscle sometimes requires a jolt to kick it into gear. Here are some ways to shock the Veteran Hack out of his complacency:

- **PUT HIM IN CHARGE OF A CREATIVE ENTERPRISE HE WOULDN'T NORMALLY TOUCH.** For example, you could ask him to create the precursor of the company newsletter. Or crown him head of the office redecorating project.
- **ASK HIM TO GIVE A GROUP REPORT ON UP-AND-COMING TRENDS.** The report *must* come with recommendations from him for modernizing your business.
- **TAKE HIM OUT OF HIS ELEMENT.** Transfer him to one of your foreign offices for two weeks and watch his creativity blossom on foreign soil. Immersion in a foreign culture may be just the thing to bust him out of his rut. If you can arrange for someone from the foreign office at roughly the same level as the Veteran Hack to temporarily trade places with him, the resulting cross-pollination of new ideas could lead to a burst of creativity in both offices.

The Golden Rule

It is highly impractical to staff your department with only A-players, as then there will be no one around to help them fulfill their visions. A-players tend to be extremely costly. And, nine times out of ten, clients don't end up buying the best work anyway. When you need someone to pull an idea out of a hat, the Veteran Hack is gifted at cranking out the work quickly. You need both hacks and geniuses around, so endeavor to expose each of them to the way the other half thinks.

CHAPTER 21

The You Wannabe (Who's After Your Job)

I once made the mistake of hiring someone who was fairly competent, and then spent hours of my precious time training her. Big no-no. Eventually, the company realized that if they just promoted her, they could have me at half my salary—and so they cut me loose.

If imitation is the sincerest form of flattery, you'd prefer to be insulted. She looks like a younger version of you. Her hair is the same color as yours; her eyes are the same color; her outfits are even knock-off versions of your outfits. She claims to have *googled* you before she ever met you, so intent was she on working for you. Flattered by her relentless enthusiasm, you eventually relented and offered her a job. Now you're questioning the wisdom of that.

She bombards you with questions and sometimes follows you around, lapping up your pearls of wisdom and salivating for more. Is she an eager acolyte who can be trusted? Or is she nipping at your heels, eagerly awaiting the first chance to topple you? When the person working for you is a bit too much like you for comfort, what are the best methods for de-cloning her?

Problem #101: She's Fresher, with Energy to Burn

At first, you're thrilled by her spunk. She really seems to care about profit margins! (You love anyone who can get jazzed up about those margins.) The You Wannabe doesn't fall asleep in meetings or even try to skirt out of the office early. She's driven. The only problem is that her rampant enthusiasm drains you, diverting you from your own work. Are you getting too old to play mentor, or are you just rusty?

Solution #101: Start Small, and Harness Her Energy

Sometimes it's better to see the trees for the forest. Preserve your stamina by focusing on the small stuff. Don't get distracted by giving your overenthusiastic employee an overarching rundown of the way the entire business operates. It will only confuse her. Instead, direct her energy by teaching her only what she needs to know in order to do her own job effectively.

HOW TO BE A GREAT LEADER

In Part 1 of this book, you met some not-so-great bosses. By studying those profiles, it was easy to glean what not to do. But what about the flip side? What does it take to become a beloved boss? Here are some pointers that can help distinguish you from the average credit-snatching, bullying, spin-doctoring kind of boss that inhabits so many corporations today. Try to keep these tips in mind as you work your way up, and hopefully you'll arrive there that much faster.

- **THINK OF YOURSELF AS A COACH RATHER THAN A BOSS.** Everyone loves coaches yet hates bosses. Have you ever stopped to consider the reason? Maybe it's because coaches embrace a team mentality. If someone on the team happens to be a superstar, the coach doesn't begrudge that person her due. A coach would never bench a superstar to compensate for his own jealousy or paranoia.
- **STRIVE TO LEAD, NOT MERELY TO MANAGE.** Ross Perot once observed, "Inventories can be managed, but people must be led." If someone needs time-management assistance, by all means, help her organize her schedule. But if that's the only thing you're doing for fellow staffers, you're not doing nearly enough.
- **DON'T BE PETTY.** The root of the word *petty* is *peti*, the same root as in the French word *petit*, which means "small." When you chastise colleagues for petty oversights you are being small-minded. Leaders need to lead large.
- **CATCH YOUR EMPLOYEES DOING SOMETHING RIGHT.** If you're from the school of M.B.W.A. (Management By Walking Around), you're bound to stumble on employees making personal phone calls and doing plenty of other things throughout the day that aren't work-related. Rather than focusing on these random acts of subversion, take care to notice someone doing something right. Did one of your people

talk an irate customer down from the ledge? Why not mention it in the next staff meeting? Better yet, ask her to give a presentation on *how* she did it so the group can learn from her success.

- **BE GENEROUS WITH PRAISE.** Everyone loves to see their name in lights. Did a team member give a rousing speech? Have her post it on the intranet system. Heck, prove that you're not a credit snatcher and write a memo in praise of her work. Employees love praise almost as much as they enjoy receiving raises and bonuses, and praise is so much cheaper to bestow.
- **WORK WITH EVERYONE ON THEIR PERSONAL GROWTH PLANS.** "Growth" does not have to mean vertical growth. Sometimes it can simply mean adding a new skill to one's arsenal. Have each staffer craft a personal goals list and make sure their goals are achievable. People love to learn.
- **WALK AMONG THE PEOPLE.** This is not to be confused with Management By Walking Around. Your charge, after all, is not to manage but to lead. *Walk Among The People (W.A.T.P.)* is about retaining your sense of humility, even if you're promoted to CEO. It means staying approachable so staffers won't be frightened to talk to you about any issues they may have. It means eschewing a cavalcade of henchmen in favor of hearing what the real people think. It means retaining your grip on reality because an army of sycophants isn't sugarcoating it. *W.A.T.P.* Try it sometime.

Problem #102: She Throws Curveballs at You All Day Long

"How do you arrive at those projections?" she lobs enthusiastically, first thing in the morning. By the afternoon, she's zinging you with considerably tougher questions, such as, "How can we develop an emotional connection with our end-customer?" A week later, she wants to know if the company is "eco-conscious." The You Wannabe is like a ball machine—relentless!

Solution #102: Set Up Office Hours When You Can Coach People

Print a schedule of times when you'll be available to answer questions or help staffers brainstorm on projects. This will dissuade other eager betties and bobs from hounding you nonstop with their pressing issues. If you have a secretary, train her to be your zealous gatekeeper.

What if you don't have someone to guard the moat? In that case, it's perfectly acceptable to pull up the drawbridge all by yourself. (It's only awkward to ask people to come back later the first hundred times. With practice, it becomes considerably easier.) Close the door to your office to communicate the message if necessary. Ease yourself of the burden of feeling like you need to "be there" for everyone else 24/7. Remember that being a mentor is not the same thing as being a private tutor. If you're not vigilant about your own time, no one else will be either.

Problem #103: Everyone Thinks the Two of You Were Separated at Birth

Recently someone on staff actually had the audacity to ask if you and the You Wannabe were related. He guessed that she might be your younger sister. As you were gently disabusing him of this scary notion, you remembered that you and she actually *do* share a few things in common. She grew up in your hometown and even attended one of your schools. Coincidence?

Solution #103: Focus on Substance over Style

Unless you asked your college for recruiting help, any passing similarity between you and your underling *is* just a coincidence. Resist the temptation to draw parallels that simply aren't there. You need someone working for you who will help solve tough problems with your clients and customers.

Why is there so much attrition and so little loyalty? Is your product line still relevant today? Are consumers more price-conscious now than in years past? It doesn't matter *what* your employee looks like if she doesn't have a brain in her head. So be certain to assign her enough stimulating work so that you can venture an educated guess about that, one way or the other.

Management Mantra

"Never hire or promote people in your own image. It is foolish to replicate your strength and idiotic to replicate your weakness."

—Dee W. Hock

Problem #104: She's Latched on to Your Coattails

She's a slick sycophant. She seconds every idea that you ever have. Behind your back, she has only the *kindest* things to say about you. Everyone considers the two of you to be attached at the hip, while you secretly fret that her hidden agenda may be to sever your ties and betray you. Should you sic the sycophant on someone else in a different department? Or go out and celebrate—because you've finally found someone who's both loyal and surprisingly competent?

Solution #104: Take Credit for Her Achievements

If the You Wannabe is talented, credit yourself for finding and grooming her. Make certain that everyone on staff is aware that she was your hire. Write staff memos publicly crediting her (which, as you now know, can only make you look better since all credit trickles up. *See* "*Trickle-Up* Theory" in Solution #36). Shovel the work off your desk and into her lap. Then get thee to the place where *you want to be*.

Problem #105: The You Wannabe Isn't You, after All

In terms of aptitude, she isn't the sharpest pencil in the credenza. If the past six months are any precedent, you can lay aside your fears that your underling will unseat you anytime soon. Her primary task was to ingratiate herself with your company's top ten accounts, and suffice it to say, she didn't. On her performance review form there's a place for you to rate her "drive," but you can't find the box marked "Deny Learner's Permit." In short, she fell far short of expectations. Dare you say it? The You Wannabe may want to be you, but, alas, she's strikingly average.

Solution #105: Teach Her to Be More Like You

If you ever received a poor review, no doubt you will dread this conversation. The last thing you want to do is to sap your underling's spirits with a yearly report card that's the corporate equivalent of a C+. (You'd never wish her to consider you mean-spirited when you're just trying to be honest.)

Studies show that over 70% of managers have difficulty giving a tough performance review to underachievers in their department. Yet doing so early on can actually be an act of kindness, as it can help give an underperforming employee a second chance.

One way to make the conversation more productive: share a personal experience where you overcame a similar challenge. Then map out a series of action steps that she can take to improve. Let her know that your door is always open for consultation (even if you have to keep it closed to prevent others from hounding you).

Don't wait until your employee's formal review to start the conversation. Instead, get into the mode of giving feedback—either positive or negative—on a more informal basis. This will help to preserve your own good reputation as someone who wants to see her people learn and grow.

HOW TO GIVE BETTER REVIEWS

Most managers today give themselves poor reviews on their ability to give them. Alas, they can take it, but they can't dish it out. Following are three ways to improve your own reviewing ability:

1. **STAND BY YOUR GRADES.** On the employee review form, there's usually a section to jot down comments along with a number grade. When giving someone an average grade on a skill, say, "organizational skills, 3," make sure that your written comment reflects *why* the person's skills are average and *how* she might better them. So often, managers do the exact opposite—giving a lower numerical mark than their written comment would imply. This "mixed grading message" just adds to confusion on the part of the person receiving the review. Don't use the written comments to take the curse off of the numerical grades or vice versa.
2. **BE FAIR.** Some managers resist giving their people the equivalent of straight A's, fearing that then their underlings will have nothing to strive for. But honestly, if the woman working for you is *that* good, she deserves to be promoted. Don't hold people back for no reason or they'll start to resent you.
3. **THINK LATERALLY, NOT JUST VERTICALLY.** What if someone on the team is acing all of her tasks? Don't automatically assume that she's a rising star. She could be a meteor, merely one nanosecond away from burnout. Or she could be

under-challenged and in need of more assignments. Test her "star quality" by giving her more work, but don't overload her. By the same token, if another employee is struggling to complete her assignments, perhaps you'll have to remove one or two of them from her roster. While every performance review spotlights just one member of the department, you need to stay focused on what's best for the whole team.

Towards Peaceful Coworker Coexistence

What if you're asked to review one of your peers—someone at your exact level in the company? Peer reviews are peerless in their ability to inspire fear among both givers and recipients. Try not to think of the peer-review process as one big popularity contest. If you need to criticize someone's performance, be constructive. Even in situations where peer feedback is supposedly anonymous, it's often a cinch to trace back the source of the complaint. Be kind.

The Golden Rule

Don't hire someone who shares your identical strengths and weaknesses, or you will either weaken your department or create a bitter rival for your own job. Instead, hire someone who is strong in the areas where you are weak. However, if you do end up hiring someone with superficial similarities, don't automatically assume that she's rooting for your downfall.

CHAPTER 22
The Spineless Sycophant

The coworker I hated the most was a sycophant. She always had plenty of gratuitous compliments for the boss. The man she was pandering to had a nickname. It was "Coattails."

If life at the office is like a game of chess, he is but a pawn. You think he's on your team, protecting your flanks, but rivals have no difficulty knocking him down. You manipulate him easily. The problem is, so does everyone else. Ultimately, his passive attitude earns him enemies—not among the bishops and knights at the office who are used to being endlessly flattered—but among his peers.

Since he never takes a controversial stand (or even lets people know where he stands), eventually his colleagues and coworkers start to resent him. If one of them gets promoted to boss, the Sycophant may find himself with a powerful enemy after all.

Most staffers, who had to take some risks to get to where they are, detest the Sycophant. They manage to see through him, whereas members of the top brass do not. Eventually, his enemies in middle management collude to topple the Sycophant, and he ends up getting his comeuppance.

Problem #106: He Can't Make a Decision

The Spineless Sycophant hates conflict. To avoid it, he sways whichever way the wind is blowing. If it's blowing your way, he's all for your idea. It's fantastic! He loves it! However, if the wind is blowing against you, he's remarkably agile at switching allegiances. As the song lyrics foretell, "The answer, my friend, is blowin' in the wind." In a crosswind, the Sycophant retreats to his office to wait it out from the comfy gray zone of his ergonomic chair. "Let's decide this tomorrow when everyone will be back" is his stalling tactic.

Solution #106: Give Him Clear, Easy-to-Follow Instructions

Make all decisions in advance and give him ironclad instructions. Know that, in your absence, he will pin any controversial decision on you.

Why bother dealing with someone like this at all, you may wonder? For starters, you can be confident that he won't make any political snafus. While he may not be the strongest player on your team, he's not totally worthless.

Depending on how adept he is at relaying information, you may be able to turn him into an effective spy. Since he never takes a risk, the higher-ups don't object to his presence in meetings. Send him to all internal powwows in your absence. Train him to drill down into the details and subtle nuances of who said what. Don't settle for a summary. You want to hear the blow-by-blow. Sycophants are often fantastic listeners. Think of yours as an invisible tape recorder in the room that can replay every single exchange back to you.

Just the Stats

According to the *American Heritage Dictionary of the English Language,* a *sycophant* is "a servile self-seeker who attempts to win favor by flattering influential people." The word derives from the Latin word *scophanta,* meaning "informer" or "slanderer." The Greek word *skophants* also means "informer."[14]

Problem #107: His Face Smiles at Executives, Then Goes Back into Place

The Spineless Sycophant has raised fawning to an art form on par with pointillism. He pointedly panders to those who consider themselves resistant to overt displays of flattery. His obsequious preening knows no limits. As he manages to hang on to his job year after year while other, more spirited types fall by the wayside, the Sycophant is living proof that flattery (in nauseating doses) will get him everywhere.

Solution #107: Have Him Teach Charm 101

Dispatch him to accompany the younger recruits in the firm to any important meetings with the top brass. The Sycophant's oily patter will grease the way to a smooth discourse, and the higher-ups can't fail to come away impressed. By nature, the Sycophant is not a good manager of others (he's too busy looking out for numero uno), but he makes a superb chaperone.

Towards Peaceful Coworker Coexistence

What if, instead of supervising the Sycophant, you find yourself in direct competition with him? Suppose that you are both equals at a company, competing over a limited pool of precious leads. His strategy is to suck up to the boss as far as she'll let him. What should your strategy be? While chances are you will never outflatter the flatterer, you can make some inroads by mirroring his technique back on him. Flatter the Sycophant. Use his own grease to butter him up big time. That way, when he succeeds in getting your boss to give him all of the good leads, the Sycophant will feel compelled to give you some of his castoffs.

Problem #108: Just How Low Will He Go?

He believes, "All is fair in love and business," and uses the vocabulary of charm to ease his way through life's daily rough spots. He sprinkles compliments like sugar and tends to say things like, "That's genius," and "Your presentation made me see bridgewear for the American working woman in a whole new light." If he can't bring himself to compliment a higher-up on one of her ideas, he'll compliment her on the way she looks that morning, or on her adorable outfits, or on her wicked sense of humor. He will stoop to new levels of gratuitous bootlicking (or self-debasement, depending on one's point of view) to become more favored among the powers-that-be.

Solution #108: His Bending and Scraping Means You May Not Have To

Work his preening to your advantage by bringing him with you to woo clients and important customers. Recognize that the manner in which the Sycophant manipulates language is skilled, and employ him to use it in pursuit of new business. You might even be able to use his ability to reflect what clients want to hear in a compelling presentation, especially if you play Devil's Advocate and deliberately present them with information they do *not* want to hear.

Position yourselves as a team, offering two different viewpoints. You might begin your meeting like this: "Jack, who tends to be an optimist, is going to describe his vision of the marketplace in the next two years. His picture looks rosy. After Jack is finished with his report, I'm going to expose you to a very different marketplace that's considerably bleaker. Together, we'll arrive at a realistic strategy for you, given the possible swings in the marketplace during the next twelve months."

Few clients will be able to resist the lure of one partner who tells them everything they wish to hear and one who tells them how things "really are" in the world out there. The Sycophant's phraseology is so exaggerated that you can deliver the unvarnished truth to your clients in a palatable way.

Any utterances from the Sycophant's lips should be treated like a propaganda report. His sentiments are all positive, all the time, unmarred by the ugly blemish of sincerity. Instead of falling prey to his flattery, ask yourself if the Sycophant could pass a polygraph test. If the answer is "no," go find someone else in your department who will give you honest feedback.

Problem #109: He Can't Defend the Fort

Riddle: what does the Spineless Sycophant have in common with French cooking? Answer: They both use way too much butter. It is this failing that makes the Sycophant dangerous to his immediate supervisors. You may think that because he's so adept at buttering up the higher-ups, he'd be the first person to detect it when the technique is used on him. Instead, he's the very last person to realize it. Is your competitor wining and dining your Sycophant to learn your company's trade secrets? Don't expect your Sycophant to guard them. They'll slip right out of his mouth.

Solution #109: Find Him a Job That's More Suitable for His Talents

The Spineless Sycophant is not a loyal soldier in your army. If he were, you'd have to buy him a fancy uniform and a bayonet. To regard him as a soldier is like asking an army man to be a midwife. (Could an army man deliver a child? Possibly. But it's probably not the job most suited to his talents.)

The Sycophant does not have the spine to stand up to outsiders. Rather, his lathering makes outsiders gravitate to him. Put him a role where his ability to tell people exactly what they want to hear will benefit your department the most. Sycophants make excellent salesmen, brokers, agents, and executive recruiters. They employ flattery to weaken their prospects and lull them into a false sense of optimism. These prospects may finally feel appreciated by someone who truly understands them. And they'll want to return the favor—by buying into what your company has to sell.

Put your Sycophant in a sales capacity, and watch your new business effort blossom. Place him in some other type of job that entails guarding secrets, and watch your new business prospects wilt faster than a plucked petunia—as your competitors learn from him everything your company is doing that they aren't.

Problem #110: You Can't Trust Him with Hush-Hush Internal Info

Tell certain people that something is "confidential," and they will carry that secret with them to the grave. Tell the Sycophant that something is "confidential," and he'll carry that secret all the way to the Watercooler Wag, where it will be shared faster than you can pop a *Cup-a-Soup* into the office microwave. BING. Your secret is out. The Sycophant's loose lips make him positively dangerous if you are entrusting him with anything that you need to keep mum. Before the words are out of your mouth, they're blasted on the company website, and there's even a blog about them.

Solution #110: Give Him the Official Press Release

Sycophants are best used to spread the official word throughout the empire. If this press release is delivered as a leak, it will have even more sway. Chances are, your Spineless Sycophant has access to different channels in the organization than you. Leak news that you want everyone to hear by giving it to the Sycophant first. Use his informer tendencies to inform on behalf of the enterprise rather than against it.

Management Mantra

"Thoughtless and futile is he who communicates his plan to the rank and file before it is necessary."

—Onasander, Greek philosopher

The Golden Rule

The Spineless Sycophant plays to people's secret fantasies about themselves. He always seems to see them exactly as they wish to be seen: brilliant, witty, and wise. Remind yourself that flattery is his modus operandi, and instead of buying into it, use him to have others buy into it.

CHAPTER 23
Suddenly Single

During the time that Winston and Paula were going at it, no work got done, as the rest of the staff just spent the whole time gossiping about them. When they finally split up, I can't tell you how relieved I was.

When most people break up with a loved one, they remind themselves that dating is a bit of a numbers game. After all, "there are other fish in the sea." By contrast, when she's in the midst of a breakup, she thinks, "Time to take a dip in the pool." The office pool, that is.

She is being most efficient by pooling her precious time and resources. And once her focus shifts to which office mates might be suitable swimming partners for her, ranking their eligibility becomes her private obsession. Your colleague could be perennially single, a serial dater, or recently separated. But in all cases, she's divorced from reality.

Today, when sexual harassment seminars are making the rounds at almost every company, what, if anything, is your obligation to a colleague who flouts the rules? If she insists on behaving irresponsibly, do you have any responsibility to her?

Problem #111: She's Hanging Out at the Pool, Checking Her Options

You can't tear her away from the adult pool as she sizes up each new male member of the department as a potential mate. You want to alert her that this isn't college: sexual harassment at the workplace is a serious issue. And should one of her swimming partners nail her (on that issue), she could even lose her job. But with her lusty *her-mones* in dire need of a cold shower, you know that somehow she'll find a way to shrug off your sage advice.

Solution #111: Warn Her That the Office Pool Is Shallower Than She Suspects

She thinks that she's swimming in an Olympic-sized pool, but she's wrong. In fact, the office pool is short, shallow, and there are few lanes open to her. Under no circumstances should she date someone who reports to her directly. Sexual harassment charges make big headlines these days. It's just not worth the career risk.

While entertaining her poolside, you might also advise her not to date the boss. Coworkers will turn on her if she receives even a soupçon of special treatment from him. They'll quickly discount her achievements, perks, and promotions. And then, if she and the boss do end up breaking up, it's a guaranteed lose-lose situation. For starters, she will have to see him every single day (not the fastest way to recuperate from heartache). If he's the vengeful type, he might even sabotage her career.

If your singleton colleague *must* date someone from the office, it should be a peer who's also single and from a different department. Even then, she would be well advised to keep the relationship under wraps.

Just the Stats

Studies show that at least 40% of working Americans have been involved with a coworker, and some studies pin the number considerably higher, up around the 60% mark. That's a litany of liaisons (all the more surprising since intraoffice dating is generally frowned upon). There are even some career coaches who feel that intraoffice relations are a good thing, since they encourage both people to hang around the office longer and work that much harder. Please note: most intraoffice relationships come to a bitter end. After the relationship combusts, there could even be career recriminations. Don't go there.

Problem #112: The Jealousy Factor

One morning, your underling, who has been engaged in a secret rendezvous with someone in the department, spots another coworker flirting with her. He tries to prevent his profound irritation from allowing his eyes to drill into innocent bystanders for the rest of the day, but unfortunately he's just not that good an actor. "What's up with Rick?" everyone wants to know. "Did Rita finally dump him?" (So much for their rendezvous being "hush-hush.")

Solution #112: Don't Feed the Green-Eyed Monster

The problem with office romances is that they're best kept secret. Discretion is not only the better part of valor; it's the mandatory part of behaving professionally.

Secrecy is all very well and good—except for the fact that then the community can't sanction the match. It's a double bind for the amorous couple. If you happen to be allies with one of the people in the relationship, never add to the jealousy factor by reporting that the coworker one cube over has also been flirting with his love interest. Instead, follow that time-honored credo, "See no evil, speak no evil." Is your colleague head over heels in lust with someone at the office? Oh, really? You hadn't noticed.

Office Dating: It's Easier to Find Someone but a Lot Harder to Make It Work

Holy Cupid, Batman. These office relationships can be sheer torture on innocent bystanders. First, your employee claims to be in love with a fellow coworker. Then she claims to love him not. Three days later, she vows she will end it with him once and for all. But by the following week, she's changed her mind again. Here's how the petals fall on falling in love at work:

- **SHE LOVES IT.** Your employee actually had a chance to learn a guy's middle name before jumping into bed with him! Compared to her other relationships, this one proceeded at a spinster's pace.
- **SHE LOVES IT NOT.** She and her paramour will always have to hide their relationship. And they'll never know whether they're being discreet enough—until it turns out that they weren't. The continual strain of hiding the relationship stresses out the relationship.
- **SHE LOVES IT.** She and her coworker have so much in common. Who cares about sports teams or movies or religion or art? When conversation runs thin, they can always talk about work!
- **SHE LOVES IT NOT.** Forget about coworkers, colleagues, and bosses. No one in the outside world approves of her relationship either. Even her Jewish mother wishes she hadn't nagged her only daughter to settle down so quickly. Dating at work is considered a social misstep.
- **SHE LOVES IT.** Work is so much more fascinating now that she's hanging around her cube 24/7, waiting for you-know-who to pop by the watercooler and blow her a big, fat air kiss.
- **SHE LOVES IT NOT.** Sending sexy emails to her office love is excessively dangerous.

- **SHE LOVES IT.** Now that she has a secret alliance with a fellow staffer, she's a font of scandalous office gossip about other people. She even knows who's bopping who down in the dusty back office.
- **SHE LOVES IT NOT.** The jerk broke up with her! Now, as she struggles to pick up her bruised ego and get on with her work, she begins to wonder how much the dalliance hurt her reputation.

Problem #113: A Coworker Crosses the Line

In theory, they agreed that they were all wrong for each other. But they had to meet several times to discuss just how ill fated the match was. Then one thing led to another, and now they're back together again, a condition that has "déjà-vu disaster" written all over it. Once again, you're asked to cover while the on-again, off-again office lovers sneak off to *Starbucks* together to stitch together their tentative rapprochement.

Solution #113: No Special Privileges

If you are a manager, you need to guard against any show of favoritism. Never agree to protect two members of your department who are having an illicit affair. If one or both of their performances (at the office) begins to dip, you will have to discuss it with them. And if their relationship seems like it's getting serious, you may even need talk to one or both of them about possibly leaving the company. Most coworkers resent political alliances built on sexual compatibility. Beyond that, dating one's coworkers may actually be explicitly against company policy. (Time to peek inside the company handbook.)

Towards Peaceful Coworker Coexistence

Are two of your coworkers falling all over each other at the copier? Are they surreptitiously groping each other at the vending machine? In the words of a certain judiciary committee, are they having "sexual relations"? Don't get involved. (If you don't have anything better to talk about, please get a life.)

Problem #114: Pillow Talk: A Colleague Is Sleeping with the Enemy

Your employee is "secretly" seeing the man at the office whom you used to not-so-secretly refer to as "Dr. Dragon" (due to his breath). Worse still, you castigated him once or twice behind his back for his grating voice and feeble people skills. The fact that your colleague would even give him a second glance, much less fall into the office-supply closet with him, is turning the gentle sitcom that is your life into a nightmare on Elm Street. What if he discovers all of the little ways that you've been slamming him?

Solution #114: Leave a Chocolate for Him on the Pillow

Once you've been hypercritical of someone, it's hard to take back the sentiment. Like writing down something in pencil, the words still leave an impression, no matter how many times you gently try to erase them. And, frankly, it's beneath you to beg your employee not to reveal all of the dastardly things that you said about her paramour. (That whole conversation will simply crystallize precisely how critical you were.)

Instead, use the fact that you know these two colleagues are allied to feed him new information through her. Just be certain to keep any compliments about him low-key and more or less objective. "I thought Rick raised the bar at the new employee training session," you might tell her. "Personally, I wasn't expecting to learn anything new, but I picked up a lot of helpful pointers from his speech. I'm thinking of having him speak at the company mission retreat."

Don't worry too much about recriminations for any backstabbing comments you made about your colleague's love interest while the two of them are still involved. Love tends to iron out a lot of ruffled feelings, with "feel-good" hormones like serotonin and oxytocin. With any luck, your underling might never relay what you and others said. However, if the two of them split up, that's when it's perfectly normal to feel wary about what she might let slip in anger.

HOW TO GET AWAY WITH AN OFFICE AFFAIR

You tried to dissuade Sally from having an affair with Stu down in accounting. But your dispassionate logic failed to convince her; and now, she and Stu can't sweep those ledgers off his credenza fast enough.

Besides leaving these two impassioned souls to commit their own mutual career hara-kiri, is there anything else that you can do—now that the proverbial deed has been done? There is. You can buy your colleague a copy of this book and tell her to check out "How to Get Away with an Office Affair" on this page. Here are the seven cardinal rules for getting away with the number-one sin in America.

1. **NEVER LEAVE OR ENTER THE OFFICE BUILDING TOGETHER—OR TONGUES WILL FLAP.** Have a client meeting outside the office? Take separate taxis.
2. **DESTROY ALL EVIDENCE.** No emails. If you must rely on technology to arrange a meeting, use voicemail. Before leaving a message, picture your love interest accidentally hitting speakerphone as he plays your message, to the loud guffaws of everyone around him. Be businesslike.

3. **ONLY GET IT ON OFF PREMISES.** Just to be clear, that means *not* meeting in any supply closets, copier rooms, stairwells, or coed bathrooms.
4. **DON'T HANG OUT TOGETHER AT THE OFFICE.** Not even for a quickie lunch in the cafeteria. People will know you're in lust.
5. **KEEP YOUR TRAVEL SCHEDULES SEPARATE.** The lure of foreign hotel rooms makes even smart coworkers do some pretty stupid things.
6. **TELL ONE PERSON, AND YOU'VE TOLD MILLIONS.** This includes people outside of your company. Every person on the planet may be six degrees removed from Kevin Bacon, but they're only one degree removed from your boss.
7. **WATCH THE MIME FACTOR.** When two people are involved with each other, they tend to mimic each other's physical and facial gestures. They may even start to pick up each other's verbal patterns. Think your coworkers will be totally oblivious to this display of verbal foreplay? Think again.

Problem #115: She's Dating Your Boss

The power dynamic has just endured a seismic shift, as your underling and boss are engaged in a tryst. Should you tell your employee to run and never look back, or offer to be one of her bridesmaids? When two of the people with whom you work most closely are improperly canoodling, what is the proper protocol on your part?

Solution #115: She's Not the Boss of You

This is one situation where denial is a perfectly valid response. Stay neutral. Just behave towards your two colleagues exactly as you have been all along. Keep your conversation business-centric and matter-of-fact. They'll both appreciate it when their relationship craters and everyone, including the mailroom guy, is chortling over their angst. You'll be the one person whom they won't be embarrassed to approach about work issues.

The Golden Rule

If a colleague of yours habitually trolls for mates in the office pool, counsel her not to sleep with the boss. For while she may temporarily gain the boss's favor, she will lose the respect of her coworkers. If two coworkers are involved and they ask you to fib about their whereabouts, don't. Never a gawker nor a gossip be.

Chapter 24

Mr. Mumble, a.k.a. The Subversive Employee

Jones was trying to act like a priest who kept the holiest of holy secrets to himself. One of his secrets was how the capital markets worked.

He's been known to play hide-and-seek with the facts. And the plain fact is, he can torture a fact until it becomes unrecognizable. Statistically speaking, his truth rate is on the low end. (Unless his whole view of the project is warped, and he's just being incredibly honest about it.)

But, while we're being frank, what difference does it make—since no one can possibly understand a word he's saying anyway? Is there a power in being muddy? A creepy Zen that derives from deliberately obscuring the facts? Or does Mr. Mumble simply throw up a haze of confusion around him in order to discourage others from trying to micromanage him? Is he being truculent? Or is he simply a poor communicator? What is the m.o. of a man who mumbles on through, and is there any way to bring his written and verbal skills all the way up to passably mediocre?

Problem #116: Stonewalling

Talking to him is like trying to pry information from a reluctant witness. "How was the meeting?" you ask. "Fine," he says, shrugging you off with his flat intonation. "Did you have a chance to ask our customer about the delayed payment?" you ask. "Sort of." "Can you elaborate?" you press, unsuccessfully trying to keep the irritation out of your voice. "Look, can't we just discuss it later?" he says.

Solution #116: Either Break the Wall with a Chisel, or Solicit the Help of a Company Spy

Do your best to assess whether his mumbling is deliberate. There may be cogent reasons why your colleague chooses to obscure the facts. If so, shaking him like a plum tree isn't going to loose the information from him. Instead, dispatch someone else to chaperone Mr. Mumble. This person can travel with him to meetings and report back to the team on outcomes and next steps. Consider asking the Sycophant to perform this necessary task. His slick demeanor may even help Mr. Mumble's meetings progress more smoothly, and you may find Mr. Mumble far more willing to open up to you. (*See* Chapter 22, *The Spineless Sycophant*.)

Problem #117: He Won't Commit Anything to Email

Ask him no questions, and he'll tell you no lies. And should you happen to ask him any questions via email, he won't honor you with a reply. He resists communication attempts of all kinds, except in person. But in person, he's not forthcoming either. (*See* Problem #116.)

Solution #117: Call a Meeting and Have Someone Write Up a Conference Report

Your underling is toying with you by blatantly resisting your authority. Prove to him that undermining you in this fashion will not work. Assign a scribe to take notes during the internal meeting and commit everything Mr. Mumble murmurs to a list of next steps. He can hem and haw. He can haw and hem. He can clear his throat, sputter, and cough. But after this meeting, at least everyone else on the project will have a clearer idea of what contributions are expected of him.

Don't vent your frustrations about Mr. Mumble to other employees. There is a certain managerial majesty in staying above the fray. On the flip side, if you find his communication style highly irksome, there is an excellent chance that others will too. If so, you will need to tackle it with him during a performance review.

Management Mantra

"I don't want to be that guy mumbling into his drink at a bar."

—Bill Murray

Problem #118: Lost Records

In the Lost and Found of corporate life, he's on the Lost side. How does this line item compare to a similar line item last year? Don't ask him! He hasn't a clue. What does the company's contract with a particular vendor say about cutting charges? He just can't remember. Sorry. Would he mind showing you how it was done last year? Unfortunately, he can't locate that particular file right now, but he'll do his best to recall it from memory. In a post-Enron world, how does Mr. Mumble continue to get away with these shenanigans?

Solution #118: View His Computerized Records by Date

The willpower of a subversive subordinate these days is no match for his computer. Computer files can help organize their creator, even against his will. If you know the approximate date of the records you're seeking, ask Mr. Mumble if you can hop on to his computer and locate them yourself. He may balk, but his resistance will be futile. If you really need access to someone's computerized records, you can generally obtain them. Even if he deletes them (and remembers to delete the deletes), they are usually housed somewhere on the company's backup server.

While you are not being paid to be someone's corporate shrink, sometimes it's also wise to spend some time trying to glean a recalcitrant employee's motivation. Is he trying to block your access to his files to spare himself the effort of having to locate them? Or is there some more sinister reason why he might be detaining you? If he's either hiding money or pocketing company profits, you will first need to conduct your due diligence and then surface your findings with someone in a position of authority such as your boss, company counsel, or the CFO.

Problem #119: He Backtracks

His favorite three words are "by the way." "By the way, our firm never factored the demolition cost into the original estimate." "Oh, by the way, that little oversight is going to cost our client tens of thousands of dollars." "And, by the way, the new invoice to them is in the mail, so you may want to screen your calls for the next week or two." By the way, you hate the way he breezily drops these bombs and then leaves you and others to pick up the pieces.

Solution #119: Instill Some Best Practices

Best practices are like preventative medicine for a wide range of unforeseeable corporate ailments. Followed rigorously, best practices can help to avoid the worst kinds of oversights.

Assign a team to craft a procedures manual with checklists clearly delineating each step, step-by-step. If there are branding issues, a procedures manual can act as a survival manual for your employees. Standardize all forms your company uses, across the board, for all clients, and automatically halve the number of oversights caused by human error.

Institute a mentor program in your company. Perhaps some of the Veterans can coach the Newbies to bring them up to speed faster. Incentivize teamwork by rewarding people for it. Discourage "Lone Ranger" behavior of all kinds.

Problem #120: The Political Hot Potato

Mr. Mumble is blathering on about something, God knows what. (*He* does, but *you* don't.) Every time you nimbly cut short the mumbler's ramble to try to clarify what he's talking about, he looks profoundly uncomfortable. You suspect that he may be suffering from hemorrhoids. Either that or he has a phobia about openness—you're not sure which. As you're weighing the two different options, one medical and the other psychological, a red flush creeps up his ample neck and fans across his jowly face. He looks like a perturbed tomato.

Solution #120: Go Offline and Off the Record

Certain politically sensitive topics are too hot to handle in a group meeting. Something may have occurred during the previous administration that can't be openly discussed in front of the whole team. It only makes sense to raise the topic with the employee in an environment where he'll feel more at ease, such as his office. Explain that you're simply trying to get to the bottom of the issue and he needs to educate you on the history of the project. Once he finally relents and opens up to you, don't take notes. Instead, listen closely, then jot down some notes only after the conversation for your own private reference.

SEVEN TIPS TO CREATE A MORE TRANSPARENT WORKPLACE

You want your people to be accountable—not just to you but to the company. Openness starts at the top. It needs to be a corporate priority and, depending on your level, you may not have enough clout to turn an oblique workplace into a transparent one. But even if you're somewhere in the middle, you don't have to feel "stuck" with the way things are.

Here are some measures to begin to open up the channels of communication.

1. **LET YOUR EMPLOYEES OUT OF THE CLOSET.** It's harder for underlings to act guarded and secretive when they are part of a team. Don't permit your people to hunker down behind closed doors. Open doors encourage an open exchange of information.
2. **MIX IT UP.** Inspire different team members to take the lead on various projects. Then they'll tackle the project as if they are running it rather than you. You can think of these teammates as "satellites." However, impose structure on the model. Everyone involved needs to receive timely feedback so they can be effective at their jobs. Monday-morning quarterback meetings and Thursday status meetings are a good start.
3. **BORROW FROM THE TENNIS ROUND-ROBIN MODEL AND DUPLICATE BRIDGE TOURNAMENTS.** Give everyone an opportunity to team up with different people. It will help them develop new skill sets. It will be easier for you to judge staffers' strengths and weaknesses when you observe how they interact with various teammates.

4. **ADOPT A DIVIDE-AND-CONQUER MENTALITY.** Even if you are the boss, know that, frequently, you will need to fill in as one of the players on the project. When that happens, it's helpful to consider yourself a peer rather than too many rungs above to be of any use.
5. **GIVE HONEST FEEDBACK IN SMALL DOSES.** If a report or presentation does not meet your expectations, explain why it doesn't in a constructive way. Did an employee do an outstanding job? Praise her, but don't be Pollyannaish.
6. **BE CONSISTENT.** Consistency may be the "hobgoblin of little minds," but it's an essential leadership tool. Your written employee performance reviews should accurately reflect what you have been saying informally about team members' performances throughout the year. Don't let your personnel reviews be overly colored by whatever has transpired during the most recent month. It's an annual review, not a monthly one.
7. **BE SENSITIVE TO LANGUAGE DIFFICULTIES.** Is there someone on staff who grew up abroad? He may not be as fluent in English as everyone else on the team. Make yourself available to discuss any special issues or difficulties he may have understanding you.

The Golden Rule

Figure out whether Mr. Mumble is being deliberately incoherent. There might be a method to his mumbling. Teaming him up with others will lessen his stranglehold over the flow of information and help you to fashion a more transparent workplace. Don't allow him or others to "sit on" information or to work in closets. Stay open, and encourage it in others.

CHAPTER 25
Your Partner, Judas

I worked with this woman who accidentally sent a nasty IM about me to me. "I'm not sure if she's slow or just lazy," the email said. When I called her on it, she apologized immediately and asked if we could meet in the [office] kitchen…so she could "explain." What could she have possibly told me that would have made it okay? After that incident, I just stopped speaking to her.

Your relationship with your work partner reminds you of an arranged marriage—one arranged by a sadistic boss. Perhaps you never even met the person with whom you were supposed to collaborate eight hours a day, every workday for the foreseeable future. Or maybe you were unfortunate enough to inherit your Judas in an ill-fated reorganization.

On paper, he's your partner, but he's not your ally. While you both share a line on your company's flowchart, the only thing flowing between you is a wave of deep distrust bordering on hostility. While you're still trying your hardest to work with him, he's telling everyone at the office how impossible you are to work with! When the person with whom you're supposed to be collaborating is conspiring against you, what is your best course of action?

Problem #121: You Both Want to Be Top Dog

You've always been the "top dog" in your relationships with previous work partners. As fate would have it, so has your new partner. Now the two of you are unwitting participants in a veritable *bitch fest,* barking at each other about the most trivial issues, such as who will be introduced first in a meeting, or who should hold the client's hand at the toy fair. If you can't find a way to work it out, you'll *both* be in the doghouse.

Solution #121: It Doesn't Have to Be a Dog-Eat-Dog World

You're supposed to be partners. Start acting like it. Split up your responsibilities, and make the lines clean. Maybe you're the "relationship person" while your partner is more of a creative hotshot. Play to each other's strengths. If separating your areas of domain won't work on a permanent basis, at least try it on a project-by-project basis. There is only one situation in which every person on a team has an identical task, and that's in a juror's box.

Management Mantra

"Divide and conquer."

Problem #122: A Hidden Agenda

You can't imagine what his agenda is, but it doesn't seem to be aligned with the company's. He may interrupt you in meetings, or shrink from getting behind an idea that you, as partners, are supposed to be selling through. You don't know whether he's self-destructive or just plain old destructive. But if you had to deconstruct it, he seems rather obstructionist.

Solution #122: Uncover the Motivation

It's easier to solve problems when you understand why they exist in the first place. Here are three questions to ponder before you map out a game plan.

1. Are the difficulties with your partner due to personality differences, differences in preferred working style, or differences of opinion relating to the work?
2. Was your partner hired by a new boss?
3. Could your partner be in place to put through *that person's* agenda?

When dealing with difficult people, it's always smart to ask yourself whether there is a *rational* reason why the two of you aren't getting along, or if the problem is personality-based.

Of the three difficulties cited in question one, differences in preferred working style are relatively easy to smooth out. Suppose that your partner enjoys noshing on a long, leisurely lunch by himself while you're more of a social butterfly. Try to be sensitive to the fact that he just doesn't want to eat with you! Stop asking him to lunch and you may solve half the problem.

Personality differences fall in the medium range of problems. If you and your partner are both type A, verbal, and passionate, you may quickly find yourselves embroiled in a turf war over who says what in meetings. Call a truce by rehearsing what you will both say in advance. This way, when the two of you aren't getting along, it will be less apparent to fellow attendees.

If the partnership just can't agree on strategies and approaches, then you may need to request to work with someone else on staff. Use this tactic sparingly or there is a 50% chance that *you'll* be labeled as "the difficult one."

And what if a new boss has been masterminding some of the problems you've been experiencing with your partner? In that case, try to do-si-do with a different partner, at least for part of the office dance. You may need to prove that it's only Judas with whom you can't get along—an easier case to make if you have a solid track record partnering with Tom, Dick, and Hilda.

Outside the narrow confines of the office, the *Beer Buddy Commandment* rules. In case you are unaware of this commandment, it's basically: *Thou Shalt Not Screw Over a Drinking Buddy.* If you are having problems working with Judas, your first line of defense should be to escort him to your local watering hole. Make an appointment, if need be, to discuss your issues. But make sure that you do it in a collegial bar that's teeming with comfort food. What if your partner is a teetotaler? Challenge him or her to a rousing match of *Wii* tennis or golf. The *Beer Buddy Commandment* is more about a toast to friendship than the number alcohol units consumed.

Problem #123: She Misses Her Ex

With partners like her, who needs rivals? You're both at loggerheads over the creative direction of a project. While you attempt to be diplomatic about your rationale, she digs her spiked heels into the colorless swath that passes as office carpeting and refuses to budge. Whenever you agree to politely disagree, she ratchets up the debate a notch, seeking outside parties to support her viewpoint. One of these sympathizers is her ex-partner, someone with whom she clearly enjoyed working in the past (and probably wouldn't mind working with again). If you express a whisper of a doubt about anything your partner suggests, she's instantly on the phone with her ex-partner, discussing it.

Solution #123: Try a Threesome

Unfortunately, the only way to break through to your new partner is by seducing her ex—verbally—with your wit, impeccable manners, and intelligent reasoning. But your logic had better be flawless. Listen to your gut. But afterward, take the time to substantiate what it tells you with irrefutable facts and figures.

Be lucid. Tell your partner that if she *insists* on running all of your combined ideas by her old partner, then it's only fair for you to meet with that person. During the appointment, clarify your viewpoint, and try to persuade them both. If her ex ends up agreeing with you, it may tame your partner's tendency to go running back to her at the first opportunity. And what if her old partner backs her up? In that case, it's time to raise the issue with the big boss.

Explain that in order to break creative differences of opinion with you, your new partner has been going outside the company fold and revealing confidential information to third parties. Mention that you even met one of the people with whom she brainstorms about sensitive company information. Have your boss raise this with your partner if necessary.

PROPER PARTNERSHIP PROTOCOL

- **INTRODUCE YOUR PARTNER AS YOUR PARTNER.** "I'd like you to meet my partner, Liza," you might say. (Try not to wince when saying the word "partner.")
- **GIVE CREDIT.** Did your partner have a brilliant idea? You'll gain major points with her if you don't hide her light under a bushel (or a bunch of mumbo jumbo about how it was a team effort.)
- **TRUST YOUR PARTNER.** That is, until you have a profound reason not to.
- **EMPLOY THE *BEER BUDDY COMMANDMENT.***
- **GO OFF-CAMPUS.** Invite your partner to your club. Have a partners-only fondue dinner. Better bonding begins outside the office.

Problem #124: He Stabs You in the Back

You're sauntering through the hallway one morning, minding your own business, whistling *Dixie,* when you overhear your partner gossiping about you. "I have no idea what ________ does. [Fill in your own name] She adds no value to the partnership." Ouch. You want to throttle him against the nearest wall, only fear that doing so might lead to a lawsuit.

Solution #124: Make Him Eat His Words

Take as long as necessary to regain your composure. You will have to remain calm during this conversation. When you're as relaxed as a yoga teacher on *Quaaludes,* float over towards your work partner and tell him that the two of you "need to talk."

Fix him with a stare. When he asks what the problem seems to be, gently close his office door and take a seat, preferably across from him so that you can continue to hold his attention with your gaze.

Explain that you overheard him bad-mouthing you. At this point, he'll probably attempt to deny it. Interrupt him mid-sentence, and watch him squirm as you repeat, verbatim, exactly what he said. "You said to so-and-so, and I quote: 'I have no idea what Patty does. She adds no value to the partnership.'" Then quickly enumerate three or four ways that you *do* add value. For example, you might say, "I keep us organized, get us to meetings, and prevent your silly temper tantrums from losing us major pieces of business. And, just a reminder: the March Madness sell-a-thon was *my* idea."

When confronted with the many contributions you bring to the partnership, no doubt your Judas will apologize. Explain that while you're grateful for his apology, it's not enough. He actually needs to repair the damage by taking back his unkind words. That entails circling back to the person to whom he uttered them and retracting them. Most likely, he'll agree to this ballsy request (if only to shoo you out of his office). Three business days later, check in with him to find out if he lived up to his word. If he claims that he simply "forgot," keep checking in with him until he follows through. This solution may feel a bit clunky and inelegant, but it works.

Problem #125A: He Gets Promoted

Your company has a no-smoking policy, but clearly, top management must have been smoking *something* to promote your ornery partner over you.

Solution #125A: Be Happy You No Longer Have to Work with Him

You have secured your much-deserved liberty from a debilitating partnership, and your job is still intact! If your partner was forever belittling your efforts behind your back, you were in an abusive work partnership. Say good luck and good riddance.

Problem #125B: You Get Promoted

It turns out that management had some vision after all. Somehow, they saw through your partner's self-propaganda and promoted you over him. Boy, are they smart!

Solution #125B: Beware Your Partner's Revenge

Your partner was bypassed for a promotion that he feels was rightfully his. Prepare for a new attack on your credibility from the same source. You may want to consider relying on your ex-partner now more than ever—now that the two of you no longer *have to* work together. For it's the only sure way to keep your eye on him. Remember Sun Tzu's brilliant credo, "Keep your friends close and your enemies closer."

Towards Peaceful Coworker Coexistence

What if you are allies with both members of a dysfunctional team? Try to be a diplomatic peacemaker rather than a lightning rod for their discontent. If the higher-ups view you as a diplomat, ultimately it could lead to your own advancement.

The Golden Rule

Many workplaces are fonts of competition. Thus, mini-teams, based on partnerships between two people, can be quite a challenge. If possible, divide and conquer your tasks as a twosome. Play to each of your strengths. As problems arise, remember the *Beer Buddy Commandment* and resolve your differences outside of the workplace.

CHAPTER 26
The Newbie

She had that deer-caught-in-the-headlights look for about six months. It scared me 'cause it reminded me of the way I used to be.

She's so wet behind the ears that you're worried water will drip onto her immaculately tailored suit and stain it. (Everyone else wears casual clothes to the office.) She's so green that just hearing the things that pop out of her mouth make you turn crimson with embarrassment. And, forget about her answers—she doesn't even know what questions to ask.

Yet in spite of the fact that she has *no idea* what she is doing, that doesn't prevent her from thinking she does. She has a reckless sort of confidence, which, when combined with equal parts ignorance, leads to a lethal cocktail mixture of mistakes. Recently, you even found yourself missing the person whom the Newbie replaced... and you never even got along with her!

When the person to whom you're supposed to be showing the ropes makes you feel like hanging yourself might be a great deal less painless, what are your best alternatives?

Problem #126: She Doesn't Want to Pay Her Dues

She's as high maintenance as a Manhattan co-op. Three weeks into the job, and the Newbie has already decided she needs a personal assistant. This makes you laugh out loud, as you have been unsuccessfully trying to get one for five years. The Newbie is a bit too enamored with delegating for your comfort. Doesn't she realize that *she's* the one to whom you're supposed to be delegating the work? Naively, she expects to attend all sorts of trade conferences whose tickets are normally reserved for those (much) higher up on the totem pole. Where does she get these Gen Y fantasies?

Solution #126: She Must Pay Them: No Ifs, Ands, or Buts

Don't spoil the Newbie, or she will develop an insufferable air of entitlement that will be difficult to quash later. You can befriend her without coddling her. Nicely explain that perks, such as tickets to expensive trade conferences, are rewards for good work and do not automatically accrue with the job.

If you work in a smaller company where everyone is expected to wear many different hats, you might try disclosing that, in this corporate environment, she is expected to be her *own* personal assistant.

An old adage warns, "Spare the rod and spoil the child." The corporate corollary is, "Spare the talk and spoil the Newbie." A spoiled Newbie eventually festers into a cantankerous Oldie and adds to the plethora of jerks already inhabiting today's corporations.

Just the Stats

With job switching at an all-time high in the U.S., more Newbies are joining companies than ever before. Be nice to your Newbie, and pray that someday in the not-too-distant future, some old-timer will pay back the karmic debt by taking an active interest in *your* development when you join a new firm. Once upon a time, we were all Newbies!

Problem #127: You're Hands Off; She's Hands On

You're a *macro manager,* with a loose, non-controlling organizational style that appeals to most underlings. But the Newbie, brought on board by someone other than you, requires a lot more hand-holding than you're used to providing. Her neediness is new to you and feels strangely childlike. How can you persuade her to become more self-reliant?

Solution #127: Be Flexible

Your employee's clinginess may disappear once she gains more confidence. First, try to allay her fears by outlining the parameters of the problem, any pitfalls you foresee, and your best recommendations for how to handle them. Then let her wander off on her own. If she asks for some guidance along the way, be open to providing it but also be honest. Tell her that once she demonstrates mastery, she will need to shoulder more responsibility.

Good communication skills are the pillars of solid relationships, so be clear about your expectations. What would constitute a smash success? What would be considered an unmitigated fiasco? Imagine that you are allowing the Newbie to roam in the woods for the first time in her life. As her counselor, you will provide a map, directions, and plenty of mosquito repellent, but you are not going to hike through the woods with her.

Towards Peaceful Coworker Coexistence

Develop empathy towards your fellow coworkers. So often, the first reaction to someone who works a little differently is to shower the person with disdain. Instead, reach back into your memory bank and channel what it felt like to be the new kid in school. Remember how much it stung to sit in that cafeteria all by yourself, and how relieved you were when someone finally reached out to you. Right now, you have the opportunity to be *that person* to the Newbie. Bring yourself to befriend her early on, and you will gain an ally and confidant.

Problem #128: She Should Be Seen and Not Heard

You have never witnessed a person so intent on sharing her thoughts when no one is keen to hear them. She should feel privileged to be in the room with these titled pinstripes; instead, she rambles on and on about *her* ideas. Her breathless cadence doesn't allow for her to be readily interrupted. Doesn't she realize there is a time to shut up and listen? And that time, well, that would be now.

Solution #128: Instruct Her in Proper Meeting Etiquette

The Newbie may not recognize that, in the corporate culture of your company, being invited to a meeting is an honor. Help her to not humiliate herself further by impressing on her the finer points of conference table etiquette. Advise her to arrive on time and bring a notepad and pen to capture important deadlines. She should not bring a snack to the meeting unless she knows that others will be. As a new hire, she should take it upon herself to absorb what the old-timers are talking about before spouting off her own opinions. Her cell phone must remain off during the entire meeting. (It's only permissible to check text messages while waiting for meetings to begin. It's incorrigibly rude to text message people during a meeting.)

Is there an exemplary employee on the team? Note her meeting etiquette, and if it's irreproachable, advise the Newbie to model her own behavior accordingly. It's always smart for Newbies to have real, live role models after which to pattern themselves. With any luck, the Newbie and the Oldie will bond and your tenure as Newbie tutor will be short-lived and uneventful.

CONFERENCE TABLE ETIQUETTE FOR SMARTIES

"Know your audience." Here's a great piece of wisdom that works across all fields. During a trial, a defense attorney would never ask a question to which he didn't already know the answer. That's knowing his audience. When a Newbie is still in training, she can't possibly know her audience well enough to have a clue as to how it will react. Therefore, she should take the opportunity to keep her ears open and mouth closed. Here are seven other don'ts for Newbies.

1. **DON'T OPINIONATE.** No one wants to hear it.
2. **DON'T B.S.** People can sniff it.
3. **DON'T FIDGET.** It makes everyone else jumpy.
4. **DON'T DOODLE—OR EXPRESS BOREDOM IN SOME OTHER FASHION.** Just how bored is the Newbie? Nobody cares.
5. **DON'T WATCH THE CLOCK.** Yes, it's 4:05 p.m. And now it's 4:07 p.m. Time crawls when it's so closely monitored.
6. **DON'T HIJACK THE MEETING.** Or use it as a forum to resolve something that's not on the agenda.
7. **DON'T ORATE.** Or everyone's eyes will flutter closed. They are getting sleepy...They are drifting off...Goodbye, audience.

Problem #129: She's a Mistake Waiting to Happen

The messages she shoots from her Blackberry are chock-full of tipos. (Incidentally, that word was supposed to be *typos.*) She hasn't mastered the difference between *Reply* and *Reply All,* and has no clue that most of the time, a reply from her isn't even necessary. When she's under pressure, her voice adopts a high, squeaky quality reminiscent of chalk rubbing against a blackboard the wrong way. Several of the top brass have already snipped that she seems to show stress at the slightest provocation. You're beginning to worry that she might never fit in.

Solution #129: Have Her Edit Herself First

Every typo subtracts major I.Q. points from someone's internal performance score sheet—that secret report card we all carry around in our heads, not just about ourselves, but about our fellow colleagues and coworkers. Fortunately, with just a click of the mouse, she can check typos in her emails and in all internal correspondence. If the typos made from her Blackberry are few and far between, have her program a signature disclaimer at the end of each communication that warns, "Sent from my Blackberry. Please forgive the typos." However, if the number of typos is excessive, advise her to ease up on using her Blackberry. It really does her a disservice.

Teach the Newbie to "go slow." Once she hits a reply to email, it's "out there." If her position at the company doesn't warrant her replying to everyone's emails, don't mince words. Simply tell her to stop hitting *Reply All.* For, at a certain point, the sheer number of internal emails will begin to annoy every single person on the cc list. Perhaps once the Newbie feels less pressure to reply to every email, she'll feel less stressed; otherwise, you will need to counsel her on that as well.

No one wants to hear her gripe about her long list of tasks. Stiff-upperlipism is the essence of professionalism.

Management Mantra

"Make each word fight for the right to stay on the page." Writing wags don't know who first coined this sage literary advice, but it's a great one to recall when editing documents. Another popular saying that makes the same point: "When in doubt, leave it out."

Problem #130: She Wants to Reinvent the Wheel

Her ego is meddling with efficiency. Deep down, she believes that she is smarter than everyone else. Even when directed to follow company templates and use the tools and libraries, she resists. She is forever starting projects with a "blank slate" rather than benefiting from all of the work that has come before her.

Solution #130: Help Her Stand On the Shoulders of Giants

Cynics may claim, "There are no new ideas," or in the words of a song by the *Barenaked Ladies,* "It's all been done before." But the plain fact is, being fresh and new is highly overrated. Even in extremely creative fields, it's often wiser to revisit what has come before than to totally ignore it. Acknowledge it. Revise it. Twist it. And you'll craft something three times sharper than the original.

Encourage the Newbie to follow Isaac Newton's famous credo and "stand on the shoulders of giants." It means that when you build on what has come before you, it's easier to achieve greatness. Presumably, some of the kinks have already been smoothed out of the project, allowing the next person who works on it to add her own touch of brilliance.

Great writers reference the classic works of literature in their own prose. Great musicians often sample other pieces of music in their new melodies or will produce a cover of a popular song. Painters frequently copy in the style of the old masters until they have perfected their own style. If standing on the shoulders of giants is good enough for these creative types, it should be standard practice for every businessperson in America.

STANDING ON THE SHOULDERS OF GIANTS, A METAPHOR THAT HAS WITHSTOOD THE TEST OF TIME

First recorded in the twelfth century, the phrase "standing on the shoulders of giants" was attributed to Bernard of Chartres. In 1159, John of Salisbury wrote in his Metalogicon:

> *"Bernard of Chartres used to say that we are like dwarfs on the shoulders of giants, so that we can see more than they."*

The point was that by capitalizing on the wisdom that others had imparted, a dwarf could see a little further than a giant.

Five centuries later, George Herbert wrote, "A dwarf on a giant's shoulders sees farther of the two." Sir Isaac Newton, founder of gravity, remarked in a letter to Robert Hooke in 1676:

> *"If I have seen a little further it is by standing on the shoulders of giants."*

As recently as 1998, Melvyn Bragg used this metaphor as the title for his nonfiction book, On Giants' Shoulders.

If you can bring yourself to improve on what has come before you, it is more likely to lead to a stellar result than if you begin every project from scratch.

The Golden Rule

Like fine wine, most Newbies mellow with age. Don't expect a Newbie to grasp the corporate culture of your company overnight. Counsel her to stay quiet in meetings, meticulously edit her own work, and help build on the work that happened before her arrival by "standing on the shoulders of giants."

CHAPTER 27
The Watercooler Wag

According to one office gossip who is proud of her calling, "I think on some level I'm secretly hoping that the rumor will get back to the subject...A lot of times that person deserves to hear what's being said about him."

She has it on excellent authority that your stuffy firm is a hotbed of romance, secret trysts, promotions, and demotions in the works. Did two people quarrel over a new employee? Is HR gunning for the big boss? Will there be a merger in the very near future? Just ask the Watercooler Wag.

She's an Information Broker, trading in people's secrets and secret fears. But while her dishes are juicy, snacking from them carries the serious risk of food poisoning. Sit down at the table with her, and it's only a matter of time before her scandalous assertions will be about you.

Should you ignore her? Counsel her to keep quiet? Start a gossip-free zone next to the company cafeteria? When the Watercooler Wag is everyone's favorite lunch companion, is there a way to stay out of sight and out of mind without appearing cold, or even haughty?

Problem #131: What's the Buzz?

The office feels deadly dull unless she's around, stirring things up with her tall tales. Her spicy recipe of enticing suppositions, romantic rumors, and impending management shakeouts makes bland, boring days conversationally riveting. You just wish you could guarantee that *you* would never be one of her secret ingredients.

Solution #131: Get Your Daily Fix from Someone Else

The Watercooler Wag jaws to everyone about everyone. She's democratic that way. Thus, there is no need to consult with her directly. For if you do, your every move will make headlines on her libelous rumor downloads. However, if you're curious about what the Watercooler Wag has been saying, just ask someone else on staff. "Hey, heard any juicy tidbits from Roberta?" you might ask. It is possible to listen without engaging.

Management Mantra

"Whoever gossips to you will gossip about you."

—Spanish proverb

Problem #132: The Word "Confidential" Isn't in Her Vocabulary

From day one, you and Brent didn't hit it off, a fact that wasn't lost on the Watercooler Wag. (Few office frictions escape her nose for malicious prattle.) Boorish Brent can't resist cutting you off every time you surface a suggestion in a team meeting.

As if sensing your mounting frustration with your coworker, the Watercooler Wag stops you in the kitchenette one dreary afternoon. "How do you feel about Brent anyway?" she asks, eyes agleam. She's caught you in a weak moment, a sugar low. Hungrily eyeing the *Snickers* bar in the vending machine, you feed the machine a dollar bill. The machine spits it back. You iron the creases from the bill with the palm of your hand while the Watercooler Wag waits patiently. She has nothing but time. Gingerly, you insert the dollar bill into the machine again. As the candy bar plunks to the metal floor of the machine with a pleasant thud, you spill all. "I find Brent arrogant," you relay, "and sometimes abrasive. Of course, that's completely confidential."

Silently, she nods her head as if to signal that she understands and then retreats to leave you to your chocolate fix.

Solution #132: Tell It to Your Nemesis

The Watercooler Wag enjoys lording the information she collects over others. If she succeeds in safeguarding your secret, then she will consider you in her debt. But it's far more likely that she will let your secret slip to whoever expresses the mildest curiosity about it.

At the point that you find yourself begging the Watercooler Wag to keep mum about something you revealed to her, a little warning sign should flash in your head. The sign says: YOU'RE VENTING TO THE WRONG PERSON. YOU'RE VENTING TO THE WRONG PERSON. By the time Brent hears about it (which he will), your little slipup could become completely contorted. But even if he hears it *exactly* the way you said it, it's still catastrophic.

Seek out Brent and ask to speak to him about the problem. Confide that you have "a small bone to pick with him." When he ushers you into a chair, simply relay that you've noticed he always manages to interrupt you in meetings. Ask if he would mind letting you finish a sentence. Don't be surprised if Brent is completely unaware of his heinous habit. Most big-time interrupters have no idea how rudely they come across to others.

Q: What separates gossip from interesting banter?

A: Subject matter. Subjects to stay away from include: romance (particularly office romance), religion, finances, health, plastic surgery operations, and (ironically) office politics.

REASONS PEOPLE GOSSIP

- **POPULARITY**—both real and imagined.
- **ACCEPTANCE.** People gravitate to gossips to learn the scoop.
- **RELEVANCE.** Gossips have their finger on the pulse.
- **POWER.** Gossips know things others don't.

REASONS NOT TO GOSSIP

- **WAGS ARE VIEWED AS UNTRUSTWORTHY.** They are less likely to receive promotions and interesting assignments.
- **IT'S UNPROFESSIONAL.**
- **IT MAKES THE GOSSIP LOOK AS IF SHE HAS TOO MUCH TIME ON HER HANDS.**
- **EVEN IDLE GOSSIP CAN MAR SOMEONE'S REPUTATION.** Sometimes that person retaliates against the talebearer.
- **GOSSIP LOWERS OFFICE MORALE**.

Problem #133: She's Not at Work to Work

Whenever you pass the Watercooler Wag, her lips are firmly affixed to another coworker's ear as she plies her with the latest drivel. Playfully, the Wag motions you to snuggle in to cozy their circle. How does she find the time to gossip, you wonder? But in fact, you are missing the point. She's at work purely to socialize, and the spreading of rumors is how she accomplishes her aim. Her favorite haunts are quiet, quasi-social niches, such as the elevator, bathroom, hallways, and kitchenette. In these spots, the less formal atmosphere acts as a giant Petri dish for her slanderous patter.

Solution #133: Master the Redirect

"Did you hear about Kevin?" and "Have you heard the latest in the Bill-Bob-Belinda escapade?" are simply the Watercooler Wag's attempts to draw you in. But just because she's trying to ensnare you doesn't mean that you have to be lured by her bait. Instead, use her bait to switch the topic. For example, you might say, "Speaking of Kevin reminds me… I have an exciting new project to discuss with you both." Or you might even try a breezy, "Bill, Bob, and Belinda? Let's not go there!" Greet all attempts to entice you with gossip with polite disinterest. Eventually, your local talebearer will get the hint.

Problem #134: Everyone Believes Her

She's bearish on your company's efforts to keep all current staff employed and vocal about her prognostications. "Layoffs are coming! Layoffs are coming!" she bells through the hallway. She overheard two top honchos discussing the impending bloodbath, so it *must* be a fact. "If I were you, I'd consider sending out your resumé," you even heard her snip to the Coddled Superstar.

Solution #134: Either Confirm or Deny

During the course of a company's history, there will be multiple swellings and retrenchments. If your company is on the cusp of a massive layoff, you owe it to the team to reveal what you know in a generalized way. Maybe one or two people will decide to leave before the dreaded ax falls, thus sparing those who really want to stay.

You can't reveal to team members who among them is on the macabre victim List; and in any event, The List may well change multiple times. But if layoffs are inevitable, a proper response is to say something to the effect that, as far as you know, "3% of staff (or whatever the real number is) will be cut, across the board, and most departments will be impacted (or whatever the fact is)."

Leadership has its responsibilities. One of them is being there to quash outrageous rumors or to confirm them. Your team members will appreciate your honesty.

Problem #135: Her Wagging Tongue Is Pointed at You

One frigid morning, a staffer whom you barely know approaches you, stares at your stomach, and says, "I understand congratulations are in order." The implication is all the more galling as you (a) are single, and (b) haven't had sex in months.

Later that afternoon, the HR manager knocks on your door, cocks her head at you sympathetically, and asks if you'd like to take the rest of the day off. From whence do these fertile rumors bud? Hmmm. Any guesses?

Solution #135: Give Her a Tongue Lashing

It is inappropriate for the Watercooler Wag to start rumors about you. If they are false, your reprimand should sting. You need to be firm enough to dissuade the behavior. That includes issuing a heated denial and a request for her to stop her libelous rumor campaign.

Even if her rumor *is* true, you don't necessarily have to deny it in order to get her to stop spreading it. You could explain that rampant rumor-mongering dampens morale and distracts teammates from getting their work done. You could cite that she's supposed to be working some of the time, not forever gossiping. You might share that gossips rarely move up quickly in companies since everyone on staff fears them.

You could even confide that her habit makes you distrust what she might reveal to others when a topic is sensitive.

Towards Peaceful Coworker Coexistence

Gossip thrives in managerial environments where information is not forthcoming. Be open with the people in your department about your expectations, long- and short-term goals, and company progress, along with any setbacks. It will do much to stem the flow of insidious gossip. Two good rules to follow: (1) share information sooner rather than later, and (2) when email communications threaten to spiral out of control, make it your mission to sit down and talk, face-to-face.

The Golden Rule

Avoid the Watercooler Wag, especially if you have something to hide or if you sense that she doesn't like you. If you must cross paths with her, direct your conversation to the world outside of your little bubble. Hey, how about those Knicks?

CHAPTER 28
The Paranoid Nut

The biggest problem I have encountered in coworkers is paranoia. Many people try to hide their shortcomings by pretending to be an expert in everything. The latter type of worker usually becomes intensely paranoid, cooking up delusions of conspiracies from both inside and outside of the enterprise.

An aura of deep-seated mistrust clings to him like the scent of tobacco to a smoker. He keeps his door closed much of the time and prefers to work in secret. Ideas he holds close to his vest, only releasing them at the last conceivable moment. Fellow staffers perceive him as standoffish.

Constantly on the lookout for signs of disrespect and supremely sensitive to abuses of power, his radar is often inaccurate and he's quick to misinterpret his findings. If anyone has an issue with any of his ideas, he has a conspiracy theory to explain it.

As a worker, he possesses some talent. But his social skills subtract major points from his promotability quotient, and you're not certain about his long-term prospects at the firm.

Can a team member survive who's anti-team? And should you do your best to encourage him to stay or leave?

Just the Stats

Paranoia, according to the Merriam-Webster dictionary, is "a tendency on the part of an individual or group towards excessive or irrational suspiciousness and distrustfulness of others." Please note the word *irrational* in the definition. While a popular adage claims, "Just because you're paranoid doesn't mean they aren't after you," in fact, this is false. If you are paranoid, then your fears are irrational and thus not justified. On the other hand, if your fears *are* justified, then by definition, you're *not* being paranoid.[15]

Problem #136: He Requires More Feedback Than Anyone Else

He is like the moon—always hovering nearby. This week, the moon happens to be in your Career House (or outside your office, anyway.) The Nut nervously waits for you, seeking an audience. When you casually inquire how things are going, he reflects your question right back at you. How do *you* think he's handling everything? he wants to know. He also pumps you for feedback about other employees, particularly those whom he believes to be his enemies.

Solution #136: Short, Informal Sessions

Get into the mode of giving this tortured employee informal feedback on a regular basis. It's the only way to lessen his feeling that everyone is seeking to oust him. Make each session as short but as meaningful as possible. And keep your reports focused solely on him. If he's doing well, that's all the information you need convey. If he requires guidance, first compliment him on what he's doing right and then frame any criticism as a simple suggestion for improvement.

Limit your contact with this person to under half an hour a day. Recognize that you can't ignore him completely (or else his paranoia will mushroom). But also realize that engaging with him has potentially debilitating side effects for you. If you can't resolve whatever needs to be addressed in a half hour, let it sit until the next day.

IS HE PARANOID? TAKE THIS SIMPLE TEST

Paranoid personality disorder (PPD) is one of a group of conditions called "eccentric personality disorders." People with PPD suffer from an unrelenting mistrust and suspicion of others.

The following checklist is not meant to substitute for a consultation with a practiced medical professional. But if your employee seems to have at least three of the following five symptoms, you may want to refer him to your company's Employee Assistance Program (E.A.P.).

1. **HE'S RELUCTANT TO CONFIDE PERSONAL INFORMATION ABOUT HIMSELF THAT IS READILY AVAILABLE.** Where does he live, again? *Well, if you promise not to tell anyone...*
2. **CONSTRUCTIVE CRITICISM UNRAVELS HIM.**
3. **HE OFTEN FEELS PERSONALLY ATTACKED.** These supposed acts of unbridled aggression aren't obvious to other people who were there to witness them.
4. **HE HAS DIFFICULTY MAINTAINING CLOSE RELATIONSHIPS.**
5. **HE PICTURES HIMSELF AS THE TARGET OF AN ELABORATE CONSPIRACY.**

Problem #137: He's Having a Breakdown

In a meeting to announce a new corporate initiative, the Nut first hears that some of his key players will be transferred to another department. His skin turns a blotchy shade of eggplant; he looks like he needs an emergency appendectomy.

Standing up suddenly, he lashes out at your boss and asserts that these moves were done "behind his back," in an effort to shrivel his power base. "This is typical of the clandestine way things happen around here," he says, brandishing his pencil like a musical baton. He slams out of the meeting, to the open-jawed astonishment of everyone else in the room.

After a moment of stunned silence, you race out the door after him, with hopes of preventing him from leaving the building. But when you finally catch up to him at the elevator bank, he looks so irate that you just dive out of his way.

Solution #137: Teach Him How to Repair Himself

The twin themes, trust and its cousin mistrust, inform a paranoid sufferer's life, so it's essential to be straight up with this employee. Be specific. Cite specific times when his outbursts worried you or other staffers. Divorce your feedback from your emotion and never take anything he says personally. For if you lose your cool, you'll both become embroiled in an impassioned standoff.

Schedule a feedback session with him as soon after his outburst as possible. It's best not to let his feelings mount. You don't have to stick to prepared remarks, but it's helpful to preplan what you might say to someone with such a low threshold for office upset.

Keep your remarks and feedback limited to *actual* events. Refuse to be pulled into a discussion about his *perceived* injustices.

Check out your company's resources through your HR department. Ask about the Employee Assistance Program. If you refer an employee to the E.A.P. and he refuses the help, you may be able to consider contact with a mental health professional a condition of his continued employment. If he had an altercation with your superior, then the two of them will also need to discuss it in detail.

Problem #138: Everyone's Out to Get Him

When another supervisor was promoted over him, the Nut stormed into your office and accused you of being "in on it" (whatever "it" was). You stared at him as if the creature before you was having a meltdown. You directed him to take the seat farthest away from the window and to exhale. He visibly shook in the chair as sweat leaked from his brow, and you felt a bit sorry for him. Once you closed your door, he proceeded to lambaste you for being in the "small, select coterie of people who always pick the safe choice." When you asked him to produce evidence, he just looked down at his lap, his lips muttering words that can't be printed here.

Solution #138: Have Your Rationale Ready

There are two issues; and unfortunately, only one of them is in your domain. They are your colleague's paranoid behavior and the fact that he feels slighted because he was bypassed. You are qualified to discuss only the second problem with him in depth. First, figure out if it's true. Was the other person promoted because his views are more aligned with those of top management? How do the two employees' results compare? Align your reasons and prepare to have an intelligent conversation with the Nut about the criteria that were used to promote his rival over him.

How Paranoia Unravels People

The paranoid often brood about problems that just aren't there. Ultimately their mistrustfulness *becomes* the problem. They will gravitate to the smallest speck of evidence that confirms their suspicion while ignoring all evidence that doesn't support it. They are emotional vigilantes—constantly on the prowl for new plots against them.

Management Mantra

"We are paid for our suspicions by finding what we suspect."

—Henry David Thoreau

Problem #139: He's Icy

The Nut runs hot and cold, two extremes of his deeply mistrustful nature, both of which are off-putting to coworkers. When he's hot, he's overheated, likely to fume and make wild accusations that have only the slimmest bearing on reality. But just as often, his internal thermostat is set to the other extreme, and he comes off as cold. He shuns intimacy, priding himself instead on his "rational" nature. Most of his coworkers don't consider him paranoid. They simply find him aloof and unfriendly.

Solution #139: Warm Him Up in School

There is little you can do about his underlying paranoia. Unless you're a licensed psychotherapist, you can't afford to sit around all day analyzing his problems. (Of course, if someone offers you $150 an hour to do so, you'll reconsider.)

But while you can't cure the cause, you can give both you and the Nut some distance from his crippling self-absorption. Take the behaviorist approach and send him to classes *during* the day. Help him brush up on his public-speaking skills. Dispatch him to seminars that teach PowerPoint and specialized computer skills. Is there a trade convention in your area? Volunteer the Nut to go in your place.

When he's thrown together with scores of new people (who clearly aren't out to get him), his aloofness may vanish. And he can continue to work for you but not interact with you on a daily basis.

One Secret of Keeping Your Job: Be Slow to Fire Others

Not everyone at the office will be easy to get along with. Personality frictions, conflicting agendas, and raging egos will butt against one another in confined spaces, causing mass claustrophobia.

If you look really hard, generally you can find some redeeming aspect about even the most difficult employee. Occasionally, of course, you won't be able to. Once in a while you will ask yourself why on earth you should have to tolerate a particular employee's noxiousness. As a manager, surely you can simply get rid of this person and extract the proverbial thumbtack from your side once and for all, right? Before you do, consider the following:

- **IS THE EMPLOYEE AN OLD-TIMER?** Has he worked at the company for over seven years? If so, chances are excellent that he's developed an entrenched system of alliances. His allies believe in him, even if you don't. Cut him loose without a strong rationale and you could inadvertently unleash the collective anger of his allies, now entirely focused on deposing you.
- **HIS AGE.** If the person is over forty, firing him carries the risk of an age discrimination lawsuit. Make certain that your reason is puncture proof and you have plenty of documentation to back it up.
- **PREGNANCY.** Firing a woman on maternity leave makes the company look particularly heartless, no matter what the circumstances were that led up to it.

All things considered, it may be easier to figure out new ways to deal with the people who are driving you crazy. A synonym for the word *firing* is *canning*—no doubt because firing even the most deserving candidate often opens a can of worms.

Problem #140: He Sees Conspiracy Theories in Benign Events

When the company declared the end of Casual Fridays, the Nut saw a deeper, darker meaning in it. He claimed it was the first sign there would be a merger. "They want us to dress better," he said, "so that when management teams come to check out the office, we'll all look more professional…as if we have a lot more clients than we actually do." You begged to differ. "Maybe they just got sick of everyone abusing Casual Fridays," you countered. "Maybe they were annoyed that everyone ignored the memos and wore blue jeans to work. Maybe they just didn't want everyone on staff to look like a frickin' slob." With a start, you realize that the last three sentences you uttered all started with the word "They," and you begin to worry that you sound like a conspiracy theorist yourself!

Solution #140: Take the Nut out of His Environment

Today's hi-tech workplace is a breeding ground for paranoia, especially if someone is already inclined. Speak on the phone, and the call could be monitored. Shoot an email, and it's stored as a matter of permanent record. Send a fax, and it can be retrieved and used as evidence forever. If an office has a paging system, it can enhance the vaguely queasy feeling that there is no escape. It's as if we are all living in a suburban, office-park nightmare, recycling one another's paranoid delusions.

If the Paranoid Nut approaches you with a wild conspiracy theory, whisk him out of the office environment as quickly as possible. Dissect the rumor outside the confines of the workplace.

Take him to lunch miles away from the company cafeteria. Or work out with him *anywhere* but in the corporate gym.

He could use the break from whatever "They" put in the company water, while the rest of your employees could use a reprieve from his ludicrous theories.

Towards Peaceful Coworker Coexistence

What if the Nut isn't your direct report but an equal? In that case, you might have the opportunity to really help him out. When he asks if you believe that a particular person on staff "has it in for him," gently laugh and tell him that he's "just being paranoid." Inexplicably, sometimes simply telling a sufferer that he's *acting* paranoid does wonders to lessen his paranoia, at least in the short term.

The Golden Rule

Working with a paranoid person will test your patience as requests for constant praise, interspersed with conspiracy updates, make him sky-high-maintenance. There is little you can do to cure the underlying condition, but you can ease the symptoms by sending the Nut away from his daily tormentors for long periods of time. Classes, seminars, and conventions are ways to have him interact less with people on staff without you having to face any possible repercussions from firing him. Place strict limits on the amount of time that you spend with him so you can stay focused on profits and productivity rather than on his personality.

CHAPTER 29
The Weak Link

He just wasn't the Derek Jeter of our team.

His fuzziness about finances borders on incompetence. He requires constant memory jogs about things others in the department only have to be told once. So why, you can't help wondering, are you the only one on staff who seems concerned? In short, why, after missing meetings, missing deadlines, missing benchmarks, and performing consistently far below average, is the Weak Link still around?

Might he have a secret strength after all? Might he be blessed with the other kind of intelligence that tops brains and even a superior track record: emotional I.Q.? Studies show that genuine likability wins out over pure skill every time. People would rather be around those with whom they enjoy spending time—even if they have to work overtime to undo their buddy's mistakes.

If a department is only as strong as the weakest link, is there any way to strengthen your Weak Link?

Problem #141: He's Disorganized

Vendor invoices slide down the rabbit hole of his memory only to mysteriously resurface in his inbox, weeks later. The top of his desk resembles a snapshot of the confusion that presumably is going on inside his head. Piles of crumpled-up bags from *McDonald's* and other detritus lie atop of papers galore. You wonder what else might be ferreting its way through the paper plates with half-eaten potato chip remnants.

Solution #141: Expose Him to Some Time-Honored Secrets of Time Management

Organization requires a system, and until that system is in place, chaos rules. Fortunately, with some discipline, it's easy for even the chronically disorganized to improve. The cornerstone of most time-management systems involves two remarkably low-tech items: a weekly calendar and a daily to-do list. (Conversely, most time-management systems break down if there is more than one calendar and multiple to-do lists. This is one case where less really is more.) The secret, for rank beginners, is to commit every single activity—both work-related as well as personal chores—to one's calendar *and* to one's to-do list.

HOW TO ORGANIZE TIME

Organization takes some discipline. But with conscientious practice, it's eminently achievable. Whether you are looking for some pointers to share with your Weak Link or feel like time is never on your side, here are ten tips to help organize the day a little smarter.

1. **YOU ARE MASTER OF YOUR DESTINY, EVEN IF YOU AREN'T.** On some primal level, you must believe that you are the CEO of your own schedule, even if you report to six people who control it in reality.
2. **FIGURE OUT *YOUR MOST EFFICIENT TIME SLOT.*** Are you most creative in the morning? Do you have bursts of adrenaline three seconds before lunch? Are you most focused in the evening when you need to laser through the piles of work on your desk? Assign yourself the most challenging tasks during your *most efficient time slot (m.e.t.s.)* and save yourself hours of unproductive head banging.
3. **FIND YOUR *LEAST EFFICIENT TIME SLOT (L.E.T.S.).*** Are you a zombie who mentally sleepwalks before 10 a.m? Schedule *that* time to shuffle over to your computer and return emails. The early morning may be your best time to accomplish low-priority tasks that won't burn up a lot of brainpower. (With the following caveat: prioritize your emails. If you are barely alive first thing in the morning, that's probably *not* the ideal moment to return an email where your company's president is cc'd.)
4. **DELEGATE WITHOUT GUILT.** If you know that you can't do something right, try not to do it at all.
5. **NEVER WRITE DOWN ANYTHING YOU HAVE NO INTENTION OF DOING.** Think you're immune? Go check your calendar right now and observe how many cross-outs you have marring its pristine pages. Writing down events that you have no interest in attending pilfers the time it takes you to write down the

entry in the first place, the time it takes to cross it out, plus all of the time it takes to ponder how much you really don't want to go. That's time poorly spent.

6. **DON'T OVERCOMMIT YOUR TIME (UNLESS YOU ARE A HOTSHOT CELEBRITY).** If you're a politico, movie star, tycoon, mogul, Hollywood agent, or kingpin of your field, you have permission to tell someone you'll be in three different places for lunch. However, if you are a mere businessperson, this behavior is taboo. Triple-booking your lunch hour is an abuse of goodwill that wastes at least three people's time.
7. **BE RESPECTFUL OF OTHER PEOPLE'S TIME.** No one really wants to hear your hole-in-one golf story again. They may act as if they do; they may laugh in all the right places; but they are only being polite.
8. **THE TOP OF YOUR DESK IS PRIME REAL ESTATE.** Don't sully it. Keep your desk space clean and clutter-free.
9. **REQUEST THE FREEDOM OF A TIGHT DEADLINE.** But build in "gestation time," plus even more time for revisions. Most ideas benefit when they are formulated quickly (to meet a deadline), but then have a chance to simmer for several days, subtly improving with additional input and minor tweaking. Think of how a delicious stew tastes even better on day two or three than on the day when it was cooked.
10. **DON'T LET YOUR TO-DO LIST DO YOU IN.** A lot of people start with a to-do list. But a daily list of chores only works beautifully if you *also* have an internal clock that can track how long each task will take to accomplish. What if you weren't born with this type of clock genetically encoded into your left wrist? Cheat and use a *real* clock. Time yourself doing certain tasks, and then, when those tasks crop up again on your to-do list, write down the estimated amount of time each will take. (Example: Make 35 telephone sales calls, two hours.)

Problem #142: He's a Genius at Spending Other People's Money

Financial irresponsibility is his forte. His inability to grasp Excel spreadsheets is only exceeded by his ignorance of budgets and line items. His fear of all things financial, coupled with his extravagant taste, means that it's only a matter of time before every project will exceed its projected budget. It's all *Monopoly* money, he believes, so he doesn't really pay it much attention.

Solution #142: Take Away His Financial Authority

Some people are financial neophytes. And frankly, they can be dangerous to keep on staff if they continue to have line-item financial responsibility. The bottom line? Delegate the job to someone with a genuine interest in the bottom line, and force the Weak Link to get approval for each and every overage. Do not delay. The last thing you need on staff is a spendthrift.

Play to people's strengths and away from their weaknesses. It's rare for employees to be equally gifted in all areas. But by considering the greater team as you hire individuals, you can build a team that is adept, agile, and multifaceted.

Problem #143: Performance Anxiety

"I'm so sorry," he says, a fetching smile fanning across his boyish features. "I thought it was due next week." Once again, he charms his way out of a pressing deadline (which, you admit, takes considerable skill). However, the person who gives him a reprieve today is less likely to feel beguiled by the Weak Link the next time he fails to meet the deadline. Whether it's because he lacks the relevant experience or because he views every project through a problem-solution lens that doesn't readily apply, it takes the Weak Link twice as long to complete his tasks as everyone else. He just can't seem to perform when there's a deadline attached to a project. Pity that's every project.

Solution #143: See What Will Bring His Performance Up

They're called "deadlines" because they make some people drop dead from the anxiety. If you have some control over these dastardly due dates, take out your metaphorical carving knife and start slicing. Will carving the *big* deadline into smaller deadlines (where less work is due at each juncture) add to the Weak Link's anxiety level or help reduce it to a more angst-appropriate level?

Does he need to be trained (or retrained) in his tasks? Certain senior-level people might resist training, stubbornly considering themselves to be "above" it. Don't be cowed by an uppity Weak Link! If he needs training, it's your job to politely insist on it.

Alternatively, you may need to find some people in the company who can take over some of the Weak Link's tasks. With fewer tasks on his plate, his performance might improve considerably. Since firing him is probably out of the question, do everything in your power to fire up his performance instead.

Self-Evaluations: How Good Are We at Reflecting on Our Strengths and Weaknesses?

There's only one tiny flaw with the "law of averages," but it's glaring. The average employee does not think of himself as "average." Blame it on hubris. Most employees believe they are doing a bang-up job, even when confronted with tons of evidence to the contrary.

You can view it as a numbers game. The top players at your company consider themselves the best at what they do, but so do most of the middle performers. Even a Weak Link may think of himself as a darned good employee!

That's why self-evaluation is actually an extremely effective management tool, although it's often controversial. The trick is to team it up with other diagnostic tools. When used in conjunction with both top-down performance reviews and peer reviews, the process allows employees to step outside the veil of narcissism so they can glimpse themselves as others do. While the reality check might be disconcerting, it can also be liberating.

Your company's legal department should heartily approve of self-evaluations. It's less likely that an employee will deem a particular performance review unfair if he receives roughly the same set of marks from both peers and his supervisor.

Management Mantra

"Knowing others is intelligence; knowing yourself is true wisdom."

—*Tao Te Ching*

Problem #144: She's Technophobic

Technically, she's the head of the management information systems department. What a travesty, then, that she happens to be absolutely terrified of the computer! The people reporting to her secretly look down on her because they regard her as a Luddite who refuses to put in the necessary time to learn the minimum required for doing her job effectively. Things work, more or less, when the Techies are around to solve the glitches. But when it's after hours and the computers are having a meltdown, so is she.

Solution #144: Boot Camp

We live in a 24/7 world where changes happen at the speed of business. It is unrealistic for someone who is managing a department that requires technical skills to *not* have a working knowledge of those skills. She needs to master the systems well enough to be able to aptly describe problems and begin to suggest diagnostic solutions. Her skill level needs to be the Techie equivalent of "broken English." That is, she doesn't have to be fluent in computerese, but someone who *is* should be able to understand her perfectly. Send her to classes that will bring her up to speed.

Problem #145: Her Life-Work Balance Sheet Is Unbalanced

On the great balance scale of work and life, the pendulum has shifted all the way to the "life" side. She used to arrive at the office on time, but recently, her life has taken on a new, dramatic twist. Her longtime nanny took a sabbatical, or the Weak Link got a puppy, or her dog had puppies that require multiple rounds of shots. Maybe the Weak Link's kids are facing disciplinary action at school for their weak grades. (Weak-Linkism *is* a genetic trait.) Or perhaps your employee suddenly has an unprecedented slew of doctors' appointments. You're delighted that she "has a life." You just wish she could squeeze some more time for work into it.

Solution #145: Don't Fight It; Flow with It

Life-balance issues can be tricky to sort through. The autocratic approach, whereby you more or less order someone to get to the office on time, is unlikely to work these days, as retaining talent has become more of a corporate priority at many companies. But if you're creative, you may be able to find a new solution that will work.

First, determine whether her life-work pendulum shift is temporary or permanent. If it's temporary (*i.e.*, her nanny quit, but the employee is frantically searching for a nanny replacement), it might be safer just to let the issue slide. You don't want to make an otherwise-valuable employee feel badly for something that she can't control.

However, if the life-work pendulum shift is permanent (she's living with a new beau who has three kids under the age of five, and they all need to be dropped off at different schools first thing every morning), you will need to broach the topic. If getting to the office on time will now be impossible for this employee, maybe there is a way that she can make it up on the other end, by staying later at night. Does your company have any daycare solutions? Try to view the problem from a fresh perspective. What if your life was suddenly as jam-packed as the IRT subway at 8 a.m.? How would you handle the situation?

Towards Peaceful Coworker Coexistence

If you happen to be peers with the Weak Link, how should you deal with her infirmity? First, recognize that everyone on staff is acutely aware that the Weak Link is just that, so don't feel obliged to cite the obvious. Help her out with her workload, knowing that doing so will only confirm people's low opinion of her.

The Golden Rule

Some staffers possess the magical gift of emotional intelligence rather than the rational, logical type of intelligence that scores well on standardized tests. Those so blessed have a strength that cannot be denied. Most people would rather work with likable people than competent, disagreeable people. If you're working with someone who is extremely likable but incredibly incompetent, it is not a good idea to cut that person from staff. She may have developed a strong system of alliances. Her allies would miss her if she left and hold the decision against you. Instead, craft new, creative solutions to the work issues that are holding her back.

CHAPTER 30
Ruby Rudest

She had a really loud voice with the most God-awful accent. From the day she arrived, we had bets on how long she'd last.

In your company's white-glove culture, she sticks out like a coarse woolen mitten. It's not that she's counterculture. She's simply uncouth. Indeed, you wonder if she's ever been exposed to *any* culture, so loud, boorish, and impolitic is she.

She bandies about strongly held opinions and insults people left and right, seemingly accidentally. Her humor has already drawn some caustic commentary from several of the organization's top brass.

In your opinion, she's a "Ruby in the rough," with emphasis on the word "rough." Will you be able to polish her enough to blend in with the rest of your genteel team? Or will she need to leave the company before she mars its spotless reputation?

In short, when the person working for you is a barbarian, what is the most diplomatic way to civilize her?

Problem #146: Frankly, My Dear, She's Too Damned Blunt

When Ruby first arrived on staff, her candid observations were like a breath of fresh air. She created scathingly funny nicknames for some of the very employees whom you most disliked. ("Mr. Mumble" and "Bald-Faced" were two of Ruby's most spirited creations.) She also had many a pointed observation about the Watercooler Wag and the Weak Link, along with the spineless wuss (Steve) to whom you now report. Ruby was also first to note that, in failing to pay back employees for their travel expenses in a timely manner, perhaps the company was trying to earn interest on the float. Pity she was overheard making some of her funniest remarks, and not everyone on staff was amused.

Solution #146: Tactfully Tell Her She's Tactless

A sense of humor can be a bit tricky asset. Something said in jest could be taken seriously, causing feelings to ruffle. Rather than leaping in to defend an underling's sense of humor, consider asking the employee in question to tone down her bluntness. These days, the *Politically Incorrect Detector Test (P.I.D.T.)* starts ringing at the slightest provocation, and employees would be well advised to dial down the humor if there is any chance that their jokes could be misinterpreted. Harassment cases abound and certain off-color remarks could even be deemed a form of bullying. If your employee has accidentally injured someone's feelings, a sincere, heartfelt apology is her best recourse.

Just the Stats

Incivility has similar costs associated with it as sexual harassment; *i.e.,* loss of productivity (while the target gossips about the slight to others on staff) and high turnover. Employees often take great pains to shun churlish coworkers. At the present time, laws banning rudeness do not exist. In the absence of a legal alternative, the means of "getting even" with the person who inflicted the harm vary widely and are difficult to quantify. Postal workers aren't the only employees who have been known to go postal.

Problem #147: She Thrusts You in Cell Hell

The snap, whistle, and buzz of her cell phone puts you on edge for the third time this week as she debriefs you with a long-winded update. You can barely hear her over the electric static, and random car-honking sounds in the background don't enhance the experience. "Are you near a landline?" you scream. "What?" she says. Crackling noises sputter and pop. Her voice fades in and out. "I can't hear you," you yell. You take a deep breath, temporarily soothing frazzled nerves, then ask, "Can I call you back on a landline?" "Did you say goldmine?" she shouts. It's like the childhood game of *Telephone*, except so much worse.

Solution #147: Teach Her to Give Good Phone

Good phone conversations are transactional. In *BusinessSpeak,* that codified shorthand that passes as English in the hallowed halls of many companies, a transactional exchange is sometimes referred to as "moving the ball from A to B." Your underling should use phone conversations to impart vital information that can't be conveyed via email. There is a reason a landline is perched on her desk. Tell her to pick up *that* phone and call you, thus dispensing with obtrusive cell phone background noise.

Teach underlings to top-line their updates over the phone and color in pertinent details in conference reports. The top line:

- **Did the meeting go well or poorly?**
- **What are the next steps?**
- **By when?**

Problem #148: Her Manners Are Beyond Atrocious

Poor old Ruby Rudest was never schooled in common courtesy. This makes her uncommonly discourteous even to *V.I.F.W.I.T.s (Very Important Folks With Impressive Titles)*. She doesn't think to hold the elevator door for those just a few steps behind her. Instead, she blithely allows the door to slam in their faces! Ruby can also be raucous. Indeed, you've heard her yelling through the mousy cubicle walls at her coworkers. She may only be shouting innocuous phrases like, "Hey, Paula, your boy toy's on the phone!" but she does so at ear-splitting levels. Based on these observations, you are not inclined to send her to an important client dinner anytime soon.

Solution #148: Be Emily Post for a Day

Counsel her to turn down the volume. Remind her that she's not at camp; other employees are trying to get their own work done in an atmosphere of peace. There are all sorts of business etiquette classes where, in a matter of hours, she can pick up the basics.

Alternatively, you could teach her some of them. While many mistakenly believe that proper etiquette is all about the right fork and glass, it's actually a system built on courtesy and respect. Courtesy means taking care not to interrupt people and keeping one's voice at a low, pleasant decibel level. Courtesy emphasizes listening over having one's points heard. It also involves treating everyone with noblesse oblige, from the big boss to the bumbling product manager to the lowly mailroom guy.

Management Mantra

"We are born charming, fresh, and spontaneous and must be civilized before we are fit to participate in society."

—Judith Martin (Miss Manners)

BUSINESS ETIQUETTE FOR NEOPHYTES

Emily Post once said, "Manners are a sensitive awareness of the feelings of others. If you have that awareness, you have good manners, no matter what fork you use."

And how does one retain that sensitivity? The author of this book notes that, like a fine diamond, there are four C's to proper etiquette, the very cornerstones on which the whole system is based. The four C's are: courtesy, consideration, cordiality, and camaraderie. For anyone whose business etiquette could use some buffing, here's a quick refresher course.

1. **COURTESY.** Avoid interrupting someone, especially if he's on an important phone call. If the call *must* be cut short due to an emergency, first silently signal the speaker with your index finger to get his attention. Next quietly mouth an apology. ("Excuse me, but...") Then quickly state the reason for the intrusion. ("The S.V.P. of North American relations needs to see you immediately.")
2. **CONSIDERATION.** Avoid using speakerphone. Nothing could be more inconsiderate. Due to our collective reliance on computers, everyone is tethered to their desks. While you're screaming into your squawk box, the seven people who sit nearest you are silently fuming about being forced to eavesdrop on your conference call. If you must have a conference call via speakerphone, first close your door, and

then set the call volume to the lowest level. It's also polite to warn those who sit nearby by posting a small sign on your door, "Conference call from 11 to 11:30. Please pardon the noise." Never use speakerphone to play back your voicemail messages unless it's after hours and you're the only person working late that night.

3. **CORDIALITY.** Say "Good morning" as cheerily as you can muster to everyone whom you pass in the hallway, even if you're having a fat day plump in the middle of a bad hair week during a root canal year. Strive to be sunny, even if it is ten degrees outside and snowing.
4. **CAMARADERIE.** Fill in for those on vacation and those who feel beleaguered. Don't keep a meticulous accounting of every favor you're owed. In a collegial group, the balance of favors due and bestowed will even out in the end.

Problem #149: She Enters Your Office without Knocking

You're on the phone in a heated conversation, when you look up to catch your underling's freckled face wrinkling down at you uncertainly. Taking a deep breath from your diaphragm and exhaling in a deliberately calm manner, you gently return the phone to its cradle. "What is it, Ruby?" you ask as sweetly as possible. As usual, she wants something incredibly trivial, such as for you to sign her delinquent timesheets.

Solution #149: Show Her the Beauty of a Handwritten Note

Teach your underling to interrupt only in emergency and Code Yellow situations. Irate clients, frantic customers, and livid CEOs qualify as "emergencies." However, even in an emergency, there is proper protocol. (*See* "Business Etiquette for Neophytes" in this chapter.)

Code Yellow situations are non-emergencies that still require immediate action. Handwritten notes work well in these situations. Instead of hovering just outside your door like a 747 awaiting landing clearance, your employee might pass you a legible note advising you of a critical issue. For example, her note might say, "John Stevens from the Paris office will be arriving in three hours. He needs an update from our department of all projects in the works. Do you want me to call an all-hands meeting at 11 a.m.?" Then you might write on the note "Absolutely," while you gracefully exit your call. Notes like this allow you to effectively multitask.

What about non-emergencies? Spell out a policy for how you wish to handle mundane, day-to-day business questions. Set up times for the two of you to confer regularly so your employee won't feel as if her concerns are being ignored.

Problem #150: She Treats Lower-Level Workers Like They're Invisible

Your secretary, not a whiner by nature, was the first to comment on Ruby's habit of treating her as if she didn't exist. She mentioned that Ruby always seemed to walk right past her without acknowledging her. Not feeling slighted by Ruby yourself, you ignored your secretary's observation, hoping against hope that one sticky situation might vanish without your intervention. No such luck. Recently, you overheard the mailroom attendant and the receptionist also carping about Ruby. The mailroom attendant observed that Ruby never made an effort to say "Hello" to him or anyone else. He even suggested that if her behavior continued, she'd never see another piece of interoffice mail!

Solution #150: Make Her See the Error of Her Ways

When workers are inconsiderate to one another, there are several different outcomes—all negative from a managerial perspective. The rudeness could escalate. Your secretary, feeling as if Ruby has ignored her presence once too often, conveniently forgets to include her on a cc list. Hence, Ruby misses an important internal meeting. You walk into Ruby's office asking why she didn't show up. Pointing to her email inbox, Ruby correctly counters that she was never invited. Insisting that your secretary "has it in" for her, Ruby then asks if *you* could alert her about all meetings rather than your secretary. This is highly unproductive behavior.

Now dribbling away even more precious time, both your secretary and Ruby share their versions of the story with others on staff.

You need to sit down with Ruby first and tell her to start treating everyone as if they're important. Instruct her to acknowledge people by name in the hallways and elevator banks. A smile of recognition or a nod of the head is also appreciated.

Circle back to your secretary and tell her that you want to keep tabs on Ruby's improvement. If your secretary doesn't detect a noticeable change in Ruby's demeanor over the next several weeks, you may need to schedule a mediation session with Ruby, your secretary, yourself, and someone from the HR department.

Who's to Blame? Untangling the Rudeness Issue

Has an employee been rude to another? As a manager who didn't overhear the exchange, it may be difficult for you to know for sure. The target may feel that a rude comment was deliberately offensive, whereas the instigator may claim the target is too sensitive or humorless. In fact, both sides of the story could be true. Look for patterns—either multiple people complaining about one employee's rudeness, or a couple of employees griping about behavior you consider offensive.

Towards Peaceful Coworker Coexistence

What if a peer slights you? Your best response is to pretend not to notice. As the stress and grind of the day churn on, the politics of politeness are often the first to disappear. You may have to remind yourself that if someone is loutish, it's his problem, not yours. As H. Jackson Brown Jr. once said, "Good manners sometimes mean simply putting up with other people's bad manners."

The Golden Rule

What isn't bred in the bone can be taught. It is possible to instruct people on staff how to be civil to one another. If someone treats one of your staffers offensively, it's best to resolve the situation before the behavior escalates. However, if someone is uncivil towards you, the best reaction is to have *no* reaction. Act as if the slight never happened. Remember the great Etiquette Paradox: it is very bad manners to tell someone she has bad manners.

CHAPTER 31
Desperately Seeking Approval

Our director is very competent and good at what she does. But people don't want to deal with her. She never says, "We had a problem and fixed it." She says "I." The group had some problem, and she's always the one who rescued it.

Her only wish is for you to approve of her. Is that too much to ask? Just look at her track record. She volunteers when no one else will. Your clients consider her nothing short of a miracle worker. And her work product just happens to be stellar—especially in comparison to everyone else's in the department. She doesn't make mistakes. She's perfect.

So why don't you thank her more often? Why can't you praise her every single day for her insightful contributions? Why aren't you telling everyone else in the department about her manifold achievements? Because she's already doing such a good job of saying she's doing a good job. That's why!

When the only thing you disapprove of is someone's bottomless need for approval, what is the right course of action?

Problem #151: Mommy, May I?

If she were a piece of punctuation, it would be an ellipsis. Would you mind terribly… if she took the entire team out for a picnic one afternoon to detangle some of the morale issues that have been plaguing the department? Might she… email you her opening remarks for the new business pitch for your approval? Are you in agreement… with her writing the all-points bulletin for the sales force? Fine, fine, fine! (Her tentativeness drives you to bark all of your answers in exclamation points.) Why does the woman always feel compelled to ask for permission?

Solution #151: Permission Granted

Show patience to a colleague who solicits your opinion. She may be trying to draw in where the lines of your responsibility end and hers begin. Are the lines fuzzy? If so, help define them for her. Commit her job description to paper if necessary. Are her constant requests for permission unraveling your concentration? Ask her to commit her questions to email or leave you a voicemail message at the end of the day.

If your employee's suggestions are generally sound, you might introduce her to the *Negative Option Clause*. This clever technique can shave the number of internal emails in half. Basically, you give her your blanket permission to follow through on her ideas—unless you direct otherwise. She leaves messages asking you to write or call her back *only if you object* to an idea. If she doesn't hear from you, she continues to leave you updates, filling you in on the vital details, which she will go ahead and execute—unless you weigh in and put a stop to it. Here's an example of a *Negative Option* voicemail message she might leave: "I'm thinking of taking the team off-campus on Thursday afternoon for a three-hour picnic, weather permitting. The purpose of the outing is to discuss some of the morale issues surrounding the departure of the two Kens. I'll need to order food and beverages for this by Wednesday morning. If you hate the idea, or can't spare people for three hours, please leave me a message tomorrow. On the other hand, if you like it, there's absolutely no need to get back to me. And by the way, I really hope you'll be able to join us."

Problem #152: The Email Queen

A day without email from her is like a national holiday. That's probably because it *is* a national holiday. To date, you haven't received an email from her on Groundhog Day, Labor Day, or Thanksgiving (for which you were truly thankful). But during most weeks, she emails you nonstop. There are some days when she emails you five, six, seven, or even fifteen times. *Please, stop the madness.*

Solution #152: Declare an Email Moratorium

First, take several steps back from your computer. Put down the cell phone that you were planning to smash into the screen. Next, decide what the real problem is (aside from the fact that you don't want to read so many damned emails from the same person every day). Is it the length of the emails, their sheer number, or the fact that at least 25% of them are completely unnecessary?

If length is the primary problem, strongly recommend that she edit all emails to under a page and use bullets to highlight her key points. What if the big issue is the vast number of emails she sends per day? Ask yourself if you'd prefer to receive one super long email at the end of each workday, summarizing her progress. (You'll need to read it with more concentration than you would multiple, shorter emails. It all comes down to your preferred working style.)

If, on reflection, you believe that most of her emails are completely unnecessary, then caution her that you only have the patience to read three of her emails a day.

Towards Peaceful Coworker Coexistence

Approval seekers tend to blast more emails per person as a way of claiming credit for some of their ideas. If one of your coworkers is using email to claim credit for one of *your* ideas, it is appropriate to gently set the record straight in email. The seamless way to accomplish this: first, find your department supervisor and give her the heads-up that the idea was, in fact, yours. Next, send an email to the group, politely expressing that you're delighted that Brent was able "to take your idea and run with it." This gambit is best used sparingly, and only if you are direct peers with the person who is trying to appropriate your credit. Don't try to claim credit for your ideas if you report to a credit snatcher. (*See* Chapter 8, *The Credit Snatcher.*)

Problem #153: Ms. Wonderful

Between singing her own praises and tooting her own horn, she is a one-woman Barbara-shop quartet. If a client meeting went awry, she was the one who single-handedly salvaged it. Did an important customer storm out of a meeting? Guess who brought him back to the table? Thank goodness you have her around to always save the day.

Solution #153: Teach Her a New Word: "We"

As Anonymous once said, "There is no 'i' in the word 'team.'" (Notice how he was never credited with his fantastic remark.) The problem with constant self-promoting is that it has an annoying, repetitive quality, much like the bleating of sheep. "Notice me, notice me," the approvee urges, and the bleat goes on, grating at fellow coworkers. Their complaints against the approval seeker will mount, and eventually, they will find a way to undermine her.

Even in highly structured, authoritarian environments where it isn't always easy to discuss life's little annoyances with one's supervisors, the team will ultimately band against the blatant approval seeker. The night will come when she really needs someone to help her out in a pinch, and no one will volunteer.

If you believe that Ms. Wonderful is an asset to the department, help her to stay around a bit longer by encouraging her to add the word "we" to her vocabulary. Sometimes this may require her to save the whole story and just report the punch line.

Management Mantra

"Talent wins games, but teamwork and intelligence wins championships."

—Michael Jordan

TOP THREE THINGS ANYONE EVER SAID ABOUT TEAMWORK

1. "We must all hang together, or assuredly, we shall all hang separately."

   —Benjamin Franklin

2. "No man is wise enough by himself."

   —Plautus, Roman playwright

3. **T**ogether
   Everyone
   Achieves
   More

   —Anonymous

Problem #154: And They Called It Puppy Love

Love is an addiction. Desperately Seeking needs your approval so badly that she'll even stalk you to get it. When you're trying to leave the office at night, there she is, blocking your doorway. She's just popping in to ask you a quick question. It won't take but a minute. Are you heading towards the fax machine? What a coincidence! She just happens to be on her way over there too. En route, she'll show you the chart she created with a perky new color palette. You like it, don't you? Yes, there is a term for this level of approval slobbering. It's called "approval harassment."

Solution #154: Make Her Stop Chasing You

Do you sometimes feel like Harriet the Spy, peeking your head just outside your door to make certain the coast is clear? Do you find yourself asking the Boss's Pet if she knows the whereabouts of the overeager approval seeker—the better to avoid her? Politely explain to the zealous bloodhound in your pursuit that you are *not* prey that needs to be hunted. Does she legitimately need to converse with you on a host of different projects? Set up a half hour once a week to discuss them in person. The rest of the time, ask her to please contact you via email.

Problem #155: She Derides the Team in Meetings

In the relentless crusade for your approval, she disrespects others in the department. She uses status meetings to rail against the work of another person. For example, she may criticize the Weak Link's financial infirmity, to the loud chortling of the group. (While you are sorely tempted to chime in, that would be a major no-no.) If another team member's work is above reproach, the approval seeker might pick on her publicly about some other flaw, hoping to push her out of your grace. As a perfect example, the approval seeker recently gave the Employee Nobody Likes but You a scented soap-on-a-rope in a group meeting, to everyone's stunned silence.

Solution #155: Subject Her to a Private Flogging

Don't allow one person's need for approval to sabotage the greater team's efforts. Tell your little approval seeker to stop comparing and contrasting herself to everyone else on the team. (That's your job. And you do it well.) Explain that the ability to "play nice" and get along with her fellow coworkers is an integral part of the formal performance review process, and that, according to this criteria, you *do not approve* of the job she's been doing. You may want to institute a peer review system to drive home the message.

Genuine team players derive some satisfaction from contributing to a functional team, rather than contributing the "diss" to "dysfunctional."

The Golden Rule

Approval seekers need continual stroking from their department heads. If the unstoppable quest for your blessing is simply a minor intrusion on your own time, work out a more pragmatic method for your underling to obtain it by introducing her to the *Negative Option Clause*. However, if the person desperately seeking your approval is disrespecting others in the department in order to make herself look better by comparison, figure out a method whereby you can reward people for being good team players and penalize those who are not.

CHAPTER 32
The Bald-Faced Liar

I once worked with a man who told me he lied 50% of the time. With him admitting that he lied that often, it was impossible to tell if he ever told the truth.

Nothing about him would surprise you—whether it was a series of fictitious jobs he held in the past, a big whopper on his resumé under the "Education" section, or the revelation that he's cheating on Uncle Sam, his wife, and the Sunday *New York Times* crossword puzzle!

He's an equal opportunity liar. He tells little white lies, medium-sized gray lies, and big black lies, although catching him an outright falsehood is difficult.

Try to tease out what really happened in a meeting, and he gives you such an incongruous spin that you can't figure out if he is simply a terrible judge or if he's deliberately misleading you. Ask him for a project's results and he cannot tell a lie. But he will anyway.

When his preposterous prevarications make your b.s. detector sound off like a car alarm, is there any way to wean him from his mendacious behavior?

Problem #156: He Lies by Omission

When it comes to Bald-Faced's upstanding character, you're a star witness—for the other side. You were in the conference room three weeks ago when the V.P. canceled the project. So how could Bald-Faced brazenly claim in an internal meeting merely three minutes ago that "no decision had been made" on the project's status? Just as a tiny squeak of disapproval began to emerge from your lips, Bald-Faced stared you down with the evil eye (two, actually) and silenced you into omission. He's not only a big, fat liar; he's turning you into one as well!

Solution #156: Let the Lie Stand

Take a deep breath and give Bald-Faced the benefit of the doubt. He may be waiting for an opportune moment to break the news to the team, and for whatever reason, feels this isn't the right time. If your team happens to be working on a new project, Bald-Faced might be pausing to assess its outcome before circling back to the V.P. to beg her to change her mind about the canceled project. In any event, the team gains little from learning the V.P. doesn't support their work. This is one case where honesty is *not* the best policy.

The person who controls the information wields all of the power. If you wish to improve your own finesse, watch those who are politically gifted and emulate them. What moment do they choose to reveal news, bad or good? And which vehicle do they use to broadcast it? Do they announce the news to the greater team in large meetings, or is everything worked out in secret cabals behind closed doors? If you seek to attain great power, be the first person to unearth information and think carefully about who should learn it and when.

Why We Lie

Everyone lies a little bit, and that's no lie.

It may be a little white lie told to spare someone's feelings, but everyone does it. We are all guilty. We start lying at a young age (around four or five) to finagle something we want or to get out of trouble.

We lie both to please people and to appease them. We lie to strengthen relationships and to maintain them. We lie to make ourselves feel better about lying to someone else.

However, oftentimes the best lies (meaning the ones that are most believable to other people) are the lies we tell ourselves.

If we can hide the truth from ourselves, it's so much easier to cloak it from others. Why do we lie? Generally speaking, because we can get away with it.

Problem #157: He Lies to Explain Away a Failed Project

He was the first person at the company to bang the green drum, and everyone, from the CEO down, got into the rhythm. Claiming that "going green" would help the company increase profits and save the planet, he stewarded a project to help cut energy consumption in some of the company's retail outlets. Unfortunately now, after further review, it turns out that this corporate initiative is extremely costly upfront and has a poor return on investment on the backend.

Is this lofty initiative—the greening of the retail outlets—destined to be quashed by a bunch of nib grinders wielding red pens? Sensing a dip in the level of enthusiasm for his pet project, Bald-Faced now claims that he "never had any intention of going green overnight" and motions for a further study to analyze the return on investment issue.

Solution #157: Allow Him to Save Face

If you call people out on the industrial carpet every time they fail, they will stop trying. Sometimes, it's important to play along and pretend that you heard something exactly as someone claims to have said it—even when you know it to be false.

It doesn't so much matter whether an employee *thinks* that something is a good idea. The key question is: is it? Your employee originally thought that going green sounded worthwhile. After further investigation, it turns out to be too pricey to accomplish in the short term. But in the long term, his idea could be brilliant.

Perhaps there's a way to begin the process without committing to it 100%—a way to "phase in" greenness. If so, you will need this employee to tackle the mission with enthusiasm. Take care not to dampen his morale.

Problem #158: He Fibs to a Client

"Everything is under control," Bald-Faced reported to your company's most important client when she called to ask him about a project's status. His lie made you cringe, as you knew for a fact that people were flying through the hallways, panic-stricken over her project.

Directly afterward, the client, enamored with Bald-Faced's confidence, called you to relay what a "phenomenal job" Bald-Faced had been doing on her business. It was all you could do to muffle that nervous cough that sprouts up whenever you feel an anxiety attack coming on.

Now you wonder how long it will take your blindsided client to discover that the project is spiraling *out of control*. When she does, you suppose that you'll just have to let Bald-Faced handle it.

Solution #158: Remind Your Employee about the Very Real Deadline

"Everything is under control" is one of those little white lies we all tell to instill confidence in the person on the receiving end. Chances are, this tiny fib will give Bald-Faced just enough breathing room from the client to actually wrest her project back under control.

However, if there is any chance the deadline will be blown, best to determine so immediately. For if you miss the deadline, then your client will learn that Bald-Faced was lying through his teeth, which could destroy her faith in your company forever. Ask Bald-Faced for a candid assessment of the project's completion date. (He's more likely to tell you the truth if you volunteer to relay the bad news to the client for him.)

When delivering news that clients don't want to hear, it's imperative to remain unflappable. You might say something like, "The project *is* very much under control, but unfortunately, it's two weeks behind schedule. Bald-Faced is going to work his magic to tighten up the schedule on the backend." It's always better to under-promise and beat your benchmarks, rather than over-promise and miss them by a mile.

Just the Stats

A study published in the *Journal of Basic and Applied Psychology* found that 60% of the participants had lied at least once during a ten-minute conversation with a stranger. On average, they told three lies during the brief interchange.[16]

Problem #159: He Covers for a Coworker

The man lies like an ill-fitting toupee. On Thursday afternoon, you overheard one of your employees telling Bald-Faced that he was planning "to play hooky" the following day. But in the Friday 9 a.m. staff meeting, Bald-Faced announced that the absent worker had caught "a raging flu." To sympathetic murmurs from the rest of the team, Bald-Faced then embellished the tale even further, claiming the coworker's illness was so bad that he had been forced to get a flu shot. Now your "deathly ill" teammate is supposedly at home recuperating and cannot be disturbed.

Solution #159: Playfully Tease Out the Facts

Once your employee returns to the office, take him aside and ask him about his personal day a couple of times. You might start with a benign, "How was your day off on Friday?" When he adamantly denies that it was "a day off," ask him, "So what *did* you do on Friday?" When he claims that he was "sick all day," perhaps query whether he *enjoyed* his time off from work. Sometimes, repeating a question a few times in different ways can gently nudge someone to disclose that he's being less than honest. Think about the techniques that litigators typically use in trials, but don't be too aggressive. The tone to hit should be one of gentle playfulness. Otherwise you'll never get your employee to confess. Once both of your employees realize that you're "on to" the lie, it may decrease their propensity to collude again.

In Case Anyone Ever Asks You…

Q: Are human beings the only creatures who deceive one another?

A: No. Chacma baboons have also been observed practicing deceptive practices. According to the Machiavellian Intelligence Hypothesis, social complexity forced our primate ancestors to become more sophisticated, mastering new forms of trickery and deception. Some primates have been spotted tricking other members of their species out of food. These primates have also been shown to form alliances in group settings. (And you thought your office was a jungle.)

TOP 10 REASONS WHY PEOPLE LIE AT THE OFFICE

A study of lying at the workplace concluded these were the top ten motivations for telling a lie.

1. As an excuse for absenteeism
2. To cover up a mistake
3. To make (the liar) look better
4. To avoid trouble
5. To protect a coworker
6. To avoid being fired
7. To get a promotion
8. To get a raise
9. To avoid doing work
10. To explain why the person was late to work.[17]

According to the Anonymous Employee website, 85% of hiring managers claim they are less likely to offer a promotion to someone who was caught lying.[18]

Problem #160: He Prevaricates to Get Someone in Trouble

Bald-Faced has an intense rivalry with someone on staff. Perhaps fearing that you prefer to work with his nemesis, Bald-Faced cooks up a nasty rumor about him, one smearing him as incompetent. Since you have been away from the office for three weeks in a row, you have no idea whether or not the insidious rumor is true. According to Bald-Faced, his rival interrupted a client "nonstop" during the last meeting. As a result, the meeting didn't go smoothly, and many of the presented ideas will need to be reworked.

Solution #160: Debrief with Other Witnesses

The most honest-sounding lies are always based on a kernel of reality that gives credence to the rest of the tale. It's not enough for you to find out the outcome of the meeting, because *that* part of the tale is undoubtedly accurate. You will need to research why the meeting turned out so poorly. Are Bald-Faced's assertions about his rival true, or are they simply fabrications of an evil, warped mind?

Sometimes you can catch someone in a lie by asking a series of probing questions. The trick is to do it in a way that doesn't make the person feel like he's on trial. You might simply start by chatting with Bald-Faced. Explain that you are conducting some "due diligence" on the meeting you missed. Ask him to recount as much as he can about it. Probe to uncover precisely what his rival said in the meeting as well as your client's reaction. Then circle around to each staffer who was in the meeting and tease out their impressions of it. In your pilgrimage for the truth, take care not to prejudice other staffers' opinions by sharing Bald-Faced's assertions with them.

When conducting this type of an investigation, the last person you should approach is Bald-Faced's antagonist (because if the rumor turns out to be false, you may never have to discuss it with him at all.) Depending on the nature of Bald-Faced's allegations, you may also want to steer clear of your client. You never want your client to feel as if you're an absentee boss who's woefully out of touch with what's happening whenever you're away. (*See* Chapter 2, *The Boss Who Doubles as the Wizard of Oz*.)

Towards Peaceful Coworker Coexistence

What if you know for a fact that one of your peers is lying about something critically important? Is there any way to make him cough up the facts? Start by communicating to those around you that you can deal with the truth. This means making it okay for people to tell you things that you don't want to hear.

Management Mantra

"Permission to speak freely." Although not officially recognized by the U.S. Army, this request is generally honored. It's a waive of protocol where anything an individual says immediately after the request will not be held against him. Give your employees the permission to speak freely around you, and fewer of them will feel compelled to lie to your face.

The Golden Rule

Lying is encoded in our DNA, and even our primate ancestors use deceptive practices. Thus, it is naïve to think that you can ever fully banish it. However, there are different levels of lying. Ignore the white lies and concentrate on those designed to destroy people's careers. Sometimes, by remaining calm and asking a series of direct questions, you can get people to admit that they fabricated the truth.

CHAPTER 33
The Waffler

The manager of our sales team told everyone "she'd know it when she saw it." The problem was, she never saw it. Her people would redo PowerPoint sales presentations over and over, basically "guessing" what she wanted.

He's all for something—until he's against it. Then, once he finally makes up his mind, there's at least a 50% chance that he'll change it back again.

His deliberations over things that have already been decided drive you to pull out each individual hair from your head, one by one, twisting them around your Mont Blanc pen just to see how quickly they will snap.

The Waffler is so wishy-washy that sometimes you wonder if he's prematurely washed up. Or is there something steely and premeditated underlying his seeming lack of conviction?

When the person under you wiggles more than *Jell-O*, is there any way to pin him to a decision?

Problem #161: He Can't Make a Decision

"Why is this blue?" he asks, frowning, as if printing the cover of a pitch book in blue is a federal offense. The last six pitch book covers have all been blue. "Why?" you ask in amazement. "You don't think we should change it, do you?" He squints at the booklet as if he's never seen that exact shade of navy before. "Maybe we *should* change it this one time," he says, hand cradling his chin. "Really?" you counter. "What color do you think it *should* be?" He promises he'll get back to you on that. Two days later, he still hasn't decided. His rampant indecision is holding up the production process.

Solution #161: Proceed without His Buy-in

Aesthetic decisions are often subjective. You should always respect someone's right to question a project's taste level or sensibility. Furthermore, certain colors may *not* fit in with your brand identity. But assuming that the original color chosen perfectly meshes with your company's brand, then change just for change's sake can be quite costly. Try to imagine the long-term ramifications, even if the particular project seems as if it's the most important one on your roster right now. If the Waffler is jaded on the color navy, promise him that you'll change the color of the *next* pitch book cover. This one needs to remain in the original color.

Problem #162: He Feels No Time Pressure

Deadlines have little meaning for him (although he has no objection to the sound of them whooshing by). He is in his own special time zone—quite apart from whether your clients happen to be located in Dallas, Detroit, Denmark, or Dubai. Urgent emails and phone calls asking him to weigh in make no impact. Calls to his close colleagues and other due diligence reveal that he is receiving the message; he just doesn't seem to be getting it.

Solution #162: Recognize That Not Deciding Is a Decision

The absence of management is a style of management, one called "cowardice." On some level, the Waffler may feel like it's not his decision to make. He may not feel strongly one way or the other. Or he may sense that he is on the cusp of a political imbroglio and would prefer to wait for someone who is more entrenched to make the big decisions.

Well, guess what? That person is you! Make the decision for him and hand it to him as a fait accompli. However, if he tries to change the outcome *after* you've stepped in to make the decision, inform him that he gave away his power to choose. When he had the chance, he voted to abstain. And now the window of opportunity is as tightly sealed as those in certain New York office skyscrapers.

Procrastinating can sometimes be a form of passive-aggressiveness. If you are overseeing someone who refuses to make a decision within a reasonable time period, you might try easing the situation by making him responsible for his own set of deadlines. Then, when he procrastinates, he will no longer be flouting your authority. He will only be sabotaging himself.

Problem #163: He Commits, Then Changes His Mind

He seems keen on one direction. But once resources are committed to it, he raises all kinds of picayune problems, impeding progress. When fellow staffers counter that his questions have already been asked and answered, he stonewalls, delaying the final decision until the next meeting. He reminds you of T.S. Elliot's J. Alfred Prufrock, with his "time for yet a hundred indecisions... and for a hundred revisions." Is he commitment-phobic or simply anti-change? And is there any way to get him to change?

Solution #163: Allow People the Freedom to Fail

Erich Fromm once said, "There can be no real freedom without the freedom to fail." In many companies today, doing something wrong tends to be punished more harshly than doing nothing at all. This has the disastrous effect of creating a corporate culture where everyone is terrified to speak out. If your culture is failure-fearing, people would rather perpetuate mistakes than admit them and change course.

Set a good example by admitting your own mistakes and self-correcting them. This will help others feel as if they can admit errors without fear of reprisal. Make every effort to create an atmosphere of continuous improvement. Occasionally, seek out people who were uninvolved with earlier decisions so you can hear a fresh take on a particular problem.

If you allow yourself the freedom to fail, others will learn and grow from your example.

HOW TO PUSH A WAFFLER OFF THE FENCE

Decisions can be complicated. Certain shortcuts help us frame our decisions in order to simplify them. If you understand how people arrive at decisions, sometimes you can locate the tipping point—that special place where it's easier for someone to make a decision than to keep putting it off.

- **FIRST IN STAYS IN.** People pay more attention to the first input they receive. Initial impressions, data, and first estimates "anchor" additional input that arrives later. If you wish to persuade a Waffler to take action, *be the first person to present your findings in a meeting.* Start with a riveting fact: "Gen-Y has more in common with the Me-Generation of the 1970s than with Gen-X."
- **CHARISMA COUNTS.** Whoever can paint a more vivid picture of the situation generally prevails. Great communicators frame the perspective from which the problem will be analyzed. Think of yourself as a charismatic litigator and craft a closing argument that will sway people's emotions.
- **THE FAMILIAR IS MORE APPEALING THAN THE UNFAMILIAR.** All things being equal, incumbents tend to win, consumers will stick with their brand of toothpaste, and a woman's hairstyle in middle age will be remarkably similar to the style she wore in high school. People tend to exaggerate the effort or emotional costs of change. Knowing that most people fear change, try positioning a new idea as a "baby step" rather than a complete departure. Make the strange familiar.

Management Mantra

"Don't fall victim to what I call the 'ready-aim-aim-aim-aim syndrome.' You must be willing to fire."

—George S. Patton

WHY GOOD PEOPLE SOMETIMES MAKE BAD DECISIONS

- **NOT ENOUGH INFORMATION TO MAKE A CHOICE.**
- **NOT UNDERSTANDING THE CHOICES FULLY.**
- **TOO MANY CHOICES.**
- **PORK BARRELING.**
- **THROWING GOOD MONEY AFTER BAD.**
- **PEER PRESSURE.**
- **GOING FOR THE SHORT-TERM, MORE POPULAR STAND OVER THE LONG-TERM, SMARTER CHOICE.**
- **SELF-SERVING POINT OF VIEW.**
- **BETTER TO DEAL WITH THE ENEMY KNOWN THAN THE ENEMY UNKNOWN.**

Problem #164: The Past Justifies the Present Trap

Too much time and energy have been expended to change direction midway, even if the original direction no longer makes any sense. Imagine that you work for a company that runs a small golf course. Ten years ago, the club was expanded to include a summer golf camp for kids. During the first few years of operation, the kiddie camp attracted many new families. But now there has been a pendulum-popping, adjust-or-bust demographic shift.

The kiddie camp is underattended, while all the original kids have sprouted into teenagers. Many people at the company wish to start a golf camp targeted to teenagers, but no one can convince the Waffler to buy in to the idea.

He continues to view the situation in terms of the investment in the kiddie camp that has *already* been made. He looks backwards, not forwards, to the detriment of all involved.

Solution #164: Set Aside the Past and Focus on the Future

Consciously set aside the past. Viewing a decision purely in terms of past investments of time, money, resources, and energy already expended is debilitating. Find new people to add perspectives on the issue that weren't considered in the past. Craft a timeline for success. Consider the upside. Only then, ascertain if there are any key components that can possibly be recycled to save money on the front end.

Problem #165: His Ego Is on the Line

Connections were contacted. Meetings were held. Strings were pulled and plucked. He poured time, money, manpower, and every other company resource into an initiative a few years back, and now his name is closely tied to it. In the interim, market research advises against pursuing the project, but he is too personally invested in it to let it go. Stubbornly, he clings to it, refusing to withdraw, even though doing so would help him salvage his reputation. (*See* Chapter 15, *The Sheltered Sultan*.)

Solution #165: It's Just Business

When a staffer becomes too attached to a particular initiative, remind him that the project isn't his "baby." He has nothing at stake in it—save for how much profit, repeat business, or new customers the proposition generates. Make him understand that he and his ideas are not one and the same. If, for whatever reason, an initiative no longer works, he needs to release it.

Towards Peaceful Coworker Coexistence

If a peer at your company has trouble making a particular decision, see if you might help him list the pros and cons of both courses of action. But don't get into the habit of making all of his decisions for him. Decision making is risky, and at a certain level, *you are being paid* to take that risk. When it comes to staffing decisions, hiring freelance help or a consultant for a short time may help to break an impasse about whether to hire someone permanently.

The Golden Rule

Some people experience a certain fear when it comes to making a decision, which is akin to paralysis. You can help lessen the fear by fostering a work atmosphere that allows people to fail with dignity. A fearless workplace helps people make smarter decisions overall, as they can be honest with you (as well as with one another) about necessary improvements.

CHAPTER 34
The Boss's Pet

I hired a new VP in my group, someone who would be my peer. Once hired, his true personality came out. He ingratiated himself with my boss and sabotaged me every chance he got, rescheduling meetings without telling me, making different recommendations to the boss than we'd agreed on. Eventually, he made himself her right-hand man. Everyone else in the company couldn't stand him.

You don't have one in your company, so you can skip this chapter. There's no one you know who is kissing up to you at the moment. (Truth be told, you wish more people would.) The only staffer who might be a bit of a sycophant is someone relatively close to you in age, who agrees with you on almost everything…

Oh gosh. Maybe you *do* have a little lapdog in your company. A pet who slurps up everything you say. But what harm could she possibly cause? She's just someone who loves you no matter what.

It's not like anyone else pays much attention to the salaries you dole out. Or the plum assignments. No one on staff is sitting there, seething with resentment…are they? If there's one person on staff who you favor more than anyone else, is there any reason to tone down your affection?

Problem #166: You Shower Her with Praise

Pets begin to resemble their owners after awhile, and yours is no exception. Your Pet is cooperative, helpful, and astute about office politics. Working closely with one so like-minded just makes the day float by a little faster. It seems only fair that you should make a special point of acknowledging her in meetings and give credit where credit is due.

Solution #166: Spread the Wealth

Employees are supremely sensitive about every acknowledgment, perk, and bonus you bequeath. If you're always rewarding only one person, team morale will tumble. Her fellow coworkers could band against her, making her more ineffective than she would be if your approval of her weren't quite so blatant. Put a leash on it.

Workers deeply resent favoritism. Plus everyone always feels, rightly or wrongly, that they are doing a spectacular job. Establish objective criteria by which to judge performance, such as the number of sales, the return on investment, and the number of new customers. Then be certain to assess each person on staff regularly.

Be magnanimous with praise, bestowing it even to those employees who you don't like. If your Pet is underperforming in certain key areas, don't mince your criticisms just because you enjoy her companionship. Reward people based on merit, not personality, and they'll pay you back by thinking of you as a decent boss.

Problem #167: She's More Fun to Confide In

Your Pet is a witty raconteur; you appreciate her fine recounting of the office bloopers and mishaps when you're not around to observe them for yourself. While she reports directly to you, you tend to view her as an equal. And her razor-sharp espionage skills have been beneficial to you on more than one occasion.

Solution #167: Start the Open-Door Policy

Open doors inspire trust and confidence. Closed doors set off waves of rumors that make employees jittery. Be democratic in the way in which you share information. Either tell people the scoop on a need-to-know basis, or call a meeting and let everyone hear the official office update at the same time. Take great pains not to let only one or two staffers into your confidence, as doing so will make everyone else seethe with resentment.

Be a commando communicator. Tell staffers what you expect of them. They will be far more loyal to you if they feel that your goals are realistic, you care about them as humans (not just as workers), and you take their opinions into account. People want to be rewarded on the basis of merit, not favoritism. (Except those who *are* being rewarded on the basis of favoritism.)

Towards Peaceful Coworker Coexistence

What if you're peers with the Boss's Pet and receive lesser assignments as a result of the high esteem in which your boss holds her? Is there any recourse? It may sound counterintuitive, but you are probably best off not complaining about the Pet directly to the boss, lest it put her on the defensive. If everyone on the team is receiving more grunt work as a result of the Pet being spared, the medley of discontent will eventually reach your boss's ears with or without your participation. And she'll have no choice but to make things more equitable for everyone. (However, if you are receiving less interesting work assignments, it is fair to tackle *that topic* with the boss. Ask for better projects, but only if you can do so without carping about the one person who *is* receiving them.)

Problem #168: She Agrees with Everything You Say

And how on earth can that be a problem, you wonder? Your Pet simply has superb judgment. She sees it your way. And, of course, that's the only way to see it. Or is it? Is she simply mirroring everything that you say in an effort to ally herself with you? Does she truly believe in your great insight and vision? It's impossible to ascertain since your Pet never challenges you on anything.

Solution #168: Seek Out Other Viewpoints

It's fine to rely on one person who shares your identical point of view—as long as you happen to be right. But what if you're wrong? As the saying goes, "Two wrongs don't make a right." But hearing the echo of your own thoughts reverberate against the Pet's lips could make you twice as likely to latch onto an unrealistic viewpoint. After all, someone else agrees with you on it. That's why brainstorming with diverse individuals who don't share your perspective often yields better ideas.

Ideas are not eggs. They won't break if you bounce them around. Share ideas with people who hold different viewpoints, and your ideas will either become stronger with the additional input or fall by the wayside.

Most ideas benefit from a good, tough winnowing process. The best ideas will bubble to the surface.

Problem #169: She's an Excellent Spy

Her little tidbits of information are your lifeline to office rumblings when you can't be around to observe the beehive. She reports accurate information, gossip, and so many facts that you feel as if you're "there." How else would you know that Amy in accounting is on the verge of quitting or that Sherry and Paul in the legal department are now legally separated? You may be out of sight, but with her input, at least you're not out of touch.

Solution #169: Get 360-Degree Feedback from Everyone Who Was There

Entrusting just one person to fill you in on the office palaver is not wise. The Pet might spin the facts or just have a woefully inaccurate viewpoint. If you were unable to attend an important meeting or conference, debrief with every person on staff who was there. While doing so will be time-consuming, you will come away with a much fuller, more nuanced feeling about what actually transpired in the room. This will make your suggestions for follow-up and any next steps much better informed.

HOW TO SPOT A BROWN-NOSER

After reading this chapter, you've made a vow not to be swayed by the treacle of flattery. You will not adopt a Pet, as doing so will simply dampen the morale of everyone else on staff. Your intentions are excellent—if, indeed, you can identify those who are sucking up to you.

The problem is, you may be blind to it. The veil of narcissism, invisible to the naked eye, is the very thing that may prevent you from seeing those who are simply kowtowing to your wishes and agreeing with you simply to come off as agreeable.

Here are some ways to identify a brown-noser when you are the target of her adulation.

- **FLATTERY.** Compliments on your mode of dress, style, charisma, charm, and sense of humor are all suspect. If someone a few rungs down from you comments on how fantastic you look, first say, "Thank you." Then silently ask yourself if the observation is even true. If it isn't, the person is simply trying to butter you up.
- **FAVORS.** Suppose that you hate driving in large metropolitan areas. Your sister, who has been living out of the country for several years, is flying into town and insists on being driven from the airport to her hotel. You mention this to an underling in passing, who informs you that she'd be delighted to pick up your sister and drive her into the city. That behavior, while nice, is entirely uncalled for. It's a blatant attempt to curry your favor. Don't take her up on it.
- **FAWNING.** According to the *American Heritage Dictionary of the English Language*, the word *fawning* means, "To exhibit affection or attempt to please, as a dog does by wagging its tail, whining, or cringing."[19] If an employee always agrees with your opinion,

chances are she's only doing it in order to gain your favor. One way to avoid this is by asking your people how they feel about an initiative *before* you weigh in to agree or disagree. This technique has been used with great success at all types of different organizations. Build stronger leaders by forcing your people to take a stand before they know where you stand.

Just the Stats

When someone appears to be treated better than others for reasons unrelated to superior work performance, that is considered *favoritism.* This may result in that person being promoted faster, receiving a better office, getting better perks, or being given a certain leeway not granted to others.

WAS AESOP WRONG?

Aesop told a fable concerning a gaunt Wolf and a well-fed House Dog. Passing the hungry Wolf in the forest one afternoon, the Dog tried to persuade him to work steadily and have his food regularly given to him. The Wolf had no objection.

"Come with me to my master," the Dog offered, "and you shall share my work."

The Wolf and the Dog walked towards the town together. On the way, the Wolf observed that the hair around the Dog's neck was worn away.

"It is nothing," said the Dog. "That is the place where the collar is put on at night to keep me chained up. It hurts, but one soon gets used to it."

"Is that all?" said the Wolf. "Then good-bye to you, Master Dog."

The moral of the tale was that it was better to starve free than to be a fat and well-paid servant.

Problem #170: Fellow Staffers Want to Muzzle the Pet

You adore your trusted office Pet, but the rest of the team claims to be allergic to her. Recently, you've heard complaints about *both* her personality and her work ethic. Staffers find her bossy and resist all of her great suggestions. Is it possible that you're going to have to reprimand your Pet—just for being her sweet, compliant, agreeable self?

Solution #170: Learn the Moral of This Story

You have created a monster. In this case, the monster isn't Frankenstein, yet fellow staffers find the creature scary indeed. If you have allowed her to get away with a work ethic that is sub par, make a great show of disciplining her in public. You need to hold her to the same rigorous standards as the rest of the team or else your competence as a manager could be in question.

If, conversely, she has been using the information gained from you in private to boss around other team members, ask yourself if you sanction this behavior. You shouldn't. You need to discuss this with her behind closed doors in the sanctity of your office. Make every effort to take her down a few notches, but know that in fact, you are to blame.

Take this opportunity to think through a real recognition plan for your employees. Try to make each plan individualized. One employee may wish to be recognized in a staff meeting. Another may prefer an email—where you copy someone in HR—so the note can be placed into her file. A third may desire a small bonus, or a gift certificate to her favorite store. Don't be shy about asking your employees how they would prefer to be recognized. With rewards such as bonuses and gift certificates, the monetary amount should be roughly equal.

The Golden Rule

Don't play favorites at the office, or those out of favor will rise up to slay the office Pet. Strive to have a reign marked by fairness. Hold everyone up to the same exacting standards and reward only those workers who surpass them.

PART 3

When the Problem Lies Within

Most people leave jobs due to personality conflicts with bosses and coworkers rather than an inability to do the task. Psychological problems, ranging from fear of success to imposter syndrome to an inability to cope with authority figures, may plague certain employees and prevent them from performing well at a particular job, or in any.

Of course, the biggest problem with The Problem That Lies Within is detecting it. Let's face it: it takes a will of iron to hold a mirror up to your soul and take responsibility for your destiny. Is your boss hypercritical? Or are you being too sensitive? Are his expectations too high? Or did you stop putting forth your best effort a long time ago? Have you been merely "mailing it in," hoping against hope that no one will call you on it? Is your boss truly a tyrant? Or are you just a rebel—with or without a cause?

If you have a history of problems at the workplace, it really pays to examine your own actions and behaviors with a magnifying glass. You may not love what you see, but it's still worth focusing on those ungainly problem areas. For managing yourself is the one area that's in your domain. And ultimately, self-management may be the key to your success more than how well you manage others (or fail to).

If you recognize yourself in any of the scenarios that follow, it could be a sign that emotional issues are hijacking you and contributing to the problems you face with others. If so, assess the problem and don't be afraid to seek help. Above all, recognize that it's okay to be human. We all are. To be human means to be flawed, sometimes deeply. No matter what your particular problem, chances are excellent that you are not alone.

CHAPTER 35
I'm Not a People Person

I'm not okay when I have to be around everyone all the time.
—*Keri Russell*

Left to your own devices, you're extremely productive. It's just *people* who always get in the way. (You wish you never had to deal with them. But unfortunately, they're everywhere. Sigh…) Secretly, you believe that people who need people are the *unluckiest* people in the world.

In your opinion, most meetings are a colossal waste of time. You want to get back to the work, without the banal banter and feeble attempts at group brainstorming that never seem to lead to anything brilliant. You're efficient, and have no desire to spend all night, night after night, working with… people.

You let 99% of your phone calls go directly into voicemail, and then do your best to reply to those messages via email. (Email is less likely to find you in a foul mood. Plus it doubles as a legal document!)

Your favorite T-shirt bears the legend: "What do I look like, a frickin' people person?"

Problem #171: I Don't Respond Well to Feedback Unless It's Positive

"No good deed goes unpunished." Whoever wrote that clever phrase *must* have worked for your boss at some point. Just take your latest experience with her on your report. You spent a whole week on the research alone, only surfacing to scuttle from your desktop computer to the office library. When it came to writing up your findings, you were as meticulous as a scientist. After triple-checking your report for clarity, you even had the on-staff proofreader comb through it for grammatical errors. You handed the manifesto to your supervisor with a flourish. Six minutes later, she approached you with a long list of issues and casually asked you to revise your report. You're so angry that you feel like telling her to write her own damned report!

Solution #171: Decompress for 24 Hours (and Deal with It Tomorrow)

If you bristle like a porcupine every time you hear something negative about your performance, your bosses will be terrified to give you good assignments. Work on developing a "poker face." That is, develop the knack for stifling any defensive outbursts and teach yourself how to *not* react—at least *not* until you've had a chance to absorb the criticism.

If you fluster easily, it may take a whole day to simmer down long enough for the feedback to sink in. What do you do while you're waiting to calm down? Take notes. The very act of note taking will force you to keep your head down as you focus on jotting down all of your boss's issues with your piece. Once you've mulled over each one, pick and choose which suggestions to follow.

Chances are, you won't have to make every last change she requested. (But if you're going to dispute any of them, you will need an airtight rationale.)

Stay humble. Humble people have a way of selling through more of their ideas.

Problem #172: I Think Most Meetings Are for Bloviators and Seat-Warmers

Meetings at your company seem to be the ideal forum for those blustery, loquacious types who spend 90% of their time showboating about some initiative that will probably never happen. By the time the bloviators have finished waxing prolific, the seat-warmers barely have the stamina to sit up, much less speak. If only you could just skip it all and read the damned conference report.

Solution #172: Recognize That Meetings Are for "Face Time," Not for Getting Work Accomplished

The next time you find yourself in a meeting that isn't all that productive, glance around the table. Are there any faces you don't normally see? The purpose of the meeting may simply be for your supervisor to rustle the whole team in front of some higher-ups. Sometimes, just "being seen" in a room helps give you partial ownership of a project without the words being said. Instead of worrying about what is not getting done while you're trapped in the meeting from Hell, focus on the "face time" that you are getting with these muckety-mucks.

On that note, what is your face doing? Is it furrowing, wrinkling, or frowning? Is it scrunching up like a fan as it wonders if it will get out of the meeting in time to catch your favorite T.V. show? It would be helpful if it could manage to look upbeat and pleasant rather than excruciatingly bored.

HOW TO BECOME A PEOPLE PERSON

You don't have to be a people person by nature to become more adept at the way you handle humans. People skills are like other skills: they can be learned. You may never blossom into office diplomat, but you can become friendlier and more approachable in an instant. And with some attention and a lot of practice, you might even become something of a people magnet. Here are some vital tips to keep in mind on that noble quest.

- **EXUDE ENTHUSIASM.** A positive attitude will draw more people to you than a negative one. Even neglaholics prefer to hang out with positive people. Feel like you have nothing to feel positive about? Fake it.
- **LEAVE YOUR GROUCH BEHIND.** Did you find your first gray hair this morning or quarrel with your beau? Are your bills mounting, with no raise in the foreseeable future? Did your drainpipe burst on your way out the door? Throw yourself a pity party. Just make sure you're the only person on the guest list.
- **COLLECT ACQUAINTANCES.** It's vital to have some close friends (who, indeed, will care most deeply about your drainpipes). But in order to be a true people person, you'll also need to cultivate a circle of acquaintances. Sometimes referred to as "weak links" only because their emotional connection to *you* is weak, acquaintances can be enormously beneficial in a job search. When you meet new people in a networking situation, trade business cards with them, and then commit their contact information to a "people file."
- **KEEP IN TOUCH, BUT NOT TOO MUCH.** Never send a new acquaintance a slew of emails, but if you discover something you think may pique his interest, feel free to share it. For example, if he mentioned that he and his wife were planning to

take a safari, you might send him a link to an interesting travel blog whose writer recently returned from one.

- **TALKATHONS ARE FOR JERRY LEWIS: LISTEN UP.** Be curious about other people's lives. Ask questions that prove you care.
- **SHOW APPRECIATION.** Everyone craves appreciation in almost limitless amounts. (Think "bottomless pit" and then some.) Show your colleagues that you're grateful to have them around. Compliment them on a job well done. (However, if the job left a lot to be desired, give constructive criticism so they can improve the next time around.)
- **DEVELOP A SENSE OF HUMOR.** Contrary to popular belief, your first name doesn't have to be *Groucho* to be quite the stand-up. Imagine yourself wearing a Groucho mask sporting bushy eyebrows and a big nose. Automatically, this disguise will give you a comic distance on your fellow man that is the essence of irony. Buy some hilarious books. Don't automatically delete the Internet jokes making the rounds. (You might try reading them first.) Develop your ear for the patter and timing of comedy.

Management Mantra

"A sense of humor is part of the art of leadership, of getting along with people, of getting things done." As Dwight D. Eisenhower's words explain, having a sense of humor is one serious asset.

Problem #173: I'm Not a Frickin' Cheerleader

No one would ever accuse you of behaving in an overly perky manner. You don't compliment people gratuitously or sing a happy tune when things are going well. It may take more muscles to frown than to smile, but the corners of your mouth turn down naturally, and wearing a permanent sulk just seems to fit you. Isn't it enough to be a tireless worker? Is it really necessary to also pretend to be so rah-rah-shish-boom-bah? Bah humbug.

Solution #173: Take Acting Lessons

According to the bard William Shakespeare, "All the world's a stage." By implication, that includes your local conference room. Improve your stage presence by investing in acting classes. Perhaps there's a program that meets on Saturday afternoons or on weeknights. Acting classes can help build confidence along with your communication skills. Having just a teaspoon of charisma will help you ace your internal presentations. Discover how to modulate your inflections until your voice develops the patina of silk. Acting training can also help you see yourself as others do, giving you a degree of self-knowledge that few possess in the corporate world.

The Golden Rule

Likability is an important motivator of others as well as a key to success. Happily, likability can be learned. Even if you're not a people person by nature, your people skills can be buffed. Start by taking an active interest in other people's lives. Vow to listen more than you talk. Practice being someone whom you wouldn't mind hanging out with, and you'll be halfway there.

CHAPTER 36

I Hate Coming to Work Every Day

The trouble with the rat race is that even if you win, you're still a rat.
—Lily Tomlin

It wasn't so very long ago that you used to love going to work each morning. But somewhere along the line, you metamorphosed from a happy worker bee into a chronic clock-watcher. Now you feel like you're part of the infrastructure, plastic Bonsai tree and all. You've held the same job for three years, six months, four days, and two and a half hours. And, baby, the thrill is gone.

You have reason to believe that growth potential at your company right now is limited, which only adds to the stasis. Sapped of energy, you worry that you're not emotionally prepared to tackle a massive job search.

Recently, a few people at the office have detected a change in you. It's not like you have received a bad review—yet. But you're worried that evidence of your chronic boredom is beginning to pop up like a jack-in-the-box that won't quit.

It's time to focus on turning around your attitude before the people around you start to turn on you.

Problem #174: I Feel Like I'm Just Going through the Motions

In the beginning, you and your job had a healthy relationship. But now the honeymoon is over, and you've started to view your job as your "ball and chain." No longer do you regard every staff meeting as a moment to shine. Staying on top of your projects has always been one of your secret strengths, and everyone still compliments you on your organizational skills. But lately, you've felt like there's nothing magical about schedules or your particular projects. You can't remember the last time your job challenged you. You're on autopilot. Or is it cruise control? Whatever…

Solution #174: Ask for an Intriguing Assignment

If you're not moving forward in your career, you're moving backward. Complacency is the first sign that you're losing your mental edge. And in the words of a famous public service ad campaign, "A mind is a terrible thing to waste."

Set up a meeting with your boss, pronto. Express enthusiasm (even if you feel like you're faking it). Phrase all requests in a positive way. "I was wondering if I might help out with that exciting new research initiative" sounds a lot more upbeat than, "I'm bored out of my mind. Save me!"

One caveat: if your boss doesn't have anything gripping for you at the moment, be patient. Work may be slowing down, and you never want to make your boss feel he doesn't have enough interesting work to keep you gainfully employed.

If possible, reroll the dice by working with new people. Try giving yourself the burst of adrenaline required to become passionate about your projects again. If you have to pretend that it's your first week at the job all over again to ratchet up your excitement level, do so. Feel too blasé to make the effort? It's time to get your mojo back. Do not "pass Go." Read the Corporate Mojo box first.

FIND YOUR CORPORATE MOJO OUTSIDE THE OFFICE

Offices have cycles. If yours is in the midst of an upswing, chances are you have little time for extracurricular activities. However, if yours happens to be in a slow period, you could be chafing with ennui. Unfortunately, boredom, like the yawn that signals its onset, is contagious. It can deplete everyone's energy for weeks, making it difficult for the whole group to recuperate as yet another person falls victim.

Instead of feeling like you're "bored with work," try reframing the sentiment. Admit that you're simply "bored with you." That's right. Convince yourself that work isn't the problem. It's your whole life that's the problem! Once you frame the issue that way, you really have no choice but to do everything in your power to bust yourself out of boredom's vicious hold.

When your life threatens to become a crashing bore, here are some ways to add a tingle of excitement to it.

- **RESHUFFLE YOUR PRIORITIES.** Tackle some of those tasks that are at the very bottom of your *Life To-Do List*. If you don't have such a list, create one. Write down one hundred things that you'd like to do before you die. Once you're finished with your list, start at number 100 and work your way up to number 93. (This will prevent you from cheating on your list by undertaking items that you're already doing, or wimping out at number 2 or 3.) Take up tango. Learn Spanish. Become a foodie editor on your own blog.

- **GIVE A DAMN.** Adopt a new charity or a pet cause. (However, be careful not to overcommit. Try giving just two hours, one night a week, and see how that meshes with the rest of your schedule before taking on more.)
- **REPLENISH YOUR SOUL.** Travel to an exotic destination halfway around the world. Voyage to castles; take a fertility tour (only if you're trying to get pregnant); compare and contrast church steeples across Europe.

Management Mantra

"Recharge your own batteries." That's your charge, no one else's. Don't sit around waiting for someone to charge your batteries for you...or you could be sitting in the same seat for a long time!

Problem #175: There's One Person Who Depresses My Chi

He sits near you, crunching wasabi nuts all day long. First, you hear the telltale crack of his teeth grinding against the nuts, followed by an occasional burp and the mandatory "Excuse me," said to no one in particular. Each nut takes him about thirty seconds to chew, and he seems to have an endless supply of them. You can't imagine why the sound of his eating bothers you so much. It's just ordinary mastication, right? But for some reason, hearing him crunch reminds you that each day is long and drawn out, with few exciting bits to savor in between the burps.

Solution #175: Find Ways to Inoculate Yourself

Every person we meet in life affects us differently. Just as there is "love at first sight," there is also "disdain at first sight." If someone at the office makes you cringe for whatever reason, do your utmost to avoid him. Don't burn a lot of mental energy worrying about *why* you dislike the person so intensely. Just skedaddle out of his way.

If someone is too loud, think of how you might cushion yourself from the noise. Depending on your company's corporate culture, you may be able to sport an *iPod* for part of the day. Seek out rooms that lend themselves to quiet contemplation. There may be an obscure conference room that's virtually unused. Check out the company library and cafeteria during off hours.

If your company allows employees to work off campus, scout for nearby public venues where you can camp out for a few productive hours. When you find your secret hiding spot, don't reveal it to others, lest the noise that drove you there in the first place shadow you.

Just the Stats

A pet peeve is a complaint about a specific behavior. This behavior might involve rudeness or personal hygiene. Let's suppose that one of your roommates never sponges down the tub after using it. If it really bothers you, then that's one of your pet peeves. Behavior that rattles you may just bounce off of someone else. (That's why it's *your* pet peeve and not your roommate's.)

Problem #176: I'm So Busy Managing the Squabble Squad, I Can't Get My Work Done

Eliza thinks Darrin is a self-promoter. Darrin thinks Eliza is a do-nothing princess whose daddy had something to do with her being his supervisor. (Her daddy used to sit on the board.) Petra is petrified to make a move without Eliza's blessing. Cecil has problems with all three of them. You appreciate that your staffers are so in touch with their feelings, but their trials and tribulations suck away the hours of your day like a vacuum cleaner on adrenaline. Can't someone manage these folks?

Solution #176: Experiment until You Find the Winning Combination

Once you reach a certain rank on the great corporate hierarchy, your job *is* to help make your colleagues' problems disappear, even if those problems are only the ones they have with one another. Your other work may not be as crucial as just having the people on the team get along.

Try laying some ground rules for good team behavior. If that doesn't work, try shaking up the team by recombining the people in different groupings. There may be two people who work together beautifully while another unit functions best as a threesome. Be flexible. There could even be two people who get along famously as long as they don't have to be office neighbors. If so, introduce them to the classic parlor game called *Musical Chairs*. Resolve to try every combination imaginable until you find one that's optimum.

If personality issues persist, don't always strive to fix the problem. Sometimes, just taking an active interest in your people's upsets and triumphs may be all the therapy required.

The Golden Rule

Offices go through busy and quiet cycles, but if you're bored, challenge yourself to view the problem as being with *you*, rather than with the job. Try to secure more interesting assignments at work, but if there are none, view the down period as an opportunity to cross off some activities on your *Life To-Do List.* Some of the people at the office who are demoralizing you with their constant bickering may need you to pay *more* attention to them rather than less.

CHAPTER 37
Imposter Syndrome

Women are certainly no strangers to faking it—we've faked our hair color, cup size, hell, we've even faked fur.

—*Carrie Bradshaw,* Sex and the City

Everyone else at the office is a cowboy, all gunning for a promotion in a brand-new territory. By contrast, you have always been perfectly content to follow the action from the fringes of the office corral.

Then, one day before you've been around long enough to earn your first holster, your boss approaches you with phenomenal news. You are going to be promoted! A whole team will report to you. At long last, you'll have a title that you won't be embarrassed to cite at cocktail parties. You'll even earn a paycheck that will keep you in cowboy boots for a long time to come.

Why does your breath catch in your throat instead of inflating your chest with pride? You should be bellowing, "Hee-haw." Instead, you feel like mounting the horse that you rode in on, and galloping the hell out of town before you're found out.

Somehow, you deceived them all into believing that you have this mysterious thing called "management talent."

Why are you convinced that you will fail before you've even tried?

Problem #177: I Feel Like a Poseur

Competence, pluck, and street smarts had nothing to do with it. Your recent promotion was simply luck of the draw. You feel as if you wear an ill-fitting mask every day to work and that it's only a matter of time until someone rips it from your face, exposing you for the incompetent Newbie you really are. You live in secret dread that others will discover how much knowledge you lack.

Solution #177: Conduct a Reality Check

The first step to changing your low self-image is tapping into your secret fears. Identify your feelings by asking yourself a series of questions to pinpoint the underlying problem. Do you feel like you're not smart enough to have merited the promotion? Are you questioning whether your boss or HR made a mistake in selecting you? On some level, do you believe that your charm was responsible for your advancement rather than your innate talent?

It's imperative to grapple with your feelings so you can distinguish them from the truth, because in this case, there's a rather large disconnect. Try committing your thoughts to a diary at home. Let your words stew for a few days, brewing in all of their negativity. Then, when you have some time to devote to the task, change those negative statements into what psychologists call "coping statements." For example, you might write, "The fact that I think I charmed my way into the promotion doesn't mean I did." Or, "I may believe HR made a mistake in choosing me, but it doesn't make it true."

The point of this exercise is to separate your automatic tendency to label yourself as an "imposter" from the reality that you are a successful businessperson who should be taking pride in her accomplishments.

Just the Stats

A person suffering from Imposter Syndrome often gives supervisors the answers he or she *believes* they are looking for, which increases the feeling of being a poseur.

Problem #178: Fear of Success

It's a paradox: the more praise you receive, the less praiseworthy you feel. You diminish your success by attributing it to luck rather than to any particular skill. "Oh, thanks," you toss off with a wan smile, "It was just a fluke," swatting away the third compliment from your boss this week on the power of your presentation skills.

Solution #178: Blame Your Parents

Freud may have slipped out of favor these days (and that's no Freudian slip). But most ids, egos, and superegos agree—the psychiatrist from Vienna was right about one thing: It's *not* your fault. It's your parents' fault!

If your career aspirations conflicted with what your parents envisioned for you, it might enhance your internal belief that, somehow, you don't deserve to be successful. Another contributing factor could be the label your family pinned on you while you were growing up. For example, if they always called you "the artsy one," while they labeled your older sister "the smart one," you may have inadvertently defied your parents' expectations by pursuing a highly intellectual field and daring to succeed in it. Perhaps you've just made partner at a law firm. Objectively, you are very successful. In spite of that, you may have difficulty balancing your success with what your parents continue to believe about you, all evidence notwithstanding.

One thing you might try as an exercise is learning how to accept a compliment. When you allow yourself to accept that the other person is *sincerely* praising you for a job well done, it helps to dispel the belief that it was all just "dumb luck." The next time a supervisor commends you for doing a phenomenal job, try just saying, "Thank you." Curb your desire to deflect the compliment or attribute it to an outside force, such as luck.

Management Mantra

"I'm a great believer in luck, and I find the harder I work, the more I have of it." Thomas Jefferson's quote is a reminder that luck and skill are inextricably connected rather than independent forces. When you work really hard, you create your own luck. Thus, attributing your success entirely to luck (as if it's a force that has nothing to do with you) makes no sense. You worked really hard, thus creating the fortuitous circumstances needed to reach a particular milestone. Be happy for your achievements.

How to Accept a Compliment

According to an old adage, "'Tis better to give than to receive." But when it comes to compliments, 'tis better to give *and* receive.

When someone notices something nice about you and comments on it, she is not anticipating that you will refute it. Suppose that you've worked tirelessly to melt those extra ten pounds before a big reunion. You subsisted on tofu for three months straight. Then one day, hallelujah, someone at the office finally notices the "new you."

"You look amazing," your colleague says. "Have you lost weight?"

"Gee, thanks," you muster. "I think these pants must just be super flattering."

Chances are, your colleague shrugs it off and keeps walking. But now, your self-doubt has subtly begun to impact the way she views you. "Maybe I insulted her," she worries, "by suggesting that she needs to lose weight." Then your kindhearted colleague makes a mental note to herself to compliment you less often.

There are two ways to view this. If your colleagues are in the habit of gratuitously complimenting you to worm their way into your favor, it may be smart to discourage their behavior by being seemingly immune to their nice words. But if you work with someone who is sincerely complimenting you, then refuting her on it sends a strange message. At best, you come off as a bit insecure. At worst, you come off as ungrateful *and* insecure.

A heartfelt "Thank you" is always in good taste. If you must embellish on those words, a simple "Thank you, I've been working hard on it" will suffice.

Depending on the nature of the compliment, you might also try "Thank you, that's very kind," "I'm genuinely touched by your sweet words," or "I'm delighted you enjoyed the present."

The next time you receive a compliment, try responding in a way that shows you appreciate your colleague's kind sentiments.

Problem #179: Survivor Guilt

There was a huge layoff at the office, and against all odds, you survived. Your boss has just congratulated you with a huge hug. She whispers in your ear that 30% of the staff was cut and that "some people are extremely upset." Echoing her sentiment, you can hear people's office doors nearby beginning to bang closed as fellow teammates gossip amongst themselves about the recent bloodletting. After your boss leaves, your phone rings. It's your favorite employee, your trusted confidant, Rita. "Do you have a second?" Rita breathes into the phone. "For you, anytime," you sing, even more chipper than usual, as you anticipate sharing with her your boss's news. Surely, Rita will be happy that you survived the massacre. Moments later, she's perched in your doorway, asking permission to close the door. You scrutinize her pomegranate-colored, tear-drenched face. Oh, no, say it isn't so! With a pang, you recall that Rita has three young kids who are dependent on her plus that slacker, otherwise known as her husband. Meanwhile, you're single with no outstanding debts.

Solution #179: Get Darwinian

It's normal to feel a twinge of survivor guilt, particularly if you disagree about who was let go. You might question management's choices, especially if you know that someone who was actively looking for a job was spared at the expense of an enthusiastic "lifer."

Management may not have been correct about all of their selections, but they were right about one thing. They were smart to keep you! Give yourself two days to commiserate with those who were cut unfairly, and then vow to lose yourself in your work. There are fewer people now to shoulder the same crushing workload, so your company needs you to stay strong. The powers-that-be selected you. Show them that they made the right choice.

The Golden Rule

While attributing your current success to luck may not have held you back so far, there *is* a point at which people will expect you to carry an air of confidence. Experiment with the various suggestions in this chapter, and if you still can't shake that imposter feeling, consider discussing it with a licensed professional.

CHAPTER 38
I'm Having Trouble Exerting My Authority

Marvin: I've been talking to the main computer.
Arthur: And?
Marvin: It hates me.

—*The Hitchhiker's Guide to the Galaxy* (movie)

Compared to your many ex-bosses, you're a saint. Unlike them, you are *not* autocratic, unfair, uninformed, sniveling, or base. Machiavellian agendas hold no allure for you. You have never dueled with anyone on staff. "Do no evil" could almost describe your personal philosophy, were it not already *Google's* most awesome tagline. You are a most benevolent ruler, if you do say so yourself.

So why is it that people just don't listen to you? Why can't they follow your lead when it comes to the top line so you won't have to make drastic cuts to preserve the bottom line?

Why can't they simply take a leap of faith and trust your judgment? Or bow to your seniority, if not your spotless service?

Problem #180: I Can't Get Their Attention

Whenever you conduct a meeting, you can feel the whole room twitching. One important team member is doodling while another's cell phone erupts into a stirring rendition of *The Star-Spangled Banner.* A third team member always manages to sneak in a long bathroom break, while others discreetly float in and out of the conference room like balloons. With all of these distractions, you have to question if your main points are getting through. You don't understand why your people can't pause long enough to listen to what you have to say when you know for a fact that it's utterly fascinating.

Solution #180: Brush Up on Your Public-Speaking Skills

Don't monologue, or your audience may try to escape! And the average conference room isn't equipped with iron gates and prison guards to stop them. To prevent a mental jailbreak on the part of your listeners, keep your speeches snappy. Pause occasionally. Engage people, by asking if anyone has any questions.

Dispense with the hypothetical and use concrete examples to illustrate your points. Draw pictures with your words. Instead of mentioning that a client was "furious," for example, substitute with, "He was red-faced with anger."

At the end of your discourse, summarize your points. Be a font of pith, and the people who work for you will start quoting you instead of running away from you at the first opportunity.

Just the Stats

The average attention span is only seven seconds long. That means every seven seconds, your focus shifts and you think about something else. You're starving. Hmmm. Wonder what's on TV later. Hmmm. Is that guy still droning on about profit margins? Hmmm. Time for a quick stroll to the vending machine. Hmmm. If your own attention span jumps faster than a Mexican jumping bean, consider the attention spans of the fidgeting folks who are supposed to be listening to you.

Problem #181: People Still See Me in My Old Role

Sometimes it feels like a token promotion. You made a startling leap during the past year, yet no one around you acknowledges it. Those above you still give you the same demeaning tasks to do as always, while those beneath you aren't exactly kowtowing to your command either. What if you've been deluding yourself this whole time and merely dreamed about your promotion, in between watching Internet clips of *The Office* and reruns of *Murphy Brown?*

Solution #181: Get Your Manager to Help Out

Some overlap between your old position and your new one is normal. It might take fellow staffers several weeks to acclimate. Some people may have even been on vacation when your promotion was announced (the nerve!) and may not have received the official press release. But if the confusion persists, it's not your job to get the word out. It's your boss's job—assuming that he was the person responsible for your promotion in the first place.

Ask him to write a memo telling the troops who is handling your old responsibilities. Then, if someone asks you to do something that's no longer part of your job description, you can pleasantly refer her to your replacement. While you're waiting for the reality of your new promotion to set in, best to be as easygoing and flexible as possible.

Problem #182: They Want to Do It Their Way

There is a disconnect between you and those who report to you that's as big as the generation gap. As young at heart as you feel, sometimes you think that you are far too old to command the respect of the twenty-somethings in your employ. Everyone on your team is so talented. But they're brash, with a headstrong desire to prove they're right that doesn't always lead to stellar results. You wish they'd master "the company way" before they tried to do it in some newfangled way.

Solution #182: Earn the Privilege to Lead

President Dwight Eisenhower once said, "In order to be a leader, a man must have followers. And to have followers, a leader must have their confidence." Always ask yourself if, like a politician currying an electorate's favor, you have the people's mandate.

No matter how much you get paid or who selected you to lead, it's your job to win over your people's hearts and minds. Start by making the people on your team feel valuable. What have they done for you lately? Be certain to thank them for it. Then look for ways to invest them in your success by sharing your power. Delegate to your strongest players, but check on the progress of all projects. Schedule weekly progress reports. You want to give your people leeway, but not so much that they feel directionless.

If your teammates succeed, give them all the credit. If they fail, take all of the responsibility. Follow in the footsteps of another American president and own your mistakes as well as your triumphs. As Harry S. Truman said, "The buck stops here."

ON EXERTING YOUR AUTHORITY WITHOUT BEING AUTOCRATIC: A USER'S GUIDE

What is that magical ingredient called "leadership material," and how can you get some of it—fast? One method is to devote yourself to getting along with your colleagues and coworkers. If you were promoted recently while others were bypassed, it's even more important for you to show your teammates that whoever chose you made the right decision.

- **BE VISIBLE.** Don't allow a new promotion to thrust you into the shadows of your cube as you struggle to stay abreast of your heftier workload. Better that you should squander your weekends catching up than to be invisible during a time when everyone expects you to be out and about more than in the past.
- **BE MORE APPROACHABLE THAN EVER.** Does someone need your help with a complicated spreadsheet? Is another staffer questioning your direction? Make an effort to visit with team members and find out.
- **MASTER THE SYSTEM OF ALLIANCES.** On paper, your secretary and the No. 2 guy in your organization are a whole hierarchy apart. But as fate would have it, he went to college with her older brother, an interesting piece of trivia that significantly closes the distance between your secretary and No. 2 both inside and outside the office. They sometimes socialize with her brother on the weekends; and at work, the two of them are allies. Devote yourself to figuring out who hangs out together after hours and you'll have a lever you can use with them at the workplace. (See the following corollary.)
- **KNOW WHO IS CONFIDANTS WITH WHOM.** Do you need to persuade someone to do something that you know he'll resist? Instead of approaching the person directly, it's often smarter to consult with his trusted confidant first. As visible as you want to be in your new, turbo-charged capacity, never forget that much can be accomplished through the real influencers at your company.

Anything that you can add to a meeting to make it more fun or more interactive will be appreciated, with an important *if*—if doing so won't make the meeting run too long. Challenge your team to a "ten ideas in ten minutes" brainstorm. Or give away a funky tote bag to the person who comes up with the most creative business building idea. Sweeten the time staffers spend together by stealing a goodie from every focus group in America, and bring plenty of *M&M's* and a *Poland Spring's* worth of bottled water to your next meeting. Even if the meeting runs overtime, you may find that no one seems to mind.

The Golden Rule

A promotion signals one or two people's confidence in your leadership prowess. Now you only have to persuade everyone else on the team that you're worthy! If your speeches are deadly, liven them up. Shorten them, lace them with interesting anecdotes, and consider including an interactive element. If people aren't treating you with the respect that you deserve, appeal to your manager for assistance. Look for new ways to share your power and increase your influence.

CHAPTER 39
I'm a Total Perfectionist

Perfectionists are their own devils.
—*Jack Kirby, comic book artist, writer, and editor*

You do sweat the small stuff.

You not only dot your i's and cross your t's, you dot your j's, cross your f's, and care how the descenders look on your q's, g's, and p's. (Anyone who doesn't is alphabetically challenged.)

You may have stopped the occasional presentation from going forward because a chart was in the incorrect font, or because there was a typo on page 49. And if that had the unfortunate side effect of having the people who report to you consider you a raving lunatic, so be it. (Lunacy is a highly underrated quality.)

In your last job, you worked in a *Fortune* 500 company with a vast network of professional resources. You were hired to import some of that "big company" professionalism to this start-up. Why can't these professionally impoverished neophytes appreciate that, like a modern-day Henrietta Higgins, you seek merely to educate them?

WHAT'S WRONG WITH PERFECTIONISM

Perfectionism might work if you were only demanding it of yourself. But unless you're an artist who works alone in a studio, you must always deal with these imperfect creatures known as human beings. Perfectionism holds others to an unrealistic standard. Then, when they fail to deliver, you feel betrayed and miserable.

If you are a perfectionist, chances are you developed a series of bad habits a long time ago that may be difficult to break. Nevertheless, with practice and forbearance, you can become less perfect, if you really try.

- **REALIZE THAT PERFECTION IS IMPOSSIBLE.** There will always be someone richer, thinner, prettier, younger-looking, or more successful than you. You don't have to invite her to become your best friend or babysit your husband. But you don't have to resent her.
- **DON'T THINK OF YOURSELF AS AN A-PERSONALITY OR A B-PERSONALITY.** Instead, consider yourself a B+ personality. "B+ people" are not underachievers. They manage to achieve their goals, balancing them with a little thing called a personal life.
- **KEEP A PIECE OF PAPER AND PEN ON YOUR NIGHT TABLE.** When you wake up in the middle of the night with a great idea, write it down. Then analyze it in the cold light of day. Is it really so wonderful? You may find that, while it's okay, it's not all the way up to brilliant. And that's perfectly okay. It's okay to have ideas that are half-baked. Someone else may be able to stick them in the oven and help them rise.
- **STOP PRACTICING CONVERSATION INTERRUPTUS.** Way back in 44 B.C., Cicero set down the rules for ordinary conversation. And do you know what Cicero said back in the day? "Do not interrupt," or in Latin, "Nolo interruptus." It was one of Cicero's key tenets. Interrupting has been annoying people since 44 B.C. Don't do it.

- **HOWEVER, FEEL FREE TO SAY, "SHUT UP, MOM."** Chances are, your mother always told you not to say "shut up." The words aren't fit for polite company. But when you say, "Shut up, Mom," you're not really admonishing your mother to be quiet. You are silencing your inner voice, the one that sounds like your mother when she's criticizing you. When your inner critic starts beating you over the head because you made a simple typo, just say, "Shut up, Mom." (Then watch her sulk because you don't call home often enough.)

Problem #183: If I Want Something Done Right, I Have to Do It Myself

You have no issue with delegating when other people do it. The problem only rears its hideous head when *you* try to delegate. Then it ends up taking way too much time on the back end, once you calculate how long it takes for you to correct all of the work that was done incorrectly.

Solution #183: Learn How to Tolerate Imperfection

The problem with being right all of the time is that you will come off as an insufferable prig to those around you. For starters, if you are always right, then by definition, they must be wrong. (Funny how no one will ever thank you for pointing this out. Truth be told, they may get rather annoyed with you.)

Instead of fruitlessly nitpicking other people's work, try to look for what *is* right about the efforts others have made. There is usually *something* that's right, even if it's the tiniest little thing. They put the presentation on white bond paper rather than orange! They wrote it in English instead of using hieroglyphics! Now you're really getting somewhere. What else was perfectly correct about the presentation? Make a list of things that were done right, and keep adding to it. Begin by appreciating what your staffers did *right,* and recognize everything they did to move the project forward.

You never want to pander to people's insecurities, but you also don't want to frighten them into believing that pleasing you is impossible.

Just the Stats

Some people become perfectionists because they learn early in life that others value them only for their achievements rather than for who they are. As a result, perfectionists tend to view themselves from the outside in, judging themselves on the basis of other people's approval. When it comes to receiving criticism, perfectionists are notoriously prickly. *(See* Chapter 42, *I'm a Supremely Sensitive Creature.*) They may also suffer sudden declines in self-confidence if they encounter a series of unlucky breaks or find themselves in a situation where their work isn't appreciated.

Problem #184: No One's Standards Are up to Mine

The ideas are so lame. The colors are washed out. The words are lackluster. The typeface is beyond Helvetica ho-hum. The humor is flat. The charts reveal no new insights. The assumptions are unclear. The projections are ludicrous. And while we're being honest, you don't care for the style of the presentation binder, either!

Solution #184: Aim for a B Instead of an A

If the work is at a D level, do yourself a favor and just aim for a B. The reason to keep your benchmarks low is because then they are eminently achievable.

Think "evolution," not "revolution." When you evolve the work gradually, it raises fewer problems with everyone—the old-timers at the company who will dig in their heels and resist change at their peril, the Newbies who may buck at countless revisions, and the clients paying the bills. Just try to bring up the work to a solid, respectable B, and few will quarrel with your mission.

Then slowly, almost imperceptibly, start trying to improve the work a tiny bit more during each round. Aim for 2% improvements rather than radical overhauls, and you'll get more people to buy in to your cause while upsetting far fewer people along the way.

Management Mantra

"No one is perfect...that's why pencils have erasers."

—Anonymous

Problem #185: I Hate to Be out of Control

Your raise, reputation, and the undying respect of your boss are all riding on the twelve people in your team pulling together seamlessly. Unfortunately, three of them are out of the country, one is out on maternity leave, and one has been incommunicado since she and Stu down in accounting were caught checking out each other's assets. But even when the whole team *is* together functioning as a unit, it's hardly a marvel of modern machinery. Parts of it sputter and creak while other parts break down constantly—a fact you never realize until it's too late because the communication function is always the first to go. You hate being dependent on others who may let you down. If modern science can clone a sheep and a horse, why can't it just hurry up and clone you?

Solution #185: Practice Serenity

Serenity is the quality of being calm or tranquil. When you attempt to mastermind other people's projects, the capacity to feel at peace diminishes. After all, no project *ever* runs perfectly smoothly. You should anticipate that there will be glitches galore, and then some. But when you have faith in people's ability to get things done, you can step back from the brink of your own desire to control everything. You can relax, because ultimately, you know that those whom you entrusted will figure out the right solution. It may not be the *perfect* solution. But it will be good enough.

Here are three serene thoughts to keep before you as you learn how to relinquish control:

1. **Stop thinking of yourself as *The Fixer*. Trust in your people to solve their own problems.**
2. **Offer guidance, not step-by-step instructions.**
3. **Ride the learning curve. Know that when you allow your people to rely on themselves, it builds their confidence. Then, the next time they have a problem, they will be more likely to try to correct it before seeking your guidance.**

The Golden Rule

The relentless pursuit of perfection is self-defeating, as its attainment is impossible. Instead, practice new ways to give up control. Don't fall into the role of master puppeteer, yanking on your employees' invisible strings while controlling their every move. Recognize that in order for your company to achieve its goals, your people will need to learn how to stand up by themselves. Allowing them to do so will not diminish your power base.

CHAPTER 40
I'm Too Smart for This Job

Only two things are infinite, the universe and human stupidity, and I'm not sure about the former.

—*Albert Einstein*

You're reporting to someone who makes your nanny look like a Rhodes Scholar.

Your supervisor has mastered the art of giving orders, but ask him any probing questions, and he'll tell you to consult with two other nitwits who don't understand the project either. Since it's impossible to get a straight answer from anyone about anything except the looming deadline, you live in secret dread that, eventually someone will ask you to actually turn in your project. But when you raise questions about it in a group meeting, everyone shuts you down, explaining that *this* isn't the correct forum for you to be asking *those* types of questions.

"What *is* the correct forum?" you ask, bewildered, only to be met with stone-cold silence.

You keep waiting for that "surreal office feeling" to dissipate, the way a new-car smell eventually does. But, if anything, your sense of existential discomfort increases the more time that you spend with these people. How much will you have to dumb yourself down in order to survive?

Problem #186: My Boss Is an Idiot

When you first met your boss, you thought it was cute that he had both *Networking for Dummies* and *The Complete Idiot's Guide to Networking* on his office bookshelf. "What a self-deprecating guy," you thought. "He must have quite a sense of humor." But since working for him, you realize that he really *is* a management information systems moron and those two books are his bibles. Your boss assigns you tasks he never had to tackle. Thus, when you ask him for direction, he's clueless. "Figure it out," he huffs at you. "It ain't exactly brain surgery."

Solution #186: Idiot-Proof Yourself

Someone in your organization knows how to do the task your boss has assigned you. Your first order of business should be to go find that person, the keeper of institutional memory, and pick his brain about how to accomplish the project. Recognize that because this person isn't your direct supervisor, the time he has to devote to your tutorial will be short. If necessary, take notes on every step so you won't have to waste his time by going back to him for more instruction later on. Then, simply complete the task to the best of your ability.

Just the Stats

Most people who have had the unmitigated joy of working for an idiot agree: you can fight 'em or you can dumb yourself down and try to work with 'em. The only thing you can't do is change 'em. However, if you can change the way that you view them, then you will have made a positive start. Remember that the problem lies *within*. You alone have the ability to change the way in which you regard "problem people." If you really are "too smart for the job," then you should be clever enough to change the way you deal with the plethora of idiots around you.

Problem #187: If I'm So Smart, Why Am I Taking Orders from People So Dumb?

If you took your boss's I.Q., then added it to the I.Q.s of his two henchmen, and divided it by three, you'd have three idiots running the asylum. Except that simple math problems confound them, and they'd probably add or subtract an idiot by mistake. Lackadaisical about deadlines, rude to clients, and even ruder to insiders, you can't help wondering why these three have the titles, windowed offices, and the stock options, while you, brilliant, quiet, courteous, and with an MBA, are working for *them*. Will the real idiot please take a bow?

Solution #187: Outsmart the Idiots: Get Them Promoted

The word "promoted" above is not a typo. Concentrate on getting your boss promoted, and trust him to take care of his idiotic cronies. Make it your raison d'être to have your boss shine in all meetings. Talk him up to the higher-ups. Wax rhapsodic about his achievements. If he does get promoted, he'll have no incentive to hold you back. (Unless, of course, he detects that you consider him an idiot. Take care to keep your disdain well hidden in a lockbox and throw away the key. Idiots can be idiot savants about sniffing other people's derision.) Work diligently to get your boss promoted. And if the stars happen to fall into proper alignment, you might even be able to take his place.

Simultaneously, you may want to pursue a policy of trying to secure him a better job on the outside. The next time your head-hunter tells you about a fantastic job opportunity, convey what a bang-up job your boss has been doing and how much you respect him. If your headhunter is like many others, just hearing your boss's name again will automatically thrust him onto her radar, and she'll check her databank for jobs at his level. (However, if she specifically asks you to recommend someone at his level for an executive search, it's wise *not* to offer his name. For if you do, it will be far too obvious that the two of you don't get along—a fact she could ultimately wield against you, should she find another candidate to take *your* place.)

Many career coaches advise those who are working for idiots to suffer in silence on the theory that the idiotic boss won't be going anywhere anytime soon. But you won't have to suffer at all—if you can help your boss either move up in the organization or out to a better job elsewhere.

Management Mantra

"I will pay more for the ability to handle people than for any other talent under the sun."

—John D. Rockefeller

Problem #188: Take This Job and...

You used to vent your frustrations in a humorous way at the office Christmas party, playing pranks on colleagues and coworkers that made everyone share a loud guffaw. But recently, your whoopee cushion jokes have put the "flat" back in "flatulence" (even if giving the Best Communicator award to the Watercooler Wag this year was a masterstroke). You have begun to ponder whether you might not be better off employing your creativity in a venture for yourself. Friends have often told you that you have an independent streak. If only you had a dollop of courage and a bankroll to go along with it.

Solution #188: Become an Entrepreneur for a Year

Everyone should try his or her hand at entrepreneurship, just to see how difficult it is. Do you despise the hours you've been putting in at your firm? Try working for yourself, and watch your hours double. Do you feel like you work at a "sweatshop"? When you are your own boss, see how forgiving you are with *yourself* about taking off extra time. Is your boss a nincompoop? See if you don't feel more graciously towards him when, as an entrepreneur, you watch your first marketing salvo falter and then have *no idea* how to resuscitate it. It's really easy to develop compassion for your current boss. Simply take a year off to go work for yourself. Doing so may help you gain the proper perspective.

Keep the door open at your company, especially if you're leaving to pursue an entrepreneurial dream. You may find that you hate working for yourself, in which case, it will be helpful to still have the respect of the your current colleagues and boss. If you don't have a new job lined up, give your company a lot of notice (at least four weeks). Offer to help find your replacement and train her. Show everyone how your intricate filing system really works. Stay in touch with people after you leave. You never know when you may be coming back.

OUTSMARTING AN IDIOTIC BOSS

- **DON'T LOOK TO HIM FOR GUIDANCE, AND HE'LL NEVER DISAPPOINT YOU.**
- **IF YOU CAN'T BRING YOURSELF TO RESPECT HIS KEEN INTELLIGENCE, AT LEAST RESPECT HIS AUTHORITY.**
- **IF POSSIBLE, COMMIT ALL QUESTIONS TO WRITING.** It can help clear up misunderstandings.
- **FIND A COMMON BOND WITH YOUR BOSS.** Does he enjoy pancakes? Perhaps suggest a "pancake power breakfast" for managers during the third quarter.
- **GIVE YOURSELF AN EXTRA ASSIGNMENT.** Try organizing the office Super Bowl pool or an Emmy nominations ballot. It will help earn you points for boosting office morale while keeping your mind off of your boss's idiocy.

The Golden Rule

When the inmates are running the asylum, you have no choice but to idiot-proof yourself and do your best to get along with them. If your boss is a poor supervisor, find someone else to teach you how to do your tasks. Is there a whole coterie of idiots to whom you report? Try to get your boss promoted, and with any luck, he'll take his henchmen with him.

Chapter 41

My Spouse/Significant Other/Children Never See Me Anymore

I don't want to achieve immortality through my work.
I want to achieve it through not dying.

—*Woody Allen*

You always thought forty-hour workweeks were for slackers. But in the beginning of your career, you drew the line at forty-five hours. Pity it turned out to be a line drawn in the sand at the beach you never had a chance to visit anymore.

Gradually, the time spent at the office consumed more and more of your waking hours. And now the bottom half of the work hourglass that symbolizes your life is over three-quarters full. If you divide your paycheck by the number of hours you work, you earn less money than a *McDonald's* worker (and without the tasty *Big Mac* and fries perk).

Is there any way to wrest your time back from the office quagmire and get thee to a class play of *Hamlet* before your kids' teacher accuses you of being Hamlet's ghost?

Problem #189: I'm Working CEO Hours without the Fancy Title

If you drew a pie chart of your pathetic excuse for a life, 92% of it would be the work slice, with only a skimpy 8% left over for your spouse and kids. Your better half complains that he feels like a "work widower," while your kids claim they feel like orphans!

Your life is so lopsided that you're more likely to bring work to bed with you than your spouse. (You're certain that your work really appreciates it, even if it *is* inanimate.)

The high-stress work diet may not kill you overnight, but clearly it isn't good for your heart or your love life.

Solution #189: Experience the Joy of Delegation

You need to learn to let things go, not just for yourself, but for the long-term viability of your company. No longer can you do it all alone. The most important thing you *can* do—even before deciding which tasks to delegate—is to figure out what your *highest value contribution* is to your company. Focus on that role. Own it.

If you are a senior-level executive, it helps to start with a vision. Your main challenge is to inspire your staff. Depending on the nature of your business, you may also need to reach out to customers, vendors, suppliers, investors, or even your public. Relationship building, by necessity, falls in your domain. Done correctly, fostering new relationships will be time-consuming.

What about all of your former tasks? Delegate them. Most functions such as product development and sales can be delegated. Even staffing can be delegated. Letting go may be difficult, but it can also be liberating. While at first it may feel as if you are jumping out of a plane without a parachute, once you let go a couple of times, it will become second nature to you.

Management Mantra

"The best executive is the one who has sense enough to pick good men to do what he wants done, and self-restraint enough to keep from meddling with them while they do it."

—Theodore Roosevelt

FIVE GOOD REASONS TO DELEGATE

1. To prevent burnout (yours, as well as other people's)
2. To develop new leaders
3. To foster team spirit
4. To tap into different members' strengths (while you delegate away from their weaknesses)
5. To stay married (to your spouse, as opposed to your job)

Problem #190: I'm an Email Junkie

There must be a twelve-step program somewhere that can help you kick this pernicious habit. You're so addicted to email that you actually look forward to reading spam! True confession: You check your email, not once, not twice, but ten times an hour, 'round the clock while at the office. During the ride home, you exhibit a bit more restraint: checking your email only twice via Blackberry. (Then again, you're driving.) Once home, you don't even bother glancing through your snail mail before booting up your laptop—just to make sure that you didn't miss anything on email. When you need to travel abroad where Internet connections are spotty, sometimes you feel as if you're going through withdrawal.

Solution #190: Go Cold Turkey

If staying abreast of your email is required for your job, chances are there is no cause for alarm. But if checking your email like a maniac isn't strictly required, then doing so at this pitch and frequency may be diminishing your ability to concentrate.

Similar to breaking other addictions, it's often easier to go cold turkey (rather than gently weaning yourself down over a period of weeks). Travel somewhere on vacation where email access will be remote. Are you tooling around Europe? Reserve a room at a hotel *without* a business center. Stay out of the Internet cafés.

Make a clean break. Force yourself to post an automatic message on your email account advising people that you are away and telling them who to contact in your absence.

Your spouse and kids carp incessantly that they never see you. You have a choice. You can wallow in your guilt or recognize that they're right and choose to change. They may be trying to tell you something that the people who work for you wouldn't dare: you don't have to do everything for it to be done right. Breaking an e-addiction will also free up more quality time for you to spend with your family. When you're with your loved ones, you can really be "with them" and not mentally popping off into cyberspace.

Problem #191: I Never Take a Vacation

Your company has a use-it-or-lose-it vacation policy. You freely admit that you've totally lost it—having willingly sacrificed your precious days off countless times during your long tenure at the firm. After putting in sixty-hour weeks, year after year, you don't feel "burned out" as much as filed down. Your personality has been filed down below the quick. No one invites you to interesting cocktail parties anymore (a stroke of luck since you wouldn't know what to talk about anyway).

Solution #191: Say "Bon Voyage" to Your Guilt

If you're a working parent, realize that many workers with kids actually sneak in a lot *more* vacation time than they are technically allotted, considering activities such as school events, day-care pickups, and doctor appointments lasting less than two hours "not really vacation." Under the circumstances, it's only fair for you to take what's rightfully yours. Guiltlessly, arrange one of those great trips abroad that you'll remember for the rest of your life. (However, know that some employers judge their employees not just on productivity alone, but also by the amount of "face time" they put in. So don't abuse the system. Just take your fair share.)

Just the Stats

Most health experts agree that it's critical to take some time off each year to revitalize mind and body. Make the time to relax before your body breaks down and forces you to change your lifestyle. When you get back you'll be even more valuable to your company because you'll feel refreshed.

The Golden Rule

Unless you are the CEO of your company, chances are you are not indispensable. Learn how to delegate and take time away from the office guiltlessly—or watch your inability to tear yourself away from your work wreak havoc on your personal relationships.

Chapter 42
I'm a Supremely Sensitive Creature

It seemed to Jerome Lindsey that disagreeable news invariably arrived when he and New York weather were in execrable moods.
—*Taylor Caldwell,* This Side of Innocence

You are like an exotic hothouse plant that only thrives with special care and nurturing. In the right circumstances, you are a marvel of nature. But if there is a sudden frost or you have to subsist without sunlight for any length of time, you could die.

Welcome to the modern office, where one can't always control one's climate. Winds of change, from a brand new boss to a harsh new directive from the old management team, often blow through the vents. A hiring freeze could put the chill on your own growth potential. Flexibility and adaptability are key considerations for your own long-term prospects.

If you don't learn how to adapt and become a bit hardier, you may not be able to survive for too many more seasons.

Problem #192: I'm Moody

If people wish to know how you're feeling, they need only glance at your face which perfectly gauges the range of emotions roiling inside you. Are you confused? Your eyebrows furrow into small *u* shapes, quickly telegraphing your critique of your boss's new incentive plan as "unclear." Are you angry? Your eyes narrow until their color dives into the black vortexes of your pupils.

Some people wear their hearts on their sleeves. You wear your emotions on your face, which is why you will never be a phenomenal poker player or office politician.

Solution #192: Mind over Mood

An old adage claims, "You are what you eat." But you don't necessarily have to be what you think. It all depends on your mood. When you're in a good mood, there's no harm in spreading it around. Most people appreciate some joviality, even if they are in a foul mood. If your mood is upbeat enough, it could even become contagious. So if you're feeling funny, give yourself the permission to be funny. Let your extraversion hang out and play.

But if your mood today would make a thundercloud look fluffy by comparison, then take steps to remove yourself from it. Gain some emotional distance from it. Think of yourself as completely independent from your frame of mind. Who is responsible for your foul mood? If it's your boss or a colleague, bolster your emotional distance from your mood with physical distance from the person who caused it. Escape from the office. Take a walk around the block. Count to 1,110. Calmly assess if you will need to discuss why you're annoyed or angry with that person, or if, with enough time, the feeling will simply pass.

What if the person who caused your distress happens to be your spouse? Recover your serenity from a polite distance. One trick is to is to become unreachable by turning off your cell phone.

Problem #193: It's That Time of the Month Again

Your emotions have a way of hijacking you and taking you hostage, especially right before your period. You're an emotional wreck, sometimes for as long as a week beforehand. The silliest things make you tear up, and the feeling of being out of control is only getting worse as you age. When there is a real reason to be upset (on top of your premenstrual craziness) sometimes your fists even clench.

Solution #193: It May Not Be PMS: See a Gyno

For most women, menopause happens at around age fifty, but every woman's body has its own timeline. Some women stop having periods in their mid-forties. Others continue well into their fifties.

Long before menopause is a phase called "perimenopause." Peri can start as early as your late thirties or as late as your early fifties. It's the process of change that leads up to menopause and lasts from two to eight years.

If you don't feel "like yourself," or if you have any questions, seeing your gynecologist may help to put your mind at rest. She might prescribe vitamins, calcium, magnesium, or even drugs to help ease your symptoms. Also query your mother about her experience with perimenopause. Some of the symptoms may include: irregular periods, hot flashes, night sweats, insomnia, mood swings, depression, headaches, heart palpitations, memory loss, and problems thinking clearly.

Maintain a low-fat, high-fiber diet that's rich in fruits, vegetables, and whole grains. Avoid alcohol and caffeine, both of which can trigger hot flashes. Exercise for at least thirty minutes a day. It can help you prevent weight gain, strengthen bones, elevate mood, and relax so that you can sleep better at night. Is your office near your home? Why not walk to work instead of always driving or taking mass transportation? Meditation and yoga may also ease the transition into menopause.

Problem #194: Did You Just Criticize Me? Ouch

The best defense is a stinging offense. Or is it?

Suppose that your boss mentions that your speech, while interesting, was too long. "How can that moron think my speech wasn't superb?" you ask yourself, eyes smarting with tears. "Has he no taste? He only heard the last ten minutes. Maybe if he had caught the other fifty-five he'd be entitled to an opinion."

Your automatic reaction is to strike back rather than listening to what he has to say. You marshal your arguments for why your speech was too long:

- Someone asked you to cover points A, B, and C.
- There were three different "audiences" for your talk, including suppliers, customers, and internal folks.
- You've been working too hard to get a good night's sleep.

Your list goes on and on. And before you consider the consequences, you start reeling it off to him, aloud.

Solution #194: Acknowledge the Criticism

You don't have to agree with your boss to acknowledge that you heard him. It's okay to be noncommittal. A decent reply might be, "I hear what you're saying. Maybe the speech *was* a bit on the long side." Or, "I'll take that under advisement, Boss." Or even (*Heaven forbid*) "You may be right."

Then do the unthinkable, and actually thank him! It can be as simple as, "Thanks for bringing that to my attention," or "Thanks for letting me know." Or, "Thanks for coming to the speech and for taking the time to critique it."

Finally, paraphrase the criticism. "Let's see if I got this right. You think that my speech, while informative, should have been about half the length. Is that correct?" Your boss will probably nod his head, dumbfounded. Most people can't accept even the tiniest bit of criticism without getting defensive, but you just proved that you were an adult about it. Your boss can't fail to come away impressed.

Management Mantra

"Criticism is something we can avoid easily by saying nothing, doing nothing, and being nothing."

—Aristotle

Criticism: How to Take It Like a Man (Even If You're a Woman)

"For every action, there is an equal and opposite reaction." Isaac Newton's third law is a good one to recall when accepting criticism. Imagine that your boss takes an action you deem unnecessary: he criticizes you. Your natural defense mechanism will be to react negatively. You will offer cogent reasons explaining why whatever you did "wrong" wasn't your fault. Your reaction then causes an equal and opposite reaction from your boss. You're so busy counter-rationalizing that he *knows* that nothing he said sunk in. This puts him on the defensive. He starts to resent that he can't be honest with you, and secretly blames you for making the act of criticizing you so unpleasant. He makes a mental note to never criticize you again (not to your face, anyway).

In one fell swoop, you've turned a mentor into someone who feels no stake in your success. You are curtailing your ability to learn and grow by being too sensitive to his remarks. Instead, force yourself to view the criticism as an opportunity for you to improve. Stay placid, impervious. Be sure to spit back to him exactly what you *think* he said. You might start, "If you don't mind, let me take a moment to repeat what you just said to make sure I understand it." His criticism may soften when he hears his own words reflected back to him.

Then, together, work out a way for you to improve. You can either ask for his suggestions or solicit his feedback on your own ideas for improvement. Since most people react defensively to criticism, this rational, less impassioned approach has huge advantages. It may even help turn a very negative review into more of a collegial exchange.

Just the Stats

Criticism is one of the few feedback tools at the workplace that can help you grow. You hear the feedback, and because it's verbal, you have a chance to comment on it. In effect, you give your feedback on the feedback. If you stay calm, pleasant, and open to criticism, your boss will come away from the exchange impressed with you, no matter what his initial take was on your speech.

The Golden Rule

Extreme sensitivity is not a trait commonly associated with success. If your sensitivity is caused by medical changes, see a doctor. However if your supreme touchiness is simply an automatic response to hearing criticism, work on your ability to listen to negative feedback without becoming defensive. With practice, you can learn how to conquer your moods so they will not control you.

CHAPTER 43
The Fuzziness Factor

Mental rest is mental rust.

—*Anonymous*

Somehow, you lost your edge.

Did it slip behind the scruffy white couch that's been doubling as a second credenza in your office? Did you, perchance, misplace it under the unwieldy pile of travel and expense reports? Or file it with that pesky Excel spreadsheet by mistake?

You're looking for your edge, but you can't find it. You're trying to reclaim it, but it's in hiding. Did you lose it in the glove compartment of your SUV during the years that you took off to be a Soccer Mom? You certainly hope not. You recently traded in that SUV for a sports car.

Did you leave your edge on some golf course during your last failed attempt at retirement? Wouldn't that be par for the course.

You have no clue where or when your edge disappeared. But you wish you could find it, as no longer being in possession of it makes getting things done rather difficult.

Problem #195: I'm a Mess When It Comes to Deadlines

In status meetings, you hear dates and deadlines, but they don't stick in your head. Then, later, when people ask how you're coming along on a project, you become unglued. Let the record reflect that you are not trying to act deliberately vague or misleading. But by your manager's tone of voice and the impatient snap of her fingers, it's patently obvious that she thinks you're disorganized.

Solution #195: Become a Calendar Girl (or Boy)

Transfer every project deadline to your personal weekly calendar. Try using different colored pens—red for urgent projects, blue for long-term projects, and green for projects requiring special attention. To avoid confusion, write down all personal appointments in black. Once you've completed a project, simply check it off in your calendar. The calendar is one vital aspect of a time management system. And the more pristinely you can keep your calendar, the more organized you will be.

Color-Code Everything

Devise a system for color-coding your projects, and always use the same colors.

Suppose that you decide all urgent projects should be coded in red. That means using a red pen to write down the project's deadline in your calendar, filing the project in a red folder, and using red Post-it Notes for any revisions. While some executives use different colored folders for different clients, it may be more beneficial to select a color based on urgency.

Visit your local office supply store, and stock up on file folders, pens, Post-it Notes, and paper clips in a rainbow of colors. Most offices have all of these organizational systems available for free, but their supplies tend to be color-challenged. For a few hundred dollars, you can correct this visual impairment by picking up a year's worth of materials at any office supply depot. You may even be able to "put in" for some of your work supplies. (Discuss it with your direct supervisor.)

Why not colorize all of your projects? It will add a plume of whimsy to an organizational system that works because it's streamlined and smart.

Problem #196: Sometimes I Get Projects Confused

L.D.H. distinctly told you that the C.T.C. project had priority over the C.I.C. project, and that they *both* had priority over the C.S.C. project. (Or was it the other way around?) Meanwhile, there's an S.V.P. on the phone asking about the C.V.T. project. You're not entirely sure if the C.V.T. project was supposed to be handled by your group in the first place. But since the S.V.P. is sort of a B.S.D., you're scared to ask him directly. Unfortunately, it's not like you can consult with anyone else either as the V.I.P.s on all four projects are M.I.A. in FLA. Your office life has morphed into a bowl of alphabet soup that spells out the word *S.N.A.F.U.*

Solution #196: N.M.A. (No More Acronyms)

Gently ask fellow staffers to dispense with the acronyms. An acronym is a set of initials that's shorthand or code for the name of a project. For example, M.O.M. (Moms on Meds) and D.A.D. (Dads against Drugs) could describe two different pharmaceutical initiatives. Some of the acronyms bandied about at your workplace may have similar groupings of letters to each other, only adding to your confusion.

Unfortunately, when everyone refers to a project by its acronym, things quickly become muddled, as then, every project has at least *two* names—its real name plus its cutesy acronym name. If you don't know what an acronym stands for, all you have to do is ask.

Encourage team members to simply refer to a project by its formal name where the words are spelled out. While it may take them ten seconds longer to use the King's English, it will save everyone else hours of second-guessing later.

Problem #197: I'm Terrible with Both Names and Faces

"What's in a name?" Shakespeare's Juliet once asked. Except that if she were asking you, you'd probably think *her* name was "Julie," "Jamie," or "June."

When you first meet people, you're so eager to make a good first impression that you often forget to register their name. Then, by the time you meet them again, you feel as if you should already know their name by heart. Adding to your embarrassment is the fact that they always remember your name perfectly. Hence, you end up greeting them the second time around with something incredibly lame such as, "Oh, hi there" (fooling no one).

Even when you ask other people to tell you the names of the new people, their names just slip in one ear and out the other.

Solution #197: Create a Mnemonic of the Person's Name

If you're new at a job, you will be meeting many people who are all new to you. Conferences, or visits to remote sales locations, are other situations that can tax your ability to keep the Bills, Bobs, and Barrys straight from the Joes, Jims, and Jerrys. Here's your best solution.

The very first time you meet someone, repeat the person's name as you shake his hand. "Hi, Bob. Very pleased to make your acquaintance." If he repeats your name, by saying something similar, you *can* get away with saying his name a second time. "Are you enjoying the conference, Bob?" Next, invent a private mnemonic of his name. A mnemonic is a way to associate two concepts. Imagine for a moment that Bob looks like a matinee idol.

You might try rhyming his name with "heartthrob." Bob the heartthrob. Or you could try "Bobby the VIP" if he's a vice-president or higher. (Take care that you don't start calling him "Bobby," though, if he prefers to be called "Bob.")

Mnemonic tricks include rhyming words with other concepts or inventing mind pictures. If you visualize Bob in the midst of an angry mob, that's using both rhyming *and* a mind picture to help you recall his name.

Management Mantra

"Sweat the details."

—Anonymous

Problem #198: When I Throw It against the Wall, Nothing Sticks

Life's a pitch and then you die (of humiliation). You contacted twenty new customers in the past month, had in-person visits with six of them, and were so confident you had received the green light from two that you actually had the chutzpah to announce the great news in a status meeting—only to have the light screech to red in both instances. Your annual performance review is in precisely four weeks, sixteen hours, and five and a half minutes. You are seriously considering crawling under a rock and camping out there until your luck changes.

Solution #198: Think of Yourself as a Work in Progress

With a track record of *zero* out of twenty new business wins, it's probably safe to assume that whatever you're doing isn't working gangbusters. While parts of your pitch may be incredibly persuasive, you're going to need to tear apart your entire presentation and put it back together again—keeping the best and throwing out the rest. This is easier to do if you are not overly attached to any particular slides or pages in your presentation.

If you work in a large firm, go find the best salesman in your department and ask him to critique your presentation. He may be able to provide some excellent pointers. Force yourself to also ask some of the potential customers who turned you down for their honest input. Ask what prompted them to choose a different company over yours, and really listen to what they have to say. If you ever deal with vendors and suppliers, solicit their input as well.

The more you can open up yourself to criticism, the better your chances will be for self-correcting. A lot of people claim that they "love to learn" when secretly they hate to be taught. View all criticism as a chance to learn and grow from the experience, even if it stretches you so much that it hurts. You can *never* afford to stop growing. You really are a constant work in progress.

What does it mean to be a lifelong learner? It means staying open to the idea of learning. Curiosity is essential. If someone invites you to do something out of your comfort zone, it means saying "yes," instead of automatically saying "no." Pepper people with questions about how things work or how they're supposed to work. Occasionally, push yourself to read a book that's completely out of the realm of your normal interests. If you always read autobiographies, pick up a juicy potboiler for a change or vice versa.

The Golden Rule

Mistakes and a run of bad luck are learning experiences. Recognize this and do your best to self-correct. No matter how many people you have working under you whose job it is to take care of the details, you can't afford to ignore them. Put a system in place to help you recall every last detail. Color-code all projects and become a slave to your calendar. Master the mnemonic and bring up your name-recognition batting average.

CHAPTER 44

Midlife Crisis, Quarter-Life Crisis, or A Funny Thing Happened on the Way to the Office

Midway on our life's journey, I found myself
In dark woods, the right road lost

—*Dante Alighieri,* The Divine Comedy

You fell off the treadmill. It happened just like this. One day, you were on the treadmill. You were keeping up with all of the other people on their own treadmills. You were running hard just to stay in place. You were in the zone. But then a thought occurred to you. For the first time since you started exercising, you asked yourself *why* you chose to get on the treadmill in the first place. What exactly was the purpose? The thought deflated you for a moment.

You decided to retire early that day, and left without even working out on the Nautilus machines. The next day, you skipped the gym. And the day after. And the day after that. Five weeks later, you packed up all of your belongings and decided to move to Alaska for some indeterminate amount of time.

You're not sure how long it will take to recuperate from falling off the treadmill, or even whether you should bother.

Just the Stats

Question: Who coined the term *midlife crisis?* Answer: Dr. Elliott Jaques, one of the world's leading psychologists and a pioneer in human development theory. But Gail Sheehy's seminal book *Passages: Predictable Crises of Adult Life* helped to popularize the term.

CARL JUNG AND THE MIDLIFE QUEST

Carl Jung was a Swiss psychiatrist who was a contemporary of Sigmund Freud's. Jung developed a system for understanding personality based on four groups of opposite behaviors: extraversion or introversion, thinking or feeling, sensation or intuition, and judging or perceiving. Meyers and Briggs also worked extensively with the Jungian model and developed an entire canon on the topic. The renowned Meyers-Briggs personality test uses these four personality indicators to arrive at sixteen different personality types, from which certain predictions can be made.

Jung believed that the central task during the first half of life is to develop one's personality. Unfortunately, doing so also means choosing one mode of behavior over its opposite. Suppose that you're a Thinker. You may develop into a superb Thinker, yet be completely out of touch with your Feeling side. The Feeling side, then, becomes repressed and forms the dark or unexplored side of your personality.

However, during midlife, there is an opportunity to reclaim the lost parts of your personality. During this time of life, there is a quest for wholeness. Using the example above, a Thinker might begin to naturally integrate more aspects of his repressed Feeling side into his personality.

The process of assimilating the repressed parts of one's personality during midlife can be the beginning of an invigorating journey. But for some people, coming to terms with their "otherness," or the parts of their personality they've never accessed before, can be extremely frightening. Denial may result, along with a Peter Pan-like refusal to grow up and take responsibility.

Problem #199: I Saw My Life Flash before My Eyes

You're late to work, frantic about catching the 8:03. By your watch, it's 8:01, and the long escalator down into the bowels of the station takes precisely three minutes. You grip the black conveyor belt handrail and caution out onto to the escalator's top metal stair. Suddenly, you feel a tiny tugging at your chest and a slight choking feeling, as the sea of people in front of you melds into a kaleidoscope of worsted wools and gray flannels. When you wake up, you're in the hospital. You've had a mild heart attack.

Solution #199: Slow Down

Our bodies sometimes communicate with us in strange ways. Yours may be pleading with you to stop pushing yourself so hard. This is a good time to reflect on your career as well as your life goals, and assess that thing that's sometimes referred to as "life balance." If you're the CEO of your company, your health crisis could be a cue that it's time to start seeking a successor. If you're a struggling middle manager, your recent scare could be a wake-up call. Perhaps you should ask yourself if the struggle is worth it. Where are you on your *Life To-Do List?* (*See* "Find Your Corporate Mojo outside the Office" in Chapter 36.) This may be the magical moment to check off one or two of those worthwhile goals.

Management Mantra

"Life is uncertain. Eat dessert first." Translation: If you keep putting off rest, relaxation, and fun until you're successful, you may find that you're denied both success and the ability to relax. Live every day as if it could be your last.

Problem #200: Burnout

If you never read another field report, that's a blessing. You couldn't care less which ways the arrows point on the fourth-quarter projection models. Office politics titillate you no longer. You are fed up and focus-grouped out. You have researched, revised, revived, reassembled, reinstituted, and reorganized once too often without even a "thank you" from the powers-that-be. Cats only have nine lives. You feel as if you've had twelve, and in your *next* life you want to write a book about it with Shirley MacLaine. Enough already!

Solution #200: Enforced Relaxation: Build Relaxation into Each Day

"Enforced relaxation" may sound a bit like house arrest, but you don't have to do it from home. You can pick *any* place that is geographically desirable as long as you commit to it. Make yourself relax by enrolling in a meditation or yoga class. Certain stretch classes may also help you unwind.

If you enjoy music, enforced relaxation may mean committing yourself to weekly guitar lessons. Depending on the nature of your relationship with your partner, it could even mean building in more time for movies, date nights, or sex. Any activity that you find relaxing is automatically on the pre-approved list, as long as you are not simultaneously attempting to close a deal, get a contract signed, or check your Blackberry!

Take a breather. Recognize that enforced relaxation will now need to become a way of life for you. It can no longer be something that you just squeeze into remnant time. No longer can you just do it on vacation.

Problem #201: I Wish I Didn't Have to Do It Anymore

You gave it your best shot. But between stroking the ruffled ego of the Coddled Superstar, enduring the rants of the Grumpy Martyr, and buying citrus cube fresheners for the Employee Nobody Likes but You, you've had it. No one could pay you enough to answer one more of the Newbie's idiotic questions or kiss up to the Spineless Sycophant for one more butterfest. Compensating for the Weak Link's deficiencies and mothering Suddenly Single through her most recent romantic fiasco has sapped the passion right out of you. Honestly, you just want to go work for someone sane and reasonable: YOU.

Solution #201: Figure Out What You Want to Be When You Grow Up

It's hard to love your life if you hate your job. If you find yourself phoning in sick when you don't have a cold, or sneaking out of work earlier and earlier just to escape from your dysfunctional colleagues, it may be a message to take a week off to sort through your options. Think of it as a retreat—a retreat from the crazy people who are running your life.

Ask yourself what you want to be. The ideal career is a balance between what you love to do, what you can afford to do, and what you're qualified to do. Reviewing your current job situation and past experience will help you shed light on your qualifications. Do you love what you do, but simply feel compelled to do it elsewhere? Or do you have a fundamental frustration with your career that no amount of money can make disappear?

Start writing lists—what you enjoy about your current job, what you hate about it, and what you liked about a particular job that you held in the past. Craft a list of your talents and skills. Create a budget: how much money do you need to maintain a comfortable lifestyle? If you get stuck on your list of talents and skills, ask your close friends to weigh in and help. You may find that some of them will have insights about you they never had the opportunity to share before.

Finally, if the answer turns out to be "start your own business," calculate precisely how long it will take to turn a profit, and *double* it. Then stick your big toe into the water, and take the plunge.

The Golden Rule

Change can be terrifying. But sometimes a health crisis or midlife crisis mandates it. And sometimes, even without a crisis precipitating change, the nagging voice inside your head just refuses to be quieted. Joseph Campbell once said, "Midlife is when you reach the top of the ladder and find that it was against the wrong wall." If you find yourself between a ladder and the wrong wall, start by asking yourself a series of questions to identify your strong likes, dislikes, talents, and needs. Give yourself the permission to explore new options. Don't begrudge yourself the hard work it takes to figure out what you want to be when you grow up.

CONCLUSION:

The Secret of Getting Along with Just about Anyone

In a perfect world, everyone at your workplace would get along famously. The strongest players would rise to become bosses, and everyone else would look up to them. People's tasks would be clearly delineated; there would never be any overlap. Those working above you would possess strong leadership skills. Those laboring beneath you would possess enthusiasm, camaraderie, and a genuine talent for their selected task.

Everyone would respect one another's time. Meetings would never run overtime. Group brainstorming would always generate productive ideas. Realistic goals would be set. Thus, everyone would meet their benchmarks, and productivity and profitability would blossom on your fertile office tundra.

No one would ever resent a fellow worker who was promoted, because he would know that at some point in the future, he would be similarly recognized. Instead of being "lonely at the top," it would be social at the top, in the middle, and even at the bottom.

In a perfect world, you wouldn't need to be diplomatic or possess the grace and social skills to smooth over any rough edges. After all, everything would already be working perfectly.

In the real world, of course, lofty goals and tight deadlines stress everyone on staff. And chronic stress has a habit of stripping away the veneer of gentility, making bosses, colleagues, and underlings snap at the most minor provocation.

One management trick is not to take anything personally. Can you rise above a petty insult that was meant as a joke but secretly hurt your feelings? Can you look a rival of yours in the eye and congratulate her for getting promoted when you were bypassed? Can you forgive an underling who went behind your back to consult with your supervisor?

Another smart management technique is to accept that people are flawed, sometimes deeply, and vow to make peace with their foibles. Can you feel flattered by a coworker's jealousy instead of resenting it? Can you accept directions from your supervisors without feeling like you are their slave? Can you forgive your Boss from Hell and maybe even consider downgrading him to the Boss from Purgatory?

You can. And with patience, practice, and perseverance, you will.

In various chapters, this book has emphasized the importance of becoming an active listener. Sometimes that will entail listening to negative feedback about your own performance. And that can be a most disheartening experience.

But consider this: every weekday, before you toss on your work uniform to spend yet another eight to twelve hours in the maze, you glance at yourself in your bathroom mirror. In that instant, whether it's while brushing your teeth, brushing your hair, or gargling, you make a snap judgment about yourself.

Now, hopefully, while you are gazing at your own reflection, you will genuinely approve of what you see. But there will also be scores of times when you won't. At these times, you will say to yourself, "Ah, I wish I could lose ten pounds, or hide that gray hair, or grow more hair, or be taller, or have whiter teeth." And in that split second of critical self-examination, you will make a decision.

Perhaps your decision will be to ignore that particular flaw for the hundredth time in a row. Or maybe, depending on the nature of your flaw, your mood, and your finances that month, you will decide to undertake some self-corrective action. But either way, you will be listening to some very tough criticism and deciding what to do about it. You won't be standing there, clutching your bathroom sink, bristling with resentment because someone told you that you could use some improvement!

If you can be brutally honest with yourself, you will find it that much easier to listen when people are trying to be honest with you. Some self-knowledge goes a long way.

If you learn only one thing from this book, may it be how to become *less* sensitive to other people's criticisms of you and considerably *more* sensitive to the way in which you deliver criticism. Or as Abraham Lincoln once said, "We should be too big to take offense and too noble to give it."

Take away that simple lesson, and there really is no need to leave your job in search of greener pastures. Of course, should someone offer you considerably more money to do your exact same job elsewhere, there's also no reason to decline. But if you are considering leaving your job to run away from a particular person—a boss, colleague, underling, or even someone in a different department who drives you crazy, rest assured, you will encounter the identical problem elsewhere. You can run, but you can't hide.

In these pages, hopefully you found the tools and strategies needed to smooth over minor grievances and look beyond certain personality tics to get along better with your fellow office mates.

Some of these gambits will work instantly. Others will need to be tweaked and refined with your own experimentation. But with conscientious practice, your relationships with most of your colleagues should improve dramatically; you'll feel both happier and more productive at the office, and instead of being part of the problem, you'll become the solution.

ENDNOTES

1. The Harris Poll #38, "Many U.S. Employees Have Negative Attitudes to Their Jobs, Employers, and Top Managers," May 6, 2005, http://harrisinteractive.com/harris_poll/index.asp?PID=568 (accessed September 14, 2007).

2. MSN-Zogby Poll, April 11–13, 2007, quoted in Rachel Zupek, "U.S. Workers Like Their Boss … Really," CareerBuilder.com, http://www.careerbuilder.com/JobSeeker/careerbytes/CBArticle.aspx?articleID=690&cbRecursion (accessed September 14, 2007).

3. For further reading, check out the Equal Employment Opportunity Commission (EEOC) website at http://www.eeoc.gov/types/sexual_harassment.html.

4. Ray, Barry, "Who's Afraid of the Big Bad Boss? Plenty of Us, New FSU Study Shows," Florida State University, http://www.fsu.com/pages/2006/12/04/BigBadBoss.html (accessed July 29, 2007).

5. "Survival of the Fittest," Wikipedia, http://en.wikipedia.org/wiki/Survival_of_ the_Fittest (accessed July 27, 2007).

6. Social psychologist and author Jerry Harvey coined the term *Abilene paradox.* For further reading, see Jerry B. Harvey, *The Abilene Paradox and Other Meditations on Management* (New York: John Wiley & Sons, 1988).
7. Helge Hoel and Cary L. Cooper, British Occupational Health Research Foundation Survey, "Destructive Conflict and Bullying at Work," Manchester School of Management, April 2000.
8. Employment Law Alliance Poll, "New Employment Law Alliance Poll: Nearly 45% of U.S. Workers Say They've Worked For An Abusive Boss, 2007," http://www.workdoctor.com/press/ela032107.html (accessed July 10, 2007).
9. *The Columbia Guide to Standard American English,* 1993, (online version); see entry "spin."
10. "Narcissistic Personality Disorder," *Diagnostic and Statistical Manual of Mental Disorders,* 4th ed., 1994, quoted at Halcyon.com, http://www.halycon.com/jmashmun/npd/dsm-iv.html (accessed August 15, 2007).
11. "Addiction in the Workplace: A Problem Worth Solving," 2007, http://www/hazelden.org/web/public/ade/40322.page (accessed August 8, 2007).
12. America Online and Salary.Com Web Survey, http://www.salary.com/sitesearch/layoutscripts/sisl display.asp?file name=&path=/destinationsearch/par485_body.html.
13. Deborah Fallows, PEW Internet & American Life Project Survey, "How Women and Men Use the Internet," December 28, 2005, http://www.pewinternet.org/.
14. *American Heritage Dictionary of the English Language,* 4th ed., 2000 (online version); see entry for "sycophant."

15. Merriam-Webster Online Dictionary, 2005; see entry for "paranoia."
16. Robin Lloyd, "Why We Lie," Live Science, May 2006. http://www.livescience.com/health/060515_why_lie.html (accessed October 28, 2007).
17. Joan D. Mahoney and James R. Meindl, Montclair State University Management Department and SUNY-Buffalo School School of Management Study, "Lying at Work: An Exploratory Study," http://www.montclair.edu/Publications/news/newsrelease499.lyin g.html (accessed October 28, 2007).
18. "Why Lying Exists in the Workplace," 2007, http://www.anonymousemployee.com/csssite/sidelinks/lying.php (accessed October 28, 2007).
19. *American Heritage Dictionary of the English Language,* 4th ed., 2000 (online version); see entry for "fawning."

INDEX

ABOUT THE AUTHOR

Vicky Oliver gives people the confidence they need to succeed—whether they're looking for a job or are trying to hang onto one. Today, her first book, *301 Smart Answers to Tough Interview Questions*, is available in the U.S., England, France, Australia, Canada, Japan, and Turkey. Her second book is called *Power Sales Words, How to Write It, Say It, and Sell It with Sizzle*. She also gives seminars on job-hunting, networking, and business etiquette.

Ms. Oliver's savvy career advice has been featured on the front page of the *New York Times* Job Market section. She has been interviewed on over 100 local and national radio programs as well as for *Esquire* magazine's Answer Fella column, the *Philadelphia Inquirer, LA Times*, and *Bloomberg* TV.

She is a frequent speaker and guest lecturer and has given seminars at the West Side Y in Manhattan, the New York Society of Security Analysts (NYSSA), and at Brown University in Rhode Island. She was designated "in-house job-hunting expert" at the Shomex Diversity Fair at Madison Square Garden. Her articles have appeared in *Adweek* magazine and on

Crain's New York Business website.

Ms. Oliver's writings and speaking engagements have put her in touch with over five thousand people in all different professions and in all walks of life: the employed, the unemployed, entrepreneurs, freelancers, retirees, college graduates, and people returning to the job market. She encourages people to contact her via email and can be reached at vicky@vickyoliver.com

A Brown University graduate with a degree in English Honors and a double major in Political Science, Ms. Oliver lives in Manhattan, where she has dedicated herself to helping others turn around their careers and their lives.